Léa Steinacker

Code Capital

A Sociotechnical Framework to Understand
the Implications of Artificially Intelligent Systems
from Design to Deployment

 **Nomos**

The author is thankful to the Swiss National Science Foundation for partly funding a survey as part of the research.

© Coverpicture: Lee – stock.adobe.com

Die Deutsche Nationalbibliothek verzeichnet diese Publikation in der Deutschen Nationalbibliografie; detaillierte bibliografische Daten sind im Internet über http://dnb.d-nb.de abrufbar.

Zugl.: St. Gallen, Univ., Diss., 2021

The Deutsche Nationalbibliothek lists this publication in the Deutsche Nationalbibliografie; detailed bibliographic data are available on the Internet at http://dnb.d-nb.de

ISBN   978-3-8487-8890-3 (Print)
         978-3-7489-2945-1 (ePDF)

British Library Cataloguing-in-Publication Data
A catalogue record for this book is available from the British Library.

ISBN   978-3-8487-8890-3 (Print)
         978-3-7489-2945-1 (ePDF)

Library of Congress Cataloging-in-Publication Data
Steinacker, Léa
Code Capital
A Sociotechnical Framework to Understand the Implications
of Artificially Intelligent Systems from Design to Deployment
Léa Steinacker
239 pp.
Includes bibliographic references.

ISBN   978-3-8487-8890-3 (Print)
         978-3-7489-2945-1 (ePDF)

Onlineversion
Nomos eLibrary

1. Auflage 2022
© Nomos Verlagsgesellschaft, Baden-Baden 2022. Gesamtverantwortung für Druck und Herstellung bei der Nomos Verlagsgesellschaft mbH & Co. KG. Alle Rechte, auch die des Nachdrucks von Auszügen, der fotomechanischen Wiedergabe und der Übersetzung, vorbehalten. Gedruckt auf alterungsbeständigem Papier.

I dedicate this dissertation to
Daniel Schillinger
(1979 – 2010)
for introducing me to the world of computers.

Acknowledgements

Around the turn of the millennium, my second cousin taught me how to code. Daniel, a computer scientist eager to share his knowledge, first trained 12-year-old me in HTML and CSS so that we could experiment with commands, classes, and color codes together. We moved on to Visual Basic which allowed me to develop small programs with inputs, outputs, buttons, and if-then loops. Mesmerized by the possibilities, I used these skills to earn my very first money designing a website. And thus, code and capital ironically merged early on for me.

Twenty years later, my journey from social justice to technological innovations brought me full circle: I am now exploring systems running on code as amalgams of many forms of capital. In my exploration of their power, I had the great privilege of being accompanied by several people without whose help this dissertation would not have emerged in quite the same way. First, I want to thank my supervisors, Damian Borth for his guidance and tireless willingness to debate with me, as well as Veronica Barassi for her insights and valuable pushback. Both took an interdisciplinary adventure ride with me that significantly shaped my thinking. Along the way, fellow researchers and dear friends engaged in illuminating discussions with me about their perspectives on how we construct technology that touches our lives. Several opened their doors to offer me immensely helpful writing retreats across the globe: Thank you to Mirco Günther in Singapore, Matt Listro in New York, Christiane zu Salm in Rottach-Egern, and Rahaf Harfoush with Jesse Morgan in Griège. Equal thanks to Antonia Baskakov for her patient eagle eyes. My deep gratitude goes to Joan Kingdom for encouraging me to play with words; to Valentin Jeutner for our ever so thoughtful discussions; to Sarah Chynoweth, who always had my back and feedback during this rollercoaster; and to Miriam Meckel for our inimitable flow in conversations about humans and machines. My family has given me unwavering support: David, Adanna, Kian, Noah, Ada, and Hilde. And none of this would have been possible without my parents, Dagmar and Gerd. I am so very grateful. Last but foremost, thank you to Ida Dizu Okadawe for facing and embracing the right now with me.

Düsseldorf, January 2022   *Léa Steinacker*

Table of Contents

List of Figures   15

List of Tables   17

Abstract   19

Zusammenfassung   21

1. Introduction   23

1.1 Ex Machina   23
    1.1.1 Calls for Action   25
    1.1.2 Institutional Responses   26

1.2 Objectives   29

1.3 Contributions   33

1.4 Overview   35
    1.4.1 Methodology   35
    1.4.2 Structure   37

1.5 Conclusion   39

2. Background: Artificial Intelligence   41

2.1 Introduction   41

2.2 A Brief History of AI   42

2.3 AI Systems Today   45
    2.3.1 Classifications and Predictions   46
    2.3.2 Rankings and Recommendations   47
    2.3.3 Generation and Alteration   50

2.4 Contextualizing Central Issues   51

2.5 Conclusion   53

3. Related Work: Technology Studies   54

3.1 Introduction   54

3.2 Determinism vs Constructivism   55
   3.2.1 Technology as Trajectory   55
   3.2.2 Technology in Context   58
      3.2.2.1 Actor-Network-Theory   60
      3.2.2.2 Large Technical Systems   62

3.3 Towards Sociomateriality   66
   3.3.1 Material features   66
   3.3.2 Constitutive Entanglement   67

3.4 Discussion   69
   3.4.1 Relevant actors   70
   3.4.2 Material features   71
   3.4.3 Sociomaterial practice and structures   71
   3.4.4 External forces   72

3.5 Conclusion   72

4. Related Work: Capital Concepts   74

4.1 Introduction   74

4.2 Capital's Economic Origins   75
   4.2.1 Money and Goods   75
   4.2.2 People and Labor   77
   4.2.3 Intangibles and Disputes   78

4.3 Capital as Social Leverage   80
   4.3.1 Interpersonal Phenomena   80
   4.3.2 Debate   82

4.4 Digital Technology and its Capitalisms   83
   4.4.1 The What: Commodifying Knowledge   83
   4.4.2 The How: Elevating Digital Technologies   84
   4.4.3 The Why: Surveilling Others   87

4.5 Discussion   93

4.6 Conclusion   95

5. Code Capital   96

5.1 Introduction   96

5.2 Code Capital: The Concept   98

5.3 The CODE Framework   100
   5.3.1 Conception   101
     5.3.1.1 Sensegiving Actors   102
     5.3.1.2 Narratives   103
     5.3.1.3 Investments and Expected Returns   104
   5.3.2 Operations   105
     5.3.2.1 Model Infrastructure   106
     5.3.2.2 User Interface   107
     5.3.2.2 Device   108
   5.3.3 Data   108
     5.3.3.1 Collection   109
     5.3.3.2 Pre-Processing   109
     5.3.3.3 Ethical Concerns   110
   5.3.4 Environment   111
     5.3.4.1 Sensemaking Actors   111
     5.3.4.2 Social Acceptance   112
     5.3.4.3 Regulatory Boundaries   113

5.4 Discussion   114

5.5 Conclusion   117

6. Impact Assessment: Facial analysis   119

6.1 Introduction   119
   6.1.1 Facial Recognition Technology and its Global Use   120
   6.1.2 Issues of Concern: Bias, Accuracy, Privacy, and Abuse 123
   6.1.3 Interaction with the Public   124

6.2 Conception   131
   6.2.1 Sensegiving Actors   132
   6.2.2 Narratives   134
   6.2.3 Investment and Expected Return   136

6.3 Operations   137
   6.3.1 Model Architecture   137
     6.3.1.1 Open-source Set-up   137
     6.3.1.2 Detection vs Recognition   139
   6.3.2 Concerns   141
     6.3.2.1 Accuracy   141
     6.3.2.2 User privacy   141
     6.3.2.3 Abuse   142

6.4 Data   142
    6.4.1 Collection   142
    6.4.2 Processing   143

6.5 Environment   144
    6.5.1 Sensemaking Actors   144
        6.5.1.1 Surveillance   144
        6.5.1.2 Public acceptance   148
    6.5.2 Regulatory Boundaries   149

6.6 Discussion   151

6.7 Conclusion   153

7. Systems Design: Text-to-Speech Synthesis   154

7.1 Introduction   154
    7.1.1 Text-to-Speech Synthesis   155
    7.1.2 Issues of Concern   156
        7.1.2.1 Automation   157
        7.1.2.2 Authenticity   158
        7.1.2.3 Participation   159
        7.1.2.4 Intimacy   159

7.2 Conception   162
    7.2.1 Sensegiving Actors   162
    7.2.2 Narratives   163
        7.2.2.1 Trust   164
        7.2.2.2 Revenue Diversification   165
    7.2.3 Investment and Expected Returns   166
        7.2.3.1 Funding   167
        7.2.3.2 Business Model   167
    7.3   Operations   168
    7.3.1 Model Architecture   168
    7.3.2 Evaluation   171
    7.3.3 User Interface   172

7.4 Data   173
    7.4.1 Collection   174
    7.4.2 Pre-Processing   175
    7.4.3 Storage   175

7.5 Environment   176
    7.5.1 Sensemaking Actors   176

7.5.2 Regulatory Boundaries 179

7.6 Discussion 183

7.7 Conclusion 185

8. Conclusions 186

8.1 Summary 186

8.2 Limitations 189

8.3 Discussion 191

    8.3.1 Theoretical Implications 191

        8.3.1.1 Accumulation 192

        8.3.1.2 Reproducibility 193

        8.3.1.3 Conversion 193

    8.3.2 Practical Applications 194

8.4 Outlook for Further Research 197

8.5 Concluding Remarks 198

References 199

Appendix 238

List of Figures

Figure 5.1 shows the CODE framework   101

Figure 6.1 shows the CODE framework as applied to
FacesOfTheRiot   131

Figure 6.2 shows screenshots of facesoftheriot.com on January 16
and February 25, 2021   138

Figure 7.1 shows the CODE framework as applied to VocallyYours   161

Figure 7.2 shows a visualization of VocallyYours TTS as shown in
one of the project's demo presentations   170

List of Tables

Table 6.1 "Do you accept or oppose the use of FRT in public?" 126

Table 6.2 "Do you think FRT increases any of the following?" 127

Table 6.3 "Do you think that facial recognition technology is more reliable or less reliable than other identification methods (e.g.: fingerprints, identity cards)?" 127

Table 6.4 "Are you concerned about any of the following issues in your country?" 128

Table 6.5 "How much do you trust governmental institutions in your country?" 128

Table 6.6 "Do you think that the government in your country has used surveillance against its own citizens in a negative way in the past?" 128

Table 6.7 "Do you generally support or oppose the use of surveillance by your government in your country?" 129

Table A: Ordered logit regression, weighted; dependent variable: social acceptance of FRT in public 238

Abstract

Advanced techniques in the field of Artificial Intelligence (AI) have been applied in commercial applications and public service across sectors to classify data, predict behaviors, and orchestrate choices. Today, experts agree that AI systems have immense economic, social, political, and environmental implications. But many recent institutional endeavors to assess them have been conceptually diffuse, overly focused on technical aspects at the cost of socialized context, and fueled by dichotomous narratives. Given the outsized influence of these sociotechnical systems, how can we capture the interdisciplinary factors that lead to their transformative effects on our social fabric? In this dissertation, I introduce my original notion of *Code Capital*, an interdisciplinary account of the intangible and material configurations that comprise an AI system's source of impact. Through the eponymous CODE framework, this new concept allows an analysis along four dimensions - Conception, Operations, Data, and Environment – to express bespoke circumstances of each system, bringing to the fore its normative forces. To test the applicability of my approach, I conducted CODE analyses of two real-life AI systems using qualitative and quantitative techniques. For my first case study on facial recognition technologies, I present empirical results from a cross-country survey I conducted with a team of researchers that underline the need to contextualize AI systems in their social embedding. My subsequent CODE analysis of a particular deployed system illustrates the framework's explanatory power for impact. I show how even thoughtful objectives risk producing unwanted outcomes and that the selection of material features has decisive effects on how the system is used. In my second case study on synthetic text-to-speech technologies, I examine the Code Capital of a system in its design phase to demonstrate how the concept can be used as a tool to guide the development process. My results show the importance of forecasting and contingency planning for potential misuse, such as the risk of identity fraud. Both case studies also emphasize the need for considering diverse representation in material design and training data to ensure inclusive participation and harm mitigation for users. Moreover, they demonstrate how centrally both the Conception and Environment dimensions contribute to the range of implications of a socially embedded AI system, which sets Code Capital apart from dominant existing approaches. Through the

Abstract

instructive CODE model, relevant stakeholders from the technological as well as the sociopolitical realm can employ a shared ontology to better anticipate and understand AI systems, with Code Capital as the novel descriptor of their potential power.

Zusammenfassung

Fortgeschrittene Anwendungen der Künstlichen Intelligenz (KI) werden im kommerziellen und im öffentlichen Sektor übergreifend eingesetzt, um Daten zu klassifizieren, Verhaltensweisen vorherzusagen und Entscheidungen zu treffen. Expert:innen sind sich heute einig, dass solche KI-Systeme immense wirtschaftliche, soziale, politische und ökologische Auswirkungen haben. Doch viele der jüngsten institutionellen Bemühungen, diese zu bewerten, sind konzeptionell diffus, fokussieren zu eng auf technische Aspekte, vernachlässigen den sozialen Kontext und werden auf dichotome Narrative reduziert. Wie lassen sich angesichts von Bedeutung und Einfluss dieser soziotechnischen Systeme die interdisziplinären Faktoren dieser KI-Systeme analysieren, die eine transformative Wirkung auf unsere Gesellschaft, unser soziales Gefüge haben? In dieser Dissertation erläutere ich den von mir entwickelten Begriff des *Code Capital*. Er verortet die Konzeptualisierung von KI-Systemen als neue Manifestation von Kapital in der Forschungstradition zu unterschiedlichen historischen Kapitalformen und beschreibt einen interdisziplinären Ansatz des Zusammenwirkens immaterieller und materieller Faktoren und Konfigurationen, die über die Auswirkungen eines KI-Systems entscheiden. Mit Hilfe des gleichnamigen CODE-Frameworks ermöglicht mein analytischer Ansatz eine Beschreibung und Bewertung von KI-Systemen entlang von vier Dimensionen - *Conception*, *Operations*, *Data* und *Environment* -, um die spezifischen Ausprägungen und Auswirkungen eines jeden Systems zu interpretieren und einzuschätzen. Um die Anwendbarkeit meines Ansatzes zu testen, habe ich CODE-Analysen von zwei KI-Systemen unter Verwendung qualitativer und quantitativer Methoden durchgeführt. Meine erste Fallstudie analysiert die empirischen Ergebnisse einer repräsentativen Mehrländerumfrage (China, Deutschland, Großbritannien, USA) zur Akzeptanz von bereits implementierten KI-gestützten Gesichtserkennungstechnologien. Meine CODE-Analyse veranschaulicht die Erklärungskraft des Frameworks: Sie zeigt, dass soziale und kulturelle Voraussetzungen die Technologieakzeptanz von Gesichtserkennungssystemen prägen und das Design der KI-Systeme entscheidenden Einfluss darauf hat, wie das System genutzt wird. Meine zweite Fallstudie über synthetische Text-to-Speech-Technologien untersucht das Code Capital eines Systems in der Designphase, um zu zeigen, wie das Framework auch als Instrument zur

Steuerung des Entwicklungsprozesses eingesetzt werden kann. Die Ergebnisse machen deutlich, wie wichtig die Vorhersage und Eventualfallplanung für die Prävention von potenziellem Missbrauch ist, z. B. für das Risiko des Identitätsbetrugs. Beide Fallstudien zeigen auch, wie wichtig es ist, von Beginn an bei der Gestaltung materieller Features und dem Sammeln von Trainingsdaten das Kriterium der diversen Repräsentation unterschiedlicher sozialer und kultureller Kontexte anzuwenden. Darüber hinaus zeigen sie, wie zentral sowohl die sorgfältige Konzeption (C) als auch die Berücksichtigung der Umweltdimension (E) sind, wenn es um die Auswirkungen eines sozial eingebetteten KI-Systems geht – zwei Dimensionen, die in den bislang existierenden Ansätzen eher unterrepräsentiert sind. Mit Hilfe des CODE-Frameworks können Akteure aus dem technologischen wie auch dem gesellschaftspolitischen Sektor nun auf ein verbindendes Bezugssystem zurückgreifen, das ihnen helfen kann, KI-Systeme besser auszugestalten und ihre potentiellen Wirkungsweisen besser zu verstehen oder gar zu antizipieren.

1. Introduction

> *"It is however pretty evident, on general principles, that in devising for mathematical truths a new form in which to record and throw themselves out for actual use, views are likely to be induced, which should again react on the more theoretical phase of the subject. There are in all extensions of human power, or additions to human knowledge, various collateral influences, besides the main and primary object attained."*
>
> Ada, Countess of Lovelace
> *Notes on the Analytical Engine*, 1842

1.1 Ex Machina

Systems that use Artificial Intelligence (AI) surround us. Having moved from research institutions to industry and real-world applications, they track actions, anticipate behavior, curate information, orchestrate choices, score individuals, and guide decision-making (Citron & Pasquale, 2014; Gillespie, 2014; Graham & Wood, 2003; Markoff, 2011; O'Neil, 2017; Siegel, 2013; Steiner, 2013; Thompson, 2014). While scientific inquiry into the building of machines that "think and act rationally" dates back to the mid-20th century (Russell & Norvig, 2010), more recently, AI applications in the form of products and services deployed by both private entities and public institutions have permeated most aspects of daily life, fueled by substantial investment in a particular fusion: ubiquitous data collection at scale, exponential computing capacity, and advanced algorithmic modeling (Miailhe, 2017; The Royal Society, 2017). On a macro-level, these applications have affected sectors from medicine (Liu et al., 2019), finance (Lenglet, 2011) and politics (Milan, 2015), to news (CW Anderson, 2013), national security (Cheney-Lippold, 2016) and policing (Moses & Chan, 2018). On a micro-level, they have altered the daily habits and social interactions of billions of people (Slater, 2013).

Experts have become increasingly sensitive to this growing impact of AI and the future-defining significance of who shapes its development (P. Stone et al., 2016). Research has examined our "algorithmic culture", where humans "have (delegated) the work of culture – the sorting, classifying and hierarchizing of people, places, objects and ideas – increasingly to computational processes" (Striphas, 2015). Several scholars have specifically expressed concern about the reproduction of human biases scaled to great effect, which in turn can exacerbate existing inequalities and discriminatory effects (Eubanks, 2018; O'Neil, 2017).[1] For example, studies have demonstrated that facial analysis technologies trained on data that skews heavily towards certain characteristics work less effectively on already vulnerable populations (Braca, 2017; Buolamwini & Gebru, 2018). Similarly, research on the delivery of job advertisements has shown that models trained to optimize for cost-effectiveness display offers related to science, technology, engineering, and math less often to female users, thereby exposing them to fewer opportunities in these fields (Datta et al., 2015; Lambrecht & Tucker, 2019; Sweeney, 2013). These examples illustrate that AI systems used at vast scale have broad socioeconomic ramifications.

Similarly, political scholars have assessed the influence of these systems on civic and bureaucratic processes, observing an "algorithmic democracy" (Campbell-Dollaghan, 2016) and "computational politics (…) engineering the public" (Tufekci, 2014). Among other applications, AI techniques like natural language processing (NLP) can be used to analyze social media posts about political candidates to predict election outcomes (Sengupta, 2020). Meanwhile, systems that employ generative adversarial networks (GANs) to produce synthetic media known as 'deepfakes' can have ethical implications for the integrity of elections (Diakopoulos & Johnson, 2019). As the U.S. National Security Commission's 2021 report on AI summarizes, the technology "will be the most powerful tool in generations for benefiting humanity" but AI systems "will also be used in the pursuit of power. (…) We must not take for granted that future technology trends will reinforce rather than erode democracy" (Schmidt et al., 2021, pp. 1–2). This caution underlines the potentially serious political effects wielded through AI systems.

Another stream of recent work has investigated the environmental and financial cost of large-scale deep learning techniques (Bender et al., 2021). For example, the computational resources needed for highly advanced NLP systems have been shown to necessitate substantial energy consump-

---

1   While not all algorithmic decision-making systems utilize machine learning techniques that qualify as AI, the argument of computational structures resulting in social effects is similar. Notably, though, some technologists are particularly concerned that exact inner reasoning of highly advanced learning systems employed to mediate publicly relevant decision-making are a "black box" at times even to their creators (Knight, 2017b; Pasquale, 2016a).

tion due to extensive training, thereby contributing to the depletion of natural resources (Strubell et al., 2019).

Evidently, AI systems comprise social, economic, political, and environmental effects with potentially vast implications for humanity. This topic has recently risen to a level of significant concern for several stakeholders. My doctoral work focuses on understanding these effects and how they emerge through the interaction of multiple sociotechnical factors.

1.1.1 Calls for Action

Spurred by the above concerns, the last few years have seen the emergence of vibrant debate and research about the unmitigated impact of AI systems. Indeed, several examples illustrate that their widespread adoption raises ethical questions with vast consequences. In 1999, Harvard Professor Lawrence Lessig declared that in cyberspace, "code is law", highlighting the beginning authority of software (1999). As scholars debate the possibilities of embedding rules into AI systems – "outsourcing its moral codification" (Donde, 2017) - the consequences of encoded morality itself could reconfigure social norms as well as legal regulations (Gasser, 2017). Lessig has since expounded on his adage: „If code functions as law, then we are creating the most significant new jurisdiction" (Lessig, 2006, p. 318). In this quest to define the new jurisdiction, some scholars have focused on accountability mechanisms (Gillespie, 2014; Groth et al., 2019), for example by calling for an "algorithmic social contract" with a "society-in-the-loop" paradigm, urging to "create and tame the new Techno-Leviathan" (2018, p. 13). Others seek to embed the fight against unwanted bias and privacy violations through AI and other digital technologies in the larger movement for social justice by calling for "data justice" (Dencik et al., 2016) to ensure "fairness in the way people are made visible, represented and treated" (L. Taylor, 2017, p. 1). Yet others elevate the need for diverse representation of demographics and backgrounds and increased inclusion practices in the field of computer science itself to combat the design of computational structures that further disadvantage traditionally vulnerable groups (Leavy, 2018). Many have called for a more interdisciplinary research agenda that complements computer science to understand the relations between AI and humans (boyd & Crawford, 2012), "showing uncertainties, alternative futures, and the implications of different interventions" (Cave et al., 2020, p. 13). One consortium of researchers has suggested an approach to study "machine behavior" analogous to a biological examination of a new species, arguing that understanding AI systems' "beneficial and detrimental effect on humanity (…) is essential to our ability to control their actions, reap their benefits and minimize their harms" (Rahwan et al., 2019, pp. 477–478). What these efforts have in common is the growing urgency they convey about the need to assess and manage the wide-ranging implications of AI systems and the role of humans in developing them.

1.1.2 Institutional Responses

Lagging behind are the institutional responses to the proliferation of AI systems, supposed to give contours of rules that will define the future of the field. But since 2015, a total of at least 117 documents related to AI principles in the form of guidelines, strategies, assessment frameworks, and regulations have begun to emerge worldwide from research institutions, governmental and intergovernmental agencies, as well as private companies (AI Ethics Lab, 2020).

Research and professional organizations were the earliest to publish systematized principles for their own or other's work. In 2015, the Icelandic Institute for Intelligent Machines[2], the country's only non-profit research institute for AI and advanced automation, prescribed its own Ethics Policy for what it called 'Peaceful R&D'. In it the Institute vowed to, among other things, not undertake activities intended to "invade personal privacy" or "be applied to unlawful activities" (Icelandic Institute for Intelligent Machines, 2015). Similarly, the U.S. multistakeholder organization Partnership On AI[3], whose main pillars of work include "safety-critical AI" and "fair, transparent, and accountable AI", released guidelines for its own research on best practices, pledging to "ensure that AI research and engineering communities remain socially responsible, sensitive, and engaged directly with the potential influences of AI technologies on wider society" (Partnership On AI, 2016). While these early instances of published principles referred to the organizations' own approaches, projects, and activities, several others developed guidelines for impact assessments to be conducted either by developers and providers of technologies themselves or by independent third parties. For example, the U.S.-based AI Now Institute[4] released an Algorithmic Impact Assessment focused on

---

2 https://www.iiim.is/
3 https://www.partnershiponai.org/
4 https://www.ainowinstitute.org/

the accountability of public agencies to examine systems that might be applied in "particularly sensitive domains" with regards to whether "they are sufficiently sophisticated to contend with complex social and historical contexts" (Reisman et al., 2018, p. 3).[5] What these frameworks share is the lack of statutory obligation to use them. They are in effect selfregulating instruments, offerings that organizations can choose to employ in the design and deployment of AI systems at their own volition.

While research and professional organizations acted the earliest, commercial companies have produced the highest number of documents (D. Zhang et al., 2021, p. 129). Several corporate actors have put forth statements and frameworks on the management of AI systems. For example, industrial giant Rolls Royce released its Alethia Framework, a toolkit to help examine AI systems on three dimensions, including social impact, accuracy and trust, as well as governance, with the explicit aim to "help build trust in artificial intelligence" (Rolls Royce, 2020). In parallel to the global rise in awareness about ethical concerns in relation to AI, executives of numerous leading technology companies like Google, Facebook, and Microsoft, have more recently been outspoken in their support for AI regulation, too (Pichai, 2020; Press Association, 2019; Vincent, 2016). While organizations like Google and Microsoft have publicly shared their own principles for Responsible AI[6], their appeals for regulation and self-declared guidelines must be considered within the context of the outsized influence their corporations have had on the proliferation of the technology (Kharpal, 2020). Google, for example, experienced widespread backlash amidst the departure of multiple members of its ethics research team after having declined to publish a paper that flagged risks of large language models and suggested mitigation strategies (Simonite, 2021). Finally, the corporate frameworks are rarely obligatory or have consequences for non-compliance.

More recently, policymakers have issued a variety of strategies, guidelines, and proposed regulations focused on AI systems, ranging from ethics recommendations to concrete laws. While countries like Singapore were early in their adoption of a national AI strategy, the European Union (EU)

---

5 Likewise, the independent Dutch organization Platform for the Information Society released an AI Impact Assessment guide to produce "an ethical and legally justifiable deployment of AI" and, notably, to help "protect the reputation and investments of the user" (Platform for the Information Society, 2018, p. 26).

6 https://ai.google/responsibilities/responsible-ai-practices/, https://www.microsoft.com/en-us/ai/our-approach

Commission has become the first agency to devise potentially binding rules on an intergovernmental level. At first, in its Ethical Guidelines for Trustworthy AI, the EU expert panel explicitly acknowledged that AI systems bring "substantial benefits to individuals and society, (they) also pose certain risks and may have a negative impact (...) which may be difficult to anticipate, identify or measure" (EU High-Level Expert Group on AI, 2019, pp. 2–4). They thus defined "Trustworthy AI" as systems that are lawful, ethical, as well as socially and technically robust (EU High-Level Expert Group on AI, 2019, p. 2). With these ethical considerations in mind, in early 2021, the EU Commission proposed the first ever legally binding framework to govern AI to "(position) Europe to play a leading role globally" (European Commission, 2021a).

The proposed law includes several aspects of noteworthiness: First, it outlines that the use of 'high-risk' AI systems, such as facial recognition and other biometric ID systems used in public, would have to be audited for approval before deployment to ensure they are, among other things, trained on unbiased data sets.[7] Such a rule for the inspection of certain systems would be the first of its kind required in the realm of AI internationally. Second, the regulation weighs banning certain systems that fulfil criteria the EU Commission deems unacceptable.[8] Again, this rule, if put in place and enforced, would be the first to forbid certain AI systems outright. Moreover, the proposed regulation requires disclosure of AI systems that produce synthetic media of any kind that would "falsely appear to a person to be authentic or truthful ('deep fake')" (European Commission, 2021b, p. 69). Given the explosive rise of GANs and deepfakes (see Section 2.3.3), this requirement of declaration is notable. Still, several analysts have criticized the regulation for its vagueness and "serious room for loopholes" (Vincent, 2021a). While some organizations would be allowed to assess themselves, other AI providers would need a third-party assessment. In the case of non-compliance, actors could be fined up to EUR 20 million or 4 % of their total worldwide annual turnover (European Commission,

---

7 According to the proposal, a European Artificial Intelligence Board comprised of representatives from every member state will be established to assist the definition and identification of what AI systems qualify as "high-risk".

8 Specifically, it stipulates that AI systems that can "be misused and provide novel and powerful tools for manipulative, exploitative and social control practices" are "particularly harmful and should be prohibited because they contradict Union values of respect for human dignity, freedom, equality, democracy and the rule of law and Union fundamental rights" (European Commission, 2021b, p. 21). This refers especially to applications for mass surveillance and social credit scoring.

2021b, p. 82).[9] As the US and China, two national powers at the forefront of AI development, currently do not have any regulatory foundations or enforceable rules for the technology, it represents a unique stance on oversight by the EU. Given that the EU had announced to invest in early-stage AI systems via its EUR 3 billion venture capital fund to better compete with the technological prowess of these nations, the ramifications of such a regulation on the innovation momentum in the Union remain to be seen. Meanwhile, other nations now follow suit.[10] For example, Australia issued a law to intervene in the news distribution business models of Google and Facebook (Porter, 2021), while India tightened the legislative grip on social media (Agarwal, 2021). In summary, "around the world, governments are moving simultaneously to limit the power of tech companies with an urgency and breadth that no single industry had experienced before" (Mozur et al., 2021). Evidently, AI systems' wide-ranging implications have recently galvanized multiple stakeholders across sectors. My doctoral work focuses on capturing the diverse configurations that give rise to these effects in a holistic manner.

1.2 Objectives

Though many efforts, movements, strategies, guidelines, and regulation drafts have emerged in the last few years to address AI systems' rising impact, we still have not found a holistic way to capture the complex interactions that lead to their societal effects. This is the central premise motivating my doctoral research: Despite AI's increasing influence in all areas of life, we lack the crucial, shared understanding of how an individual system constitutes various assets that can exert impact. If left unaddressed, this crucial shortfall would mean the continued unmitigated proliferation of

---

9 Significantly, the regulation completely excludes AI systems that are "developed or used exclusively for military purposes" (European Commission, 2021b, p. 39).

10 Indeed, within the same month of the EU Regulation's release, the U.S. Federal Trade Commission (FTC) released a blog post emphasizing that the FTC Act "prohibits unfair or deceptive practices" of AI systems and reminding that it is "illegal for a company to use a biased algorithm that results in credit discrimination on the basis of race, color, religion, national origin, sex, marital status, age, or because a person receives public assistance" (U.S. Federal Trade Commission, 2021). At the executive level, the Biden Administration has appointed several experts known for anti-trust stances critical of technology conglomerate market domination.

the social, economic, environmental, and political effects created through AI systems. Given the microcosm of each AI employed under a unique set of circumstances, we need an explanatory model of interdisciplinary nature to reflect the iterative interaction between a particular system and its social contexts.

Since I began my research in 2016, the field investigating the implications of AI and the debate about various approaches have grown immensely (see Section 1.1 and Chapter 2). Still, I see a significant gap between the ambitions and conceptualization of responses to AI and their operationalization. Specifically, three factors contribute to this gap. First, the preceding sections gave a glimpse of the many labels that have emerged, including Responsible AI (Arrieta et al., 2020; Clarke, 2019; Sambasivan & Holbrook, 2018), Trustworthy AI (Brundage et al., 2020; Floridi, 2019; Wing, 2020), and Ethical AI (Eitel-Porter, 2021; Hibbard, 2014; B. Mittelstadt, 2019; Siau & Wang, 2020), to name just a few.[11] As a Google executive summarized, "balkanized, inconsistent regulations won't help and could actually make things worse" (Mozur et al., 2021).[12] Currently, the plethora of terms that have been put forth indicates diffusion and a lack of international and intersectoral cohesion. Given that their effects transcend national borders, this lack of coordination is problematic.

Second, many of the approaches for assessing impact so far concentrate either on auditing the underlying algorithmic models of AI systems or the necessary safeguards for handling data. While both dimensions are key to AI techniques such as machine learning, in isolation of the social fabric that gives rise and responds to the system, these elements miss critical context. This prevalent, narrow focus on computational effects "does not fully capture the open, context dependent, and unobservable nature of harms across the wide range of AI infused systems" (Boyarskaya et al., 2020). For example, intentions for an AI system inform objectives which define algorithmic models. Underlying economic incentives can affect these intentions. Similarly, cultural norms inform perceptions which guide human interactions with technologies regardless of initial intentions. Current

---

11 For a lighter take on the range of platitudinous vocabulary used to frame the debate, MIT Technology Review's *Big Tech's Guide to Talking About AI Ethics* includes comedically astute definitions such as *"accountability*: the act of holding someone else responsible when your AI system fails" or *"beneficial*: a blanket descriptor for what you are trying to build. Conveniently ill-defined" (Hao, 2021).

12 He continued, "But done right, well-aligned rules can promote innovation, increase competitiveness and help consumers and small businesses" (Mozur et al., 2021).

frameworks to account for the implications of AI insufficiently consider how these sociotechnical systems are embedded in various social structures and practices. Additionally, many of them concentrate on regional issues related to AI, with a particular focus in the Western world. Again, given their cross-cultural ramifications, AI systems can only be understood when embedded in interaction with humans.

Third, AI's growing impact as a mediator in society has spurred both utopian and dystopian public visions. Across ancient myths, literary classics and sci-fi blockbusters, various narratives have illustrated and shaped our human fascination with and expectations of machine intelligence (Cave et al., 2020; Zarkadakis, 2015). Both before and after the coinage of AI in 1956 (see Section 2.2), fictional and non-fictional accounts have envisaged the creation and human interaction with intelligent automata, often addressing notions of control, autonomy, conflict, and societal governance. Narratives of AI oscillate between the extremes of hope and fear, either overly optimistic or pessimistic about what the technology might achieve (Cave et al., 2018). Some visions concentrate on the possibilities of machines' potential resemblance to human consciousness and how this may complement (E. A. Lee, 2017) or dominate (Bostrom, 2014; Harari, 2016) human cognitive abilities. Some focused on its present-day impact herald it as an equalizing force for businesses (Tans, 2018) and a more efficient and legitimate form of governance (Sætra, 2020). Others predict the wide-spread elimination of jobs in its wake (K.-F. Lee, 2017), warn of its influence on public knowledge (Gillespie, 2014) and governance (Danaher, 2016). Common descriptions in the media tend towards abstraction by treating the impact of various AI applications in blanket terms such as "the biggest event in human history" (Russell, 2019), "upend(ing) the global economy" (S. Weber & Stanton, 2019), "changing the future of higher education" (Marcus, 2020), or driving "the end of privacy as we know it" (Hill, 2020a). Instead of analytical utility such generalizations foster descriptive obscurity. Such binary descriptions between hype and doom currently form the central debate that impacts the public's perception, adoption, and implementation of new AI applications.

This trinity represents what is missing: a lack of conceptual cohesion, social context, and multidimensional narratives. The goal of my doctoral research is to respond to this gap. Specifically, my work is motivated by the recognition that AI comprises technological and societal progress as much as it bears economic, social, environmental, and political consequences whose genesis have not yet been sufficiently articulated. My overarching research questions is: **How can we capture the factors that lead to AI's**

transformative effects on our social fabric? To systematically guide my research, I structured it into the following sub-questions which I address in the subsequent chapters respectively:
- What do the evolution of AI, current applications, and central issues raised tell us about the societal power shifts triggered by these systems?
- How can insights from Science and Technology Studies (STS) inform an approach towards evaluating an individual AI system?
- How does a notion of capital help conceptualize the various forms of leverage that AI can embody?
- What dimensions are needed to articulate the configurations of assets that constitute AI's power shift?
- How can such a framework be applied to an AI system already deployed in the real world?
- How can this framework guide the design phase of an AI system?
- What are the stakeholder implications of introducing such an explanatory model?

Sharing a vocabulary of how AI affects us would be of significant impact. While the academic discipline of AI has a long, interdisciplinary history, the recent, rapid spread of its applications has received attention from numerous outside stakeholders, too. With my background in public policy, my interdisciplinary research attempts to engage with the computer science community as well as the social scientific community concerned with the study of technologies. Specifically, I propose to explore how AI reconfigures our social fabric by considering it through an influential perspective from across disciplines: the lens of capital. As I derive insights from differing approaches to AI, balancing interdisciplinarity throughout my doctoral work has proven challenging. A social scientific perspective requires reflexive considerations about the role of the researcher and the issues raised. Reflexivity itself necessitates a generally common ground of shared definitions. Certain terms, however, such as *environment, material features*, or even *bias*, have acquired different meanings in the computer science discipline and the social sciences. I thus took it as my task to be explicit, where necessary, about my chosen interpretations to clarify frames of reference. Navigating the research in a way that would result in the most useful contributions while bridging accessibility across fields was imperative. My overall aim is to develop a cohesive, interdisciplinary approach for developers, policy makers, business leaders, activists, and those who are affected to communicate so that all stakeholders can better anticipate the risks of AI systems and sustainably leverage their benefits.

1.3 Contributions

With these objectives and interdisciplinary ambitions in mind, my doctoral research offers four central contributions. First, I introduce my original concept of Code Capital and the concomitant framework of CODE. By examining the literature on technology studies on the one hand and the evolving interpretations of capital on the other, I arrive at the idea for Code Capital. It is novel because it synthesizes these two distinct fields to represent the range of socially embedded configurations inscribed into AI systems and expresses them through the four dimensions (C, O, D, E) of the framework. I define Code Capital as the account of an AI system's potential impact in bespoke circumstances, bringing to the fore its inherent normative forces.

As my second contribution, I present a case study on facial recognition technology (FRT) that demonstrates the applicability of the CODE framework to an already deployed AI system. As part of this study, I conducted an international survey on social acceptance of FRT in China, the US, Germany, and the UK together with a team of researchers. These empirical results contribute to the growing body of research that seeks to understand the adoption, implementation, and consequences of FRT. In addition to the other dimensions I explore, they form part of the practical application of Code Capital as an analytical tool.

Third, through a second case study on synthetic voice generation, I show the applicability of the framework as an instrument to anticipate and deliberately shape outcomes in the process of designing an AI system. As part of this study, I participated in the initial idea development for a text-to-speech technology called VocallyYours. This intimate involvement in combination with additional research allowed me to closely follow the emergence of the project and the decision-making along the way. As a whole, the case study shows the potential of Code Capital in the process of AI development.

Fourth, I draw conclusions about the useful implications of Code Capital as a concept and framework. I synthesize and illustrate how a more refined understanding of consequences can benefit various stakeholders. Given the current debate about the societal impact of AI systems, my contributions aim to bridge relevant disciplines and are of both theoretical and practical importance for entrepreneurs, computer scientists, policy makers, academics, and citizens.

Key concepts

Two terms throughout my thesis are important to define upfront: AI and, relatedly, AI systems. First, as I will detail in Chapter 2, artificial intelligence and its definitions have a storied history. In their seminal textbook on the topic, computer scientists Stuart Russel and Peter Norvig contrast and compare four different approaches to AI: acting humanely (Kurzweil et al., 1990; Rich et al., 2009), thinking humanely (Bellman, 1978; Haugeland, 1989), thinking rationally (Charniak, 1985; Salin & Winston, 1992), and acting rationally (Nilsson, 1998; Poole et al., 1998). Eventually they argue for the latter: AI, in their conception, is an attempt to build agents that take the best possible - or rational – action in a situation (Russell & Norvig, 2010, p. 2). While theirs is a common definition from a computer science perspective, my doctoral research takes on an interdisciplinary lens. As such, I consider AI to embody more than rational computational action alone. As will become clear through my argument, I consider AI to encompass social decisions and technical practices, norms and institutions, politics, psychology, and culture. As Microsoft researcher and co-founder of the AI Now Institute Kate Crawford writes: "Artificial intelligence is both embodied and material, made from natural resources, fuel, human labor, infrastructures, logistics, histories, and classifications. (…) In this sense, artificial intelligence is a registry of power" (Crawford, 2021, p. 8).

Second, as I have chosen the term "AI system" as the unit of analysis, it is important to clarify the distinctions between the notion of an AI *agent*, *application* and *system* as each refers to important, individual definitions in the realm of computer science. An *agent*, according to Russel & Norvig's definition, is the entity that perceives input through sensors and acts upon it through actuators (Russell & Norvig, 2010, p. 34). An *application* is a particular AI technology put to use. For example, facial recognition is an application of advanced image analysis algorithms. For the purpose of my research, I define an AI *system* as representing the deployment of an application – which includes the agent – within a particular context. That means it includes social infrastructures and human actors who choose certain material features to embed the AI in its specific environment, as well as those who interact with this embedding. Together, these configurations constitute what I define as the AI system as a whole.

1.4 Overview

Next, I outline both the mixed methods approach I chose for my research and the structure of my dissertation overall.

1.4.1 Methodology

Given the interdisciplinary perspective of my work, I employed a mixed methodological approach throughout my doctoral research. First, through a review of two distinct theoretical fields and their synthesis with the professional insights I have gained into numerous empirical examples of AI systems, I embedded and constructed my original framework. It is informed by the long-standing study of how humans influence the machines they make and vice versa, as well as the evolution of capital and its relation to digital technologies. As a journalist who covers emerging technologies and their socioeconomic implications, and as an innovation practitioner and entrepreneur leading processes of innovation with digital media, I was able to complement my theoretical thinking with practical experience.

Second, I enriched and adapted my framework based on the two case studies I conducted. As elaborated upon in Chapter 6, the first case study on facial recognition technologies (FRT) included a cross-cultural examination of social acceptance, a study I ran together with a team of co-researchers. While most examinations of FRT acceptance by the public had previously largely focused on one national setting at a time, our work covered four countries: China, Germany, the UK, and the US. As an online survey, our questionnaire was disseminated during August and September 2019. Conducted by a Berlin-based firm that cooperates with providers in each of the four countries, the survey employed a river sampling method, drawing both first-time and regular survey participants from a base of 1-3 million unique online users through mobile applications. Eventually, our survey reached respondents through more than 100 apps out of a network of over 40,000 participating partners resulting in a sample of 6,633 respondents from all four countries in total, sampled based on age, gender and region. More details on the methodology can be found in Chapter 6. We were able to derive several interesting insights from the empirical results that informed my understanding of the entire case study: For example, we found significant differences in citizens' perception of consequences due to the technology, which included privacy violations, discrimination, surveillance, convenience, efficiency, and security. While almost half of all

German and US respondents expect FRT to increase privacy violations, only about 1 in 3 of Chinese participants do. Meanwhile, perception of an increase in discrimination was low across the board, despite research showing that accuracy rates for FRT are significantly worse for vulnerable populations (Braca, 2017; Buolamwini & Gebru, 2018; Ngan & Grother, 2015; Scheuerman et al., 2019). Our ordered logit regressions with social acceptance of FRT used in public as our dependent variable and privacy threat perception, consequences of FRT, and national issue concerns as our independent variables, show that the interpretation of privacy threat is a strong and significant negative predictor of acceptance. This finding is statistically significant across all four countries and in each setting individually. In addition, a majority of respondents in all four countries expect FRT to increase security. This emphasizes that in the nations studied, the perceived main trade-off of FRT appears to be between security and privacy. Moreover, our analysis shows that the perception of terrorist threats is a significant positive predictor for acceptance of FRT in public across all four countries. Concerns about terrorist threats are influenced by media coverage and framing, which in turn affect the narrative of an AI system purported to help hold domestic terrorists accountable like the project I discuss in more detail in Chapter 6. Therefore, together with the aforementioned results, this insight was a point of great relevance for the case study. The particular results I present as part of Chapter 6 were partly published in a workshop presentation at the 2020 International Conference on Machine Learning (Steinacker et al., 2020) and the limitations I elaborate on in Chapter 8 were included in a conference paper at the 2020 International Communications Association (Steinacker et al., 2020). Additional results of the overall study were subsequently published in the Journal of Public Understanding of Science (Kostka et al., 2021b).

Third, for both case studies, I conducted semi-structured interviews with three key participants involved in each project. Generally, my approach to these interviews were based on grounded theory (Glaser & Strauss, 2017; Strauss & Corbin, 1998). Common methods for such qualitative work include coding and categorizing interview transcripts. Specifically, it meant discovering underlying meaning by inductive reasoning in the accounts given by my research subjects. Concepts like "accountability" or "anthropomorphization" thereby emerged from the data. Inspired by my further reading of sociomateriality, however, I also attempted to move beyond representational accounts to consider the interview as a relational practice in which the researcher, the research subject, and various material features find themselves in a dynamic of entanglement (Barad, 2007; Jones

& Jenkins, 2008; Kallinikos, 2010; Leonardi, 2011; Orlikowski & Scott, 2008; Pickering, 2010). Practically, this meant I endeavored to include the performativity of sociomaterial practices during the interview process (Bodén, 2013; Hultin, 2019). Given that these interviews occurred during lockdowns induced by the COVID-19 pandemic and across international borders, I was bound to conduct them remotely. Nonetheless, I tried to combine the conversations with an "ethnography of infrastructure" (Star, 1999), meaning a study of the details of material features, decisions, and practices. As Star writes, "many aspects of infrastructure are singularly unexciting (...) It takes some digging to unearth the drama inherent in system design creating" (Star, 1999, p. 377). As best I could, I included these aspects in my virtual encounters. For example, in interviews for Chapter 6, rather than relying on the theoretical recounting of my main interview subject, I directly engaged the creator of the project with the infrastructure of the system he had built: Together, we examined the website set-up, looked at parts of the code, and traced back the experience of manually verifying the results of automated clustering. In Chapter 7, I included participants' reactions to demo audio tapes of synthetic voices in my understanding of their representational accounts. Integrating such features into my qualitative research enabled me to consider my subjects in a situated material engagement (Barad, 2007) and better combine it with my own analysis of the material infrastructure.

1.4.2 Structure

Having introduced the problem and questions driving my research as well as the methods I used, I will structure the rest of my dissertation as follows. In Chapter 2, I set the background for my premise. In offering the history of the term and field of AI, I aim to show its interdisciplinary origins and internal points of contention. Through several examples, I also illustrate the broad range of impacts that AI systems in practice may exert and how they can shift power relations. I thereby show that AI systems have morphed into a tectonic shift of power and a central concern of developers, business leaders, policymakers, social scientists, and activists alike.

In Chapter 3, I ground my research within the sociological study of technology. My review of the literature chronicles the historical development from determinism to constructivism and outlines various approaches of evaluating the genesis and impact of technological artifacts and systems. This second chapter demonstrates that the invention, introduction, and integration of technology into society has consistently spurred debate about how the tools we make emerge to shape our reality. I situate my approach within a sociotechnical perspective that considers technology as socially embedded and constitutively entangled with sociomaterial factors.

Next, in Chapter 4, I explore the evolution of the term capital to understand it as a descriptor of asset arrangements that can turn into socioeconomic leverage. In adding a review of various notions of capitalism in the age of digital technologies, I show that AI systems have transformed the economy in several ways including means of production and dissemination, collective institutions and individual behaviors. A society driven by AI systems will become increasingly reliant on intangibles and immaterial capital forces. This chapter demonstrates that capital's development from a label for financial resources to a representation of wide-ranging influences resembles that of our grasp of technology's genesis and impact from an inevitable, physical force affecting society, to a socially enacted, socially acting set of configurations.

In Chapter 5, I combine my theoretical and empirical insights to introduce my original notion of Code Capital. I present both the concept overall and the analytical framework with its eponymous CODE acronym that entails the four dimensions: Conception, Operations, Data, and Environment. Two ways of employing the framework best clarify its analytical potential: First, it can be used to understand how the configurations of an already deployed AI system manifest as implications. Second, it can guide the design of a system in development by projecting potential effects offering trajectories to adjust the system. This chapter offers my synthesis of relevant interdisciplinary factors constituting an AI system into an original contribution of theoretical and practical utility.

In Chapter 6, I apply the CODE framework to a first case study, a project called FacesOfTheRiot, that involves facial analysis. I embed this examination in the context of the cross-country empirical study that I conducted together with a team of researchers on international variations in why technology used in public places to analyze facial features is socially accepted or rejected. Next, based on my own investigation and several interviews with key participants, I then consider the four dimensions of the framework to illustrate how the particular AI system of FacesOfTheRiot emerged and how its individual configurations interact to create impact. This chapter shows the applicability of Code Capital to provide a concrete, holistic understanding of the implications that flow from a tool used to assist law enforcement in prosecuting individual citizens and how this project raises questions of legality, privacy, accountability, and justice in relation to AI.

I use the second type of application for the framework in Chapter 7 by analyzing a project called VocallyYours, a text-to-speech technology. After contextualizing the efforts in the broader realm of voice synthesis, I examine the four dimensions of CODE based on interviews with key participants and my own analysis as an early member of the team who conceived of the project. With this case study, I show that the framework can serve as a design guide for the development of AI systems to anticipate if their impact aligns with their objectives and to better manage outcomes. By offering recommendations that could sway the trajectory of the system's consequences, I demonstrate that endeavors like VocallyYours must heed thresholds of consent, inclusion, and self-declaration to ensure that questions of identity, deception, bias and trust are treated with consideration.

Finally, in Chapter 8, I draw conclusions and synthesize the contributions of my work. I argue that if Code Capital becomes standard practice, we may develop a common ground of logic, analysis, and discussion for policymakers, business leaders, developers, activists, and citizens affected in the larger context of AI management.

1.5 Conclusion

In this chapter, I laid out the relevance, and objectives of my research, including its main goals, contributions, key concepts, methodology and structure. According to Stanford University's One Hundred Year Study on AI, "longer term, AI may be thought of as a radically different mechanism for wealth creation in which everyone should be entitled to a portion of the world's AI-produced treasures" (P. Stone et al., 2016, p. 8). The first half of my chapter surveyed the efforts to anticipate, regulate, and manage these AI-produced resources, including their beneficial and detrimental impacts. Evidently, several stakeholders consider this topic one of pertinence, including developers, scientists, business leaders, policymakers, and activists. Even those central actors who played a significant role in exploiting the unmitigated implications of AI systems have more recently called for oversight and improved management.

But a lack of conceptual cohesion, social contextualization, and multidimensional narratives about AI contribute to a significant gap: None of the current approaches consider holistically how AI systems emerge in the first place with human visions, priorities, operational decisions, labor efforts as well as environmental resources inscribed within them. In my doctoral work, I examine a more interdisciplinary, integrative, and proactive process of assessing how an AI system emerges and exerts impact. I explore how the social, technical, and material aspects of AI beget each other, which crystallizes the role for human actors to participate. I argue that only if developers, policy makers, business leaders, activists, and those voluntarily and involuntarily affected by AI systems can communicate about the capital of AI with a common ontology, we will have a sustainable future with the technology. In the following chapter, I begin by providing background to the history and status of AI systems today before I ground my work within the social study of technology in Chapter 3.

2. Background: Artificial Intelligence

"Whereas in science theories are expected to model reality,
in technology they are also tools for altering reality
– for better or for worse."
Mario Bunge
Social Science Under Debate, 1999

"What he had not realized is that extremely short exposures to a relatively
simple computer program could induce powerful delusional thinking in
quite normal people. (...) The computer programmer is a creator of universes
for which he alone is the lawgiver. (...) No playwright, no stage director,
no emperor, however powerful, has ever exercised such absolute authority to
arrange a stage or field of battle and to command such unswervingly dutiful
actors or troops."
Joseph Weizenbaum,
Computer Power and Human Reason, 1976

2.1 Introduction

Brief and ubiquitous as it is, the acronym of AI might suggest one clear definition. But the term itself and the field it represents have a storied evolution. In this chapter, I describe the interdisciplinary origins of AI,[13] and the broad range of societal arenas in which AI systems can have consequential impact. To further establish the context for my doctoral work, I aim to demonstrate that the sociotechnical forces of AI have transformed into tectonic shifts of power that have sparked the interest of stakeholders across sectors and industries.

---

13 It is beyond the scope of this dissertation to give a detailed, comprehensive historical account of all inventions and developments in this field, especially as many others, like Pamela McCorduck, have done so. My goal is to illustrate the interdisciplinary origins and long-standing human fascination with creating intelligent machines overall and give examples of the many influences and interpretations of the field.

2.2 A Brief History of AI

It all began with a fusion of numbers and poetry. In the first half of the 19th century, British mathematician and writer Ada, Countess of Lovelace, became the first person to publish the idea that a computing machine had potential beyond mere calculation through symbolic substitution (Fuegi & Francis, 2003). In her translation and review of an originally French article about the Analytical Engine, conceptualized by her collaborator Charles Babbage, Lovelace included insightful commentary on what she herself called "a new, a vast and powerful language (…) developed for the future use of analysis" (Menebrea & Lovelace, 1842, p. 23). Her integration of algorithmic instructions to be coded into the hypothetical engine was the first of its kind and became "a ground-breaking description of the possibilities of programming the machine to go beyond number-crunching to 'computing' in the wider sense" (Fuegi & Francis, 2003, p. 16). Yet Lovelace continuously proclaimed the superiority of human agency, calling the computer "not a thinking being, but simply an automaton which acts according to the laws imposed upon it" (Menebrea & Lovelace, 1842, p. 5). She later mused with an acquaintance that she planned to build a mathematical model for the emergence of thoughts in the brain and feelings spurred by nerves. While this idea is less discussed, it is perhaps of equal relevance for the emergence of the field of AI: In an uncanny prediction of the neural networks of the 21st century, Lovelace called it "a calculus for the nervous system" (Woolley, 2015, p. 305).

Even long before the 19th century, homo sapiens philosophized about and experimented with machinery to perform certain human-like tasks. "Ours is a history of self-imitation," writes Pamela McCorduck in *Machines Who Think*, "to the point of madness we have reproduced ourselves in the flesh" (McCorduck, 2004, p. 3). Indeed, as early as in *The Iliad*, Homer introduces the term "automaton" for several machines, made by the god Hephaestus, who endows them with human-like powers: "There is intelligence in their hearts, and there is speech in them and strength, and from the immortal gods they have learned how to do thing" (Lattimore & Baskin, 2011, p. 386). In the 13th century, Spanish theologian Roman Lull developed what he called the Ars Magna, a description of an apparatus to logically combine notions of knowledge to address questions of metaphysics, morals and even natural science. Lull, in turn, seems to have been inspired by an earlier version of a "thinking machine" called *zairja*, constructed by a group of Arab astrologers (McCorduck, 2004, pp. 10–11). Both were "based on the assumption that human thought could be mechanized" (McCorduck, 2004, p. 37). Gottfried Leibnitz wrote about the 'calculus ratiocinator', alternatively interpreted as a theoretical calculation framework or the logical foundation for and predecessor of the digital computer (Wiener, 2019). Later, fictional characters such as E.T.A. Hoffman's mechanical robot Olimpia in *The Sandman* (1967) and Mary Shelley's *Frankenstein* (1869) raised central questions about our relationship to inventions that might be called artificially intelligent.[14] The common denominator of all these accounts, whether fictional or theoretical, is their attempt to grasp and imitate the workings of the human mind through automatons. But indeed, it was Ada Lovelace who proved visionary in her imagination for machines' capacities, rendering her Notes "a description of a general-purpose computer and its potential that would not be superseded for a century" (Ferry, 2015, p. 1731).[15]

Galvanized by various war efforts, in the early 20th century, Germany, the United States, and the United Kingdom were each working to develop the most potent technologies, explicitly linking their endeavors to the construction of computing machines who could reason (McCorduck, 2004, p. 62). It was German engineer and computer scientist Konrad Zuse who built the Z4, the first commercial digital computer, and developed *Plankalkül*, the first high-level programming language that Zuse intended for solving not only mathematical but even symbolic problems (McCorduck, 2004, p. 61). Just a few years later, British cryptographer Alan Turing argued in his seminal paper *Computing Machinery and Intelligence* that a computer would one day be able to cognitively surpass humans (1950). Through what he termed 'the imitation game', Turing would become the namesake for the field's most influential and controversial threshold experiment to ostensibly identify an AI system: the Turing Test (Saygin et al., 2000). Around that same time, US computer scientist John McCarthy together with prominent colleagues convened the first conference on an emerging field that they termed "Artificial Intelligence" at Dartmouth

---

14 Incidentally, Shelley was inspired to write her story after a prompt to invent a scary narrative from none other than Lord Byron, the father of Ada Lovelace (McCorduck, 2004, pp. 20–21).

15 Through Lovelace's wit and sarcasm her notes clarify that these impactful considerations were her own instead of Babbage's: "Whether the inventor of this engine had any such views in his mind while working on the invention, or whether he may subsequently ever have regarded it under this phase, we do not know; but it is one that forcibly occurred to ourselves on becoming acquainted with the means through which analytical combinations are actually attained by the mechanism." (Menebrea & Lovelace, 1842, p. 21)

University. In their proposal, they declared that "an attempt will be made to find how to make machines use language, form abstractions and concepts, solve kinds of problems now reserved for humans, and improve themselves" (McCarthy et al., 2006). Directly afterwards, in the 1960s, several notable programs, like Joseph Weizenbaum's natural language processor ELIZA, heralded a new level of human-machine interaction. In retrospect, the Dartmouth Conference had coined a term in the academy that had grown out of centuries of international thought and invention, and out of mythology, philosophy, mathematics, psychology, and neuroscience (Russell & Norvig, 2010).

What followed first, however, was slow progress on both funding and advancement of AI technologies during periods in the 1970's through the early 1990's. Indeed, "AI remained an area of relative scientific obscurity and limited practical interest for over half a century" (Haenlein & Kaplan, 2019). This was partly due to hyperbolic expectations and frustrations with the speed of developments. But around the turn of the millennium, the pace picked up again due to numerous computational wins in gaming that signaled breakthroughs in machine learning, the central subset of AI techniques: In 1997, IBM's Deep Blue beat the human world champion in chess and in 2015 Google's AlphaGo defeated the internationally leading player in the more advanced game Go (Haenlein & Kaplan, 2019). Today, the exact interpretation of what qualifies as AI (and even as 'intelligence' itself) is still virulently debated.[16] Both the concept and myriad applications, however, are firmly embedded in the daily lives of billions of people around the world and "the fruits of the AI revolution are now all around us. (...) We are engaged in a permanent dance with machines, locked in an increasingly dependent embrace" (Levy, 2010).

In the next section, I illustrate the many applications and influential spheres of AI systems. Both mirror aspects of the field's past as described above in terms of their wide range and existentialism, as Pamela McCorduck summarizes:

> I like to think of artificial intelligence as the scientific apotheosis of a venerable cultural tradition (...). Sometimes we forget that most sciences began with ideas that seem a bit loony to us now but were sound enough in their own time. (...) We harbor that mysterious but ancient

---

16 While the vision of a hypothetical synthetic being able to successfully learn any human task in any given context is referred to as Artificial General Intelligence (AGI), the distinct type of diverse sociotechnical agents currently employed is considered Artificial Narrow Intelligence (ANI) (Pennachin & Goertzel, 2007).

urge to reproduce ourselves in some essential but extraordinary way. Artificial intelligence comes blessed with one of the richest and most diverting histories because it addresses itself to something profound and pervasive in the human spirit. (…) True to its speculative origins, artificial intelligence poses a set of grave moral questions while, true to its claims to be a science, it promises answers to puzzles about the nature of intelligence (McCorduck, 2004, pp. 34–35).

2.3 AI Systems Today

Several arenas have seen a surge of AI applications. Specifically, three factors have intensified their recent widespread integration into society: increasing data collection at scale, exponential computing capacity, and advanced algorithmic modeling (Miailhe, 2017; The Royal Society, 2017). Together, these developments [17] constitute "a profound change at the levels of epistemology and ethics, (…) (reframing) key questions about the constitutions of knowledge, the processes of research, how we should engage with information, and the nature and the categorization of reality" (boyd & Crawford, 2012, p. 665). According to Stanford University's Human-Centered AI Institute's Annual Report, global investment in AI in 2020 increased by 40 % relative to 2019 for a total of USD 67.9 billion (D. Zhang et al., 2021, p. 93). While AI systems are used in every sector and industry, the following illustrative examples encapsulate the ubiquity and their diverse functions in societal dynamics. Though all of these systems employ machine learning techniques and some even overlap in their method, for the purpose of structuring, I have categorized the examples into applications that serve to classify and predict, rank and recommend, and generate and alter. I chose these instances because they are noteworthy either due to the technological progress they represent or because of how they affect societal processes and relations – or both.

---

17 Some refer to the recent combination of increasing data volumes, computing power, and analytical techniques as the collective phenomenon of Big Data (Bollier, 2010; Manovich, 2011).

2.3.1 Classifications and Predictions

First, recent advances in machine learning techniques alter the course of scientific discovery, as they can simulate and predict biochemical structures and processes. For example, being able to determine the complex molecular structure of unique proteins allows inferences about many of their functions, a central challenge in biology known as the "protein folding problem". But experimentally examining how a protein might fold has taken up significant resources of time and money in the past. Instead, Google DeepMind's[18] AlphaFold used computational structure prediction (Senior et al., 2020). Trained on a publicly available dataset of 170,000 protein structures, its latest version AlphaFold 2, an attention-based neural network system, achieved a median score of 92.4 in the Global Distance Test when compared to the experimentally determined ones (DeepMind, 2020; Jumper et al., 2020). These improved methods of 3D prediction could accelerate the many crucial scientific endeavors in which molecular structures play a major role, such as drug discovery and protein design (Callaway, 2020). Similarly, during the worldwide response to the COVID-19 pandemic, several technological solutions emerged to support biochemical research efforts. As part of the COVID Moonshot initiative that crowdsources molecular designs from international scientists to accelerate the development of an antiviral, AI startup PostEra[19] offers machine learning capabilities to run simulations. These modeled routes for chemical synthesis may speed up the drug discovery process (D. Zhang et al., 2021, p. 77).

In another instance, similar algorithmic prediction models have begun to enter the realm of law enforcement. Known as 'risk assessments', they are designed to forecast the likelihood that a criminally charged individual will commit crimes in the future based on aggregated data of the past. While these recidivism prediction instruments have been used by judges in determining criminal sentencing, a 2016 investigation by the investigative journalism outlet ProPublica demonstrated that such predictions are surprisingly unreliable in forecasting future incidents and bear significant racial bias (Angwin et al., 2016). Moreover, in several countries the practice of 'predictive policing' has gained traction. A mixture of past criminal, geographic, and socio-structural information combines to simulate what locations are prone to become criminal hot spots and which individuals

---

18 https://www.deepmind.com
19 https://covid.postera.ai/

might become offenders or victims. Based on these calculated risk assessments, local law enforcement officials may adjust their policing strategies, deciding where to patrol, who to subject to surveillance, and who to target as a suspect. While in the US, such predictive tools may also incorporate "everything from minor crime reports to criminals' Facebook profiles" (Hvistendahl, 2016), German variants reportedly exclude any personal information related to individuals. Nonetheless, by 2016, a number of German cities reported employment of predictive policing tools (Hamann, 2016). In an instance of real-time event and risk detection, the AI company Dataminr[20] had detected and flagged a pattern of disconcerting social media posts through its big data analysis platform First Alert, which suggested potentially dangerous behavior to occur in Washington D.C. on January 6th, 2021 (Z. C. Cohen & Wild, 2021). While the exact models are often proprietary and confidential, evidence on whether such risk assessments in fact support crime reduction remains scarce (Hvistendahl, 2016). As human actors infer options for action from the predictions offered by AI systems, their impact in the context of justice is of very tangible individual and collective consequence.

Similar AI systems used in the sphere of education may affect the assessment of and access granted to students. When in 2020, the British government employed algorithmic prediction to make up for cancellations of high school exams during the COVID-19 lockdowns, the statistical model by the Office of Qualifications and Examinations Regulation (Ofqual)[21], designed to avoid grade inflation and teacher bias, automatically lowered the grades of almost 40 % of students compared to what their educators had anticipated. Notably, disadvantaged learners were more likely and wealthier ones less likely to be impacted (Adams & McIntyre, 2020). One father of an affected child called the skewed results "collective punishment by statistics" (Pidd, 2020).

2.3.2 Rankings and Recommendations

Various AI systems forecast consumer choices to create recommendations based on estimating ratings for items previously unseen by users (Adomavicius & Tuzhilin, 2005). For example, citizens around the world consult various search engines for information seeking and news consump-

---

tion. In Germany, Alphabet's Google[22] holds 83.97 % of the market share for desktop searches and 97.37 % of mobile searches (Statista, 2021). One survey found that 60 % of German internet users obtained their news content via Google (Statista, 2018). While the specific heuristics that define the Google ranking algorithm remain opaque, its sorting results can bear significant consequences for the reality of information distribution. What started mostly as a structured quantification of importance when Sergey Brin and Larry Page designed the algorithm (Page et al., 1998), now combines over 200 factors that determine a page's relevance and popularity. It crawls through troves of data to assign a prioritization value to those websites it deems applicable, relevant and of authority within the context of the search queries. An examination of 300 million clicks on various Google results concluded that the first result page attracted 91.5 % of clicks, with 32.5 % on the very first result, and the bottom item on the first page drawing 140 % more clicks than the first item on the second page (Chitika Insights, 2013). In this example, algorithmic priorities can transfer into attention currency. In addition to their informational distribution potential, such search rankings can have offline behavioural effects as shown by the 'search engine manipulation effect' (SEME). One analysis of five experiments in two countries found that biased search ranking displaying varying pieces of information about electoral candidates could shift the voting preferences of undecided voters by 20 % or more, concluding that search ranking biases can be masked so that participants show no awareness of manipulation (Epstein & Robertson, 2015).[23] Thus, while these AI systems contribute to a democratization of the access to knowledge, their algorithmically prioritized information reality may translate to considerable societal clout.

Likewise, recommendation platforms such as Yelp[24] sort restaurants, hotels, and activities. Underlying these rankings, AI models calculate relevance based on several factors with significant ramifications. One study found that a one-point improvement of a hotel's reputation on a five-point scale meant it could raise prices by 11 % without a reduction in bookings (C. Anderson, 2012). Another found that the marginal effect of a 1-star

---

22 https://www.google.com

23 Most poignantly, as the authors note, "these phenomena occur apparently because people trust search engine companies to assign higher ranks to the results best suited to their needs, even though users generally have no idea how results get ranked" (Epstein & Robertson, 2015, p. 1).

24 https://www.yelp.com

change on consumers' willingness to pay ranged from 7 %-17 % (Adomavicius et al., 2018).

Meanwhile, the music streaming platform Spotify[25] uses a combination of collaborative modeling, natural language processing, and convolutional neural networks to recommend highly personalized playlists for users (C. Johnson, 2015). A study of the platform found that listening behavior that followed these recommendations was correlated with reduced consumption diversity (A. Anderson et al., 2020).[26] Evidently, such AI-driven intermediaries "dramatically alter the relations between the firm and the customer" (Phillips et al., 2016, p. 21) by influencing the dynamic between those who supply, those who display and sort the supply, and those who demand.

Given the vast scale of some of the leading companies that algorithmically rank and recommend content, the particular composition of their underlying AI systems can carry significant effect. An audit of over 330,925 videos on Google's video streaming platform YouTube[27] demonstrated that users watched increasingly more extreme content (Ribeiro et al., 2020), supporting the hypothesis that its algorithmic recommendation engine may lead to socio-psychological radicalization (Tufekci, 2018). Similarly, as a major social network platform with 3 billion users worldwide, Facebook's[28] content optimization for engagement has had noteworthy consequences for what is prioritized in its Newsfeed as it favors content that humans are psychologically more prone to click on. During the 2016 U.S. election cycle this resulted in leading fake election news stories creating more overall engagement on the site than the top-performing election stories from 19 major news outlets combined (Silverman, 2016). Given the reach of its optimized Newsfeed, the company's January 2021 decision to ban a head of state from the platform for the first time and its oversight board's affirmative ruling on the ban in May of the same year "will have implications far beyond US politics (...). Tougher rules could now be looming for other politicians, too" (Delcker, 2021). Indeed, "Facebook's policy decisions often have outsized geopolitical and social ramifications, even though no one has elected or appointed Mark Zuckerberg and his

---

25 https://www.spotify.com

26 Another study of various top playlists that the platform curates itself showed that inclusion on such lists increases song stream volume by almost 20 million and equals between $116,000 and $163,000 in value (Aguiar & Waldfogel, 2018).

27 https://www.youtube.com

28 https://www.facebook.com

staff to run the world" (Halpern, 2021). As these examples show, the behavior of millions of users on such AI-driven platforms can translate into commercial value, socioeconomic reconfiguration, and shifts of intersocial relations and even democratic processes.

2.3.3 Generation and Alteration

Another set of AI systems has the capabilities to alter or generate digital artifacts. Specifically, GANs can create changed or entirely new media (Goodfellow et al., 2014). For example, the autoregressive language model GPT-3 employs deep learning on 175 billion parameters of data to generate novel text (Brown et al., 2020; Floridi & Chiriatti, 2020). One application of GPT-3, called Sudowrite[29], offers to compose original text passages as a continuation of individual user input. Its effects on the processes and jobs involving language could be significant; the model has been used to create texts ranging from medical descriptions to computer code to legal formulations (Sotala, 2020). Indeed, "the consequences are vertiginous. (...) Whatever field you are in, if it uses language, it is about to be transformed. The changes that are coming are fundamental to every method of speaking and writing that presently exists" (Marche, 2021).

In the realm of imagery, Nvidia's[30] StyleGAN uses deep learning frameworks to generate images of artificial faces (Karras et al., 2019, 2020), a feat used to create the website ThisPersonDoesNotExist[31], which showcases ostensible portraits of people who, in fact, are not real. Likewise, Adobe's Sensei[32] system creates synthetic video scenes indistinguishable from authentic footage to the human eye, eliminating or tweaking objects without visible trace, even changing the content of live feeds as they are streaming. The company touts that "it enables removing unwanted things from a video by imagining what would appear if these unwanted things were removed" (Adobe, 2017). Similarly, the project LostTapesOfThe27Club[33] used GANs to artificially produce entirely new songs, including melodies as well as vocals, in the style of musicians like Amy Winehouse and Kurt Cobain, who passed away years prior. Though the latter project was pur-

---

29 https://www.sudowrite.com
30 https://www.nvidia.com
31 https://www.thispersondoesnotexist.com
32 https://www.adobe.com/sensei.html
33 https://www.losttapesofthe27club.com

portedly developed to raise awareness of mental health concerns, these examples illustrate the potential wide-ranging impact of AI systems that can computationally edit or originate digital artifacts. For example, a rise in such synthetic media creation contributes to a phenomenon known as 'deepfakes' (Chawla, 2019; Fletcher, 2018; Maras & Alexandrou, 2019; Nguyen et al., 2019), distorting the distinctive lines between fact and fiction into a 'hybrid reality' (Meckel & Steinacker, 2021).

While by far not an exhaustive list, these three sets of examples illustrate that the technological functionalities of AI and the way humans have put them to use touch realms from medicine to law enforcement to hospitality, from the distribution of information to the creation of language, images, and audio itself.

2.4 Contextualizing Central Issues

In some respects, the epistemological frenzy surrounding AI mirrors that of previous technology trajectories: Investigations of the invention, introduction, and integration of new technologies over time have centered on the central questions of how the technology emerges and how it affects the human systems it is embedded in. Before I elaborate on the evolution of these approaches in Chapter 3, it is important to reiterate that the incorporation of AI techniques into so many societal realms constitutes some substantial shifts. AI systems can automate processes and unlock human discovery of complex phenomena, but they reconfigure several social dynamics in the process. While some have written about the specific ethical challenges raised by AI systems in fields such as health care (Char et al., 2020) or the military (Svenmarck et al., 2018), many others have analyzed aspects that cut across applications such as reproducing social biases (Zou & Schiebinger, 2018), excluding already vulnerable groups (Morris, 2020), and perpetuating privacy violations (Korolova, 2010). They, in turn, build on much social scientific research exploring similar issues with Big Data and digital technologies more generally (Bollier, 2010; boyd & Crawford, 2012; Davis, 2012; Van Hoof et al., 2007; Zimmer, 2010). To give a sense of the breadth and gravity of issues related to the societal reconfigurations brought about by AI systems, I will recapitulate three major ones discussed in the field.

First, instead of assuming neutrality, we must interrogate the "imagined objectivity" (Benjamin, 2019) of these systems. Algorithmic models are inscribed with values and priorities of their developers (Brey & Søraker,

2009; Friedman & Nissenbaum, 2017; Nakamura, 2013; Wiener, 1988). Even if unintended, they can inadvertently produce outcomes that disproportionately discriminate and can be diffuse and difficult to identify (Barocas & Selbst, 2016). This is exacerbated by the opacity of many AI systems, especially when applied to socially consequential processes such as credit card fraud detection or recidivism risk assessments (Burrell, 2016; Schermer, 2011). Drawing on theories of justice and empirical economics, some experts have called to center the analysis of AI systems on inequalities and the distribution of power, specifically asking: "Who gets to set the objective function and why?" (Kasy & Abebe, 2021, p. 580). While AI techniques are applied to categorize knowledge and forecast behavior – mechanisms that constitute individual and collective perceptions of reality and conceptualizations of the world (Floridi, 2014) – the many subjectivities and normative forces enshrined in AI systems must be investigated.

Second, as AI systems assist or execute decision-making processes that used to be conducted by human actors, questions of responsibility and liability for consequences are as of yet largely unresolved (Barfield, 2018; Tutt, 2017). Given that AI systems rely heavily on inductive inferences and correlations, traceability of exact causes for outcomes, especially for machine learning systems, becomes difficult (B. D. Mittelstadt et al., 2016). One study showed that people less readily considered an AI agent tasked to launch or cancel a missile strike to be embedded in social structures and thus applied different patterns of blame and moral judgment for its actions compared to those of a human decision-maker (Malle et al., 2019). On the one hand, international regulations about what constitutes unlawful actions taken or aided by AI systems are still work in progress. On the other hand, regardless of lawfulness, AI techniques are used in critical situations such as optimizing a power grid (Rudin et al., 2011), guiding an unmanned aerial vehicle in a military setting (De Swarte et al., 2019), and profiling suspects for arrests (Garvie, 2019; Perkowitz, 2021). It is essential to understand the configurations that might lead to unwanted outcomes in different contexts and how we assess responsibility and practice accountability, especially as AI systems are deeply entangled with social systems.

Third, the proliferation of AI systems has compounded and created socioeconomic divides. Key underlying business models have augmented the economic might of the AI industry, as "the 10 largest tech firms, which have become gatekeepers in commerce, finance, entertainment and communications, now have a combined market capitalization of more than $10 trillion. In gross domestic product terms, that would rank them as the world's third-largest economy" (Mozur et al., 2021). Even more significantly, one of the central assets of these business models – the performative measurement, governance, and valuation of user metrics (Birch et al., 2021) – represent a major information asymmetry between those whose data have been collected and those with decision-making authority (Tene & Polonetsky, 2013). Some AI systems "tread a fine line between supporting and controlling decisions" (B. D. Mittelstadt et al., 2016, p. 9), thereby challenging notions of privacy, choices and individual autonomy (Ananny, 2016). Given that, as intermediaries, AI systems reconfigure the relations between those who demand and supply, those who rule and are affected, the socioeconomic forces fueling and flowing from them must be taken into account.

Throughout my practical experience and academic research into various AI systems, I have come to understand the common thread linking several issues raised by their ubiquity to be one of power (Crawford, 2021; Kasy & Abebe, 2021). Their integration into several processes and relations endows AI systems with a set of assets – in the form of normative forces, operational choices, data asymmetries, and a social embedding – which can be turned into substantial influence in societal arenas. Interrogating how these assets come to be configured is at the heart of my doctoral research.

2.5 Conclusion

After demonstrating the relevance of my research focus in Chapter 1, I spent the previous sections of Chapter 2 tracing the interdisciplinary origins of AI and demonstrated humans' long-standing fascination with the vision of such machines. Three sets of examples then served to encapsulate the technological possibilities and societal applications of AI systems today. Finally, I synthesized and contextualized the major issues raised by much prior social scientific research. Given the lack of conceptual cohesion, social contextualization, and multidimensional narratives that I have identified surrounding their implications, my doctoral work builds upon substantial existing research efforts but examines AI systems through a new lens. It combines work from two different fields to capture the factors that lead to transformative power shifts. In Chapter 3, I will first ground my work in the social study of technology before turning to perspectives on capital as a form of power in Chapter 4.

3. Related Work: Technology Studies

*"To draw attention today to technological affairs
is to focus on a concern that is as central now
as nation building and constitution making were a century ago."*
Thomas Hughes
Technological Systems and Momentum Change, 1983

*"I take the boundaries between persons and machines to be discursively
and materially enacted rather than naturally effected and to be available,
for better and worse and with greater and lesser resistance, for refiguring."*
Lucy Suchman,
Sociomateriality, 2007

3.1 Introduction

Human history is as much about our species as it is about the tools we create. We originated the hammer, the printing press, electricity, the automobile, and mobile communication – and each changed us in turn. By the mid-20th century, technology, derived from the Greek *techne* ("art, craft") and *logia* ("word, speech") to denote a "discourse on the arts, both fine and applied", had crystalized to represent the processes, techniques, and instruments by which humans "(seek) to change or manipulate (their) environment" (Buchanan, 2005). Throughout history, the invention, introduction, and integration of new technologies into society has spurred debate about two central issues: the technology's genesis and impact (Kline, 2015). How do these devices come to be and how do they affect the human systems they are embedded in? With the recent rapid rise of AI systems and the widespread implications that I outlined in Chapter 1 and 2 these two questions have renewed urgency. AI technologies affect our lives in myriad ways. Yet researchers, policymakers, and practitioners strain to define a concrete understanding of how, specifically, these systems emerge to shape our reality. To make relevant forecasts for an AI's future trajectories and decisions about rules of engagement, we need a joint approach to such a sociotechnical system. First, it is important to understand the past course of technology analysis and to discern what aspects of previous approaches remain of particular analytical value when applied to AI. Such a review underlines how the discipline grew to appreciate the social embedding of technology creation and diffusion.

In this literature review, I survey how seminal theoretical perspectives in Science and Technology Studies have addressed the analysis of both genesis and impact of sociotechnical systems. Specifically, I discuss the overarching arguments and methods of Technological Determinism and the Social Study of Technology. I first explore how the former conceptualized technology as the driving force of history and society with intrinsic logic and impenetrable autonomy. Next, I trace back the constructivist lens on technology and assess the various characteristics of Actor Network Theory, Large Technical Systems, and interpretations of Sociomateriality. My goal is to show the evolving interpretations of how the social and the technical constitute each other, and how this dynamic influences a technology's impact. In closing, I synthesize those insights that most aptly inform my original concept and framework presented in this dissertation. In the next chapter, I then introduce the evolving definitions of capital and capitalisms to show that a similar development took place: over time, the appreciation of the social aspects of capital matured and the unfolding definition encompassed more holistically the ways in which it manifests as impactful.

3.2 Determinism vs Constructivism

This section outlines the major differences between determinist and constructivist approaches to evaluating the role of technology. While the former, largely speaking, considers technology to be the central authority shaping culture, the latter situates a technology's trajectory from invention to circulation within social structures and relations.

3.2.1 Technology as Trajectory

A much-debated Marx quote emerged as a pithy synopsis of Technological Determinism. In *The Poverty of Philosophy*, originally published in 1847, the German socialist revolutionary remarked: "The hand mill gives you society with the feudal lord; the steam-mill, society with the industrial capitalist" (K. Marx, 1971, p. 109). This oft-cited adage linked with other Marxian statements about the forces of production shaping the relations of society led a number of observers to challenge Marxism's famed descriptor as "economic determinism": They declared his theory of history as one of *technology* in the driver seat (Hansen, 1921; Ogburn, 1936; Burns, 1969; Heilbroner, 1967; Shaw, 1979). For the purpose of their analyses, proponents appear to equate Marx's "material productive forces" with the collective concepts of modern day technology (Kline, 2015) and to attribute to them "powers that (border) on idolatry" rendering technology "an autonomous agent of social change" (L. Marx, 1994, p. 237).

Disciples of what became known as Technological Determinism fall along a spectrum of hard and soft extremes (L. Marx & Smith, 1994, p. xii). Even those with some interpretive reservations surmise that Marx saw in technology "the *primary independent variable* [emphasis added] active in all of history" (Winner, 1977, p. 79). In their 1994 reader *Does Technology Drive History?* Leo Marx and Merritt Roe Smith summarized the wide-ranging ramifications of this theory at its extreme:

> Society as a whole becomes increasingly dependent on large, intricately interrelated technical systems. The whole network – a system of systems, or a megasystem – becomes the indispensable technological armature of the economy. Its continued functioning is a precondition for the reproduction of the entire social order (1994, p. xi).

At least four renditions of Technological Determinism can be identified (Kline, 2015). Bimber distinguishes between Norm-Based Accounts, Logical Sequences Accounts, and Unintended Consequences Accounts (1990); Fischer adds the Impact-Imprint model (1994). Purveyors of a normative approach assert that society abdicates too much political, ethical, and social power to the logic and objectives – or "ideology" – of efficiency and productivity, promoted by technologists who pursue the "rationalization of the conditions of life" (Habermas, 1970, p. 57; Ellul, 1904). Technology is a force autonomous in its advance and deterministic in its influence then, "when the norms by which it is advanced are removed from the political and ethical discourse," when its goals "become surrogates for value-based debate over methods, alternatives, means and ends," and when "society (has) adopted a hegemonic cultural mind-set" (Bimber, 1990, p. 337).

By contrast, Logical Sequences Accounts focus on the progression and explicit impact of technological advancement on cultural and social change (G. A. Cohen, 1978; Miller, 1984). In essence, they claim that there is a fixed sequence to, first, how a particular technology develops and, second, how it "imposes a determinate pattern of social relation on (...)

society" (Heilbroner, 1967, p. 340). Notably, while the normative approach is based on the potency of social practices, this latter perspective affords machines an "internal technological logic which is independent of cultural factors" (Bimber, 1990, p. 339). Indeed, Heilbroner labels technology "a mediating factor" of history, which takes the form of "an autonomous process, "mysteriously" generated by society and thrust upon its members in a manner as indifferent as it is imperious" (Heilbroner, 1967, p. 345).

Thirdly, Bimber's definition of Unintended Consequences Accounts includes those that consider the grave implications of technology that transpire "unsought and uncontrolled" (Bimber, 1990, p. 339). According to this interpretation, these effects, neither planned nor foreseen, occur outside of the authority of human will. Similarly, while Langdon Winner does not subscribe to a framework of technological change as "a law-bounded process grinding to an inevitable conclusion" (Winner, 1977, p. 88), in his seminal work *Autonomous Technology* he describes unantici- pated ramifications of technical innovations as inimical to the notions of "choice" and "control" in a democracy: "Societies face the distinct possibil- ity of going adrift in a vast sea of 'unintended consequences'" (Winner, 1977, p. 89).

Lastly, Claude Fischer criticizes as the Impact-Imprint Model the notion that physical characteristics and capabilities of a technology translate to predictable, one-dimensional socio-cultural effects – that they are imprint- ed onto their users (1994). Rather, he argues, the variation in uses of technology matters, so the same qualities can result in differing implica- tions. Thereby, he specifically denounces "billiard ball" approaches, a term from William Ogburn, in which "a technological development rolls in from outside and 'impacts' elements of society, which in turn 'impact' one another" (Fischer, 1994, p. 8).

Since its inception, both semantic and theoretical discourse about Tech- nological Determinism has abounded. First, the underlying reading of Marx is vehemently contested. Inferring little to no human influence on the course of social change through technology overlooks the fact that Marx himself includes labor power – of humans – in defining forces of production. In response to Heilbroner's affirmative *Do Machines Make History?* (1967), MacKenzie concluded that labor power explicitly signals "conscious human agency as a determinant of history" and thus "it is people, as much as or more than the machine, that make history" (1984, p. 477). Indeed, CJ Arthur, editor of the 1970 edition of *The German Ideology*, goes so far as to clarify in the introduction:

> To treat such historical developments as though they were nothing but the passive reflection of an autonomous technological development is to fall into the most simplified and vulgar kind of evolutionism. Quite clearly, in the Marxist analysis of revolutionary change, the essential point is that reference has to be made to class struggles, political conflict, and ideological arguments. The revolution itself may well be the precondition of a subsequent flowering of technology (K. Marx & Engels, 1970, p. 34).

Second, in addition to disputing its controversial Marxist underpinnings, scholars have sought to disprove or refine both aspects of Technological Determinism: They have challenged the assertion about a fixed, internal technical logic, as well as the prescribed social impact claim (Bimber, 1990; Kline, 2015). While the subsequent rise of the Social Construction of Technology produced a number of case studies challenging the technical definition (see below), various champions of Technological Determinism themselves avow concessions with regards to society's role in it. Langdon Winner professes that "patterns of technology are themselves largely influenced by the conditions of the societies in which they exist" (1977, p. 76). Heilbroner acknowledges that "an independent 'social' element unavoidably enters the scene in the *design* of technology (...). In this way the machine will reflect, as much as mold, the social relationships of work" (Heilbroner, 1967, p. 342). Meanwhile, the impact part of the equation remains heavily debated. Heilbroner's final point appears prescient regardless of theoretical conviction:

> What seems certain (...) is that the problem of technological determinism – that is, of the impact of machines on history – will remain germane until there is forged a degree of public control over technology far greater than anything that now exists (1967, p. 345).

3.2.2 Technology in Context

Partly as a critical response to Technological Determinism, in the 1970s, the Social Study of Technology emerged out of the Sociology of Scientific Knowledge and the History of Technology. Inspired by Berger und Luckmann's seminal 1966 *The Social Construction of Reality* and most widely known as Science and Technology Studies (STS), the approach has emphasized the reciprocal effects of the social environment on both the design and usage of technological artifacts and vice versa. Two works in particular initiated what Steve Woolgar termed sociology's "turn to technology" (1991): First, Donald MacKenzie and Judy Wajcman's 1985 *Social Shaping of Technology* argued that to understand the survival and success of certain technologies compared to others, it is vital to examine the effect of the social world around them. Against determinism's "limited set of options: uncritical embracing of technological change, defensive adaptation to it, or simple rejection of it," they considered the core of STS to be

> a belief that the content and direction of technological innovation are amenable to sociological analysis and explanation. (...) It rejects the notion that technology is simply the product of rational technical imperatives; that a particular technology will triumph because it is intrinsically the best (Wajcman, 2002, p. 351).

In 1987, Wiebe Bijker, Thomas Hughes, and Trevor Pinch's *The Social Construction of Technological Systems* outlined three major approaches within STS: First, integrated social constructivism focuses on the evolution of a technological artifact itself. This approach argues that physical objects of innovation are not explanations of social phenomena in and of themselves; instead, objects need to be analyzed within their social world. As Pinch and Bijker put it: "The success of an artifact is precisely what needs to be explained. For a sociological theory of technology it should be the explanandum, not the explanans" (1987, p. 24). As they delineate three stages of analysis, they draw, on the one hand, on concepts from the Empirical Program of Relativism, a school of thought examining the social construction of scientific knowledge including their open interpretability (Collins, 1981). On the other hand, they draw on the Social Construction of Technology, which states that "the developmental process of a technological artifact is (...) an alternation of variation and selection" (Pinch & Bijker, 1987, p. 28). According to Pinch & Bijker, the first phase of constructivist analysis recognizes "the interpretive flexibility of technolog ical artifacts" (1987, p. 29) and investigates the varied options, selected and unselected, that led to their cultural construction through design and adoption. This exposes "a 'multidirectional' model, in contrast with the linear models used explicitly in many innovation studies and implicitly in much history of technology" (Pinch & Bijker, 1987, p. 28). To understand why some interpretive options are chosen over others, the constructivist approach considers the relevant social groups associated with the artifact. Pinch & Bijker define this concept as "institutions (...) or unorganized groups of individuals" where all members "share the same set of meanings, attached to a specific artifact" (1987, p. 30). These could be but are not limited to consumers, users, producers, or opponents of an innovation. Their significance as a group is due to the crucial role they play in defining the "problem" that the technological artifact ostensibly seeks to solve. Notably, the authors acknowledge that "this is also where aspects such as *power* or *economic strength* [emphasis added] enter the description, when relevant" (Pinch & Bijker, 1987, p. 34).

After this first step of analyzing the interpretive flexibility of a technological artifact according to the relevant social groups and the problems they define, the next phase considers "the role that different closure mechanisms may play in the stabilization of technological artifacts" (Pinch & Bijker, 1987, p. 40). Closure of a so-called problem can either occur through rhetorical means – for example through marketing claims that the problem has been addressed by the artifact – or through redefinition of the problem itself (Pinch & Bijker, 1987, p. 44). The third and last stage of their analysis is "to relate the content of a technological artifact to the wider sociopolitical milieu" including norms and values (Pinch & Bijker, 1987, p. 46).[34]

3.2.2.1 Actor-Network-Theory

A second approach to STS, Actor-Network Theory, was significantly developed by Madeleine Akrich, Michel Callon, Bruno Latour, and John Law. One of its core concepts is the assumption that any component of a system – actors, artifacts, or institutions – is made up of a "heterogeneous network" of nature and society and that any study of a system must uncover and analyze the relations between such "network complexities" (Law, 2001, pp. 858–859):

> Instead of thinking in terms of surfaces – two dimensions – or spheres – three dimensions – one is asked to think in terms of nodes that have as many dimensions as they have connections. (...) ANT claims that modern societies cannot be described without recognizing them as having a fibrous, thread-like, wiry, stringy, ropy, capillary character that is never captured by the notions of levels, layers, territories, spheres, categories, structures, systems (Latour, 2017, p. 370).

---

34 In 1992, as a follow-up volume to the 1987 group effort, Bijker and Law edited *Shaping Technology, Building Society* to expand on some of the previous concepts .

As part of this conception, ANT demands that each aspect of the network, whether human or not, deserves the same type of analysis, an idea the authors call the "principle of generalized symmetry" (Law, 1987). Applied to technological analysis, it considers a machine "a set of roles played by technical materials but also by such human components as operators, users and repair-persons" (Law, 2001, p. 858). This agnostic non-distinction between human and machines is the most noteworthy analytical feature of ANT. One common criticism leveled against it is that "because ANT treats humans and non-humans on the same footing, (…) it does not pay attention to such distinctively human and apparently subjective factors as cultures and practices" (Sismondo, 2009, p. 71). Moreover, although proponents of ANT proclaim to concern themselves with "the mechanics of power" (Law, 2001, p. 854), the approach has been arraigned for ignoring structural inequalities and the social categories that typically accompany power analysis among human actors such as race, class, and gender (Sovacool & Hess, 2017).

A second core ANT concept is that of the reciprocal influence of agency and structure, each exerting a detectable effect on each other. It leads to the ANT definition of an *actant* as any entity that generates such noticeable impact – again including human and non-human objects (Law, 1987). The approach recognizes the social aspects of how a technological artifact comes into being, as Madeleine Akrich puts it: "Many of the choices made by designers can be seen as decisions about what should be *delegated* to a machine and what should be left to the initiative of human actors. In this way the designer expresses the scenario of the device in question – the script out of which the future history of the object will develop" (Akrich, 1992, p. 216). Moreover, it acknowledges the power of such decisions based on both technical and social visions:

> Engineers who elaborate a new technology as well as all those who participate at one time or another in its design, development, and diffusion constantly construct hypotheses and forms of argument that pull these participants into the field of sociological analysis. Whether they want to or not, they are transformed into sociologists, or what I call *engineer-sociologists* [emphasis added] (Callon, 1987, p. 83).

And yet in contrast to some other ANT case studies, John Law has specifically advocated a move away from the focus on extraordinary individuals (e.g. inventors) and instead argued for integrating a larger understanding of the network surrounding them: "Napoleons are no different in kind to small-time hustlers, and IBMs to whelk-stalls[35]. And if they are larger, then we should be studying how this comes about – how, in other words, size, power or organization are generated" (Law, 2001, p. 854). Similarly dislodging designers as the sole determinant of a technology's impact, Akrich's work focused on their role in the development of technical objects in conjunction with the role of users. Specifically, her field studies have illustrated the impact developers wield through the "scripts", or visions of future use, that they "inscribe" into the technical content of a device, and how these in turn are adopted or denied by the behavior of users:

> If we are interested in technical objects and not in chimera, we cannot be satisfied methodologically with the designer's or user's point of view alone. Instead we have to go back and forth continually between the designer and the user, between the designer's projected user and the real user, between *the world inscribed in the object* and *the world described by its displacement*. For it is in this incessant variation that we obtain access to the crucial relationships: the user's reactions that give body to the designer's project, and the way in which the user's real environment is in part specified by the introduction of a new piece of equipment (Akrich, 1992, pp. 208–209).

Akrich's argument underlines "the obduracy of objects", a notion of irreversibility that is "established in the confrontation with users" (Akrich, 1992, p. 207) and stabilizes over time. Or as Latour has articulated: "Technology is society made durable" (Latour, 1990). Overall, ANT's analytical process provides the notion of a network assemblage that focuses "on the relational aspects among engineers, inventors, analysts, politicians, artifacts, manufacturing techniques, marketing strategies, historical context, economics and social and cultural factors" thereby highlighting that "technology emerges and diffuses through an interstitial milieu of material objects and immaterial epistemologies" (Sovacool & Hess, 2017, p. 720).

3.2.2.2 Large Technical Systems

A third seminal STS approach is historian Thomas Hughes' structure-centered theory of Large Technical Systems (LTS). It has been dubbed the

---

35 This is a British term referring to "the simplest task or enterprise" (Tréguer, 2018).

"social science systems approach" due to its "non-engineering version" of sociotechnical analysis (Hirsh & Sovacool, 2006). In his 1983 *Networks of Power: Electrification in Western Society*, Hughes laid out the case for understanding technological enterprises beyond their engineering framework as a combination of technical feats and social factors, as "heterogenous professionals and organizations" that become "interacting entities in systems (...) as if they are part of a seamless web" (Hughes, 1986, p. 282). This signified a move from "internalist" historical accounts of technologies whose chronological narrative, like deterministic approaches, failed to properly embed innovations in their social, political, and economic context. Hughes sought to counteract this by neither merely describing the emergence of technologies nor explaining a range of circumstantial categories, but by more accurately investigating "if context constructs content, if content shapes context, or if there is an interaction" (Hughes, 1986, p. 283). An LTS lens, he argued, presents an "interactive model" best equipped to understand technological systems by replacing a perspective of "inside and outside, content and context, and the hierarchical, or dependency, relationship" (Hughes, 1986, p. 285) with one recognizing that „technological systems contain messy, complex, problem-solving components. They are both socially constructed and society shaping" (Hughes, 1987, p. 51). Throughout, he emphasized the need to contrast and compare successful innovations with cases where innovation was expected but did not occur.

Fundamentally, LTS recognizes a system as a "seamless web" made up of components that are "under a central control and interact functionally to fulfil a system goal, or to contribute to a system output" (Hughes, 1986, p. 287). If any individual component fails, so would the system goal. Hughes' systems metaphor "stresses the importance of paying attention to the different but interlocking elements of physical artifacts, institutions, and their environment and thereby offers an integration of technical, social, economic, and political aspects" (Bijker et al., 1987, p. 5). Within this structure, system builders – ie., those holding centralized power over various components – form one of LTS' main analytical categories, bearing similarities to Law's notion of "heterogeneous engineers" (Law, 1987). Systems are "cultural artifacts" that "embody the physical, intellectual, and symbolic resources of the society that constructs them," so technology represents "both causes and effects of social change" (Hughes, 1983, p. 2). For example, in his analysis of large-scale electricity systems, the considerations and decisions of critical individuals that influenced the nature of the system – engineers, inventors, managers, financiers, consultants – feature prominently. Hughes found a "holistic vision", a "drive for integration and synthesis" and "controlling aspirations" in system builders to be vital factors of success (Hughes, 1986, p. 286).

Secondly, borrowing a military term for a backward protrusion in a line of battle, Hughes popularized the notion of *reverse salients*, "those components in an expanding system in need of attention, such as drag, limits to potential, emergent friction, and systemic efficiency" (Hughes, 1987, p. 73). A reverse salient can then be reformulated "as a set of critical problems, which when solved will correct it" (Hughes, 1987, p. 74). Hughes considers these points of conflict vital to the LTS approach as they might point to a system's conservatism versus a more radical innovation: "When a reverse salient cannot be corrected within the context of an existing system, the problem becomes a radical one, the solution of which may bring a new and competing system" (Hughes, 1987, p. 75). In one LTS analysis of the mobile music business in Japan and Korea, the authors identified copyright management institutions as what they called a "social reverse salient" (Takeishi & Lee, 2005).

Another core LTS concept is that of momentum, the impetus shaped by "business concerns, government agencies, professional societies, educations institutions, and other organizations" to create a "perceptive rate of growth or velocity" and, in a more established system, provide "an inertia of directed motion" (Hughes, 1983, p. 15). This LTS version of path dependency differs to the inevitable trajectory of determinism because momentum can be affected by "a confluence of contingency, catastrophe and conversion" (Hughes, 1989, pp. 470–471) and, importantly, "human stakeholders play important roles in channeling momentum" (Hirsh & Sovacool, 2006, p. 82). Indeed, LTS does not consider evolving systems as "driverless vehicles carrying society to destinations unknown and perhaps undesired" (Hughes, 1983, p. 462). Instead, "though they may not always realize the consequences of their actions – contributing to forces that alter momentum in unanticipated ways – people remain at the core of technological systems because of their concern for political control, influence, money, and power" (Hirsh & Sovacool, 2006, p. 82).

Finally, according to the LTS approach, systems evolve through a number of phases (Joerges, 1988). First, an invention proceeds through development, ideally culminating in an innovation put to use. Second, during the transfer to a different context it may change its contours, also known as its technological style, "the widely varying shape 'one and the same' technology takes under different geographical, political, legal and historical conditions" (Joerges, 1988, p. 12). In the third phase the innovation experiences periods of growth and faces competition, which leads to consolidation. While at outset the central system builders are "technical inventor-entrepreneurs", in the later stages, "manager-entrepreneurs" and "financier-entrepreneurs" become more dominant (Joerges, 1988, p. 13).

With this model, Hughes encapsulates an examination of the identifiable actors that shape technological systems and their structural features and conflicts. Hirsh and Sovacool have summarized the LTS understanding of technological emergence as follows: "Systems develop through human managers' control of elements to exploit the existing social environment. Systems acquire momentum, and they resist alteration as they mature" (2006, p. 73). Evidently, the metaphorical bases of ANT and LTS bear manifold similarities. Their main difference appears to lie in the overarching unit of analysis:

> A system (...) has an environment – a remaining outside – that a network does not. The organizers of networks leave nothing outside (...) that would affect the network. In systems, the environment is made up of influences and forces that affect, and are affected by, the system, but are not controlled by it (Hughes, 1986, p. 290).

This points to a fundamental distinction in understanding the world outside of the technological system to be analyzed and therefore its potential power: An acknowledgement that even for system builders some forces remain ungovernable.

The approaches outlined in Section 3.2.2 above gave rise to an understanding of sociotechnical systems. The definition of such an assemblage is best encapsulated by Hughes' summary that these systems "are both socially constructed and society shaping" (Hughes, 1987, p. 51).[36] As the next section shows, more recent STS scholarship has evolved from an analytical frame of the sociotechnical to the sociomaterial, with a focus on entanglement that implies they are inextricably linked.

---

36 As a discipline, sociotechnology is described mainly as a way for problem-solving. More specifically, it refers to the study of how to affect social systems through technology: "(It) studies ways of maintaining, repairing, improving, or replacing existing social systems (...) and processes (...); and it designs or redesigns social systems and processes to tackle social issues (...). Whereas science (...) studies the world, technology devises ways to change it: it is the art and science of getting things done in the most efficient way. If preferred, technology devises rational ways of leaping from *is* to *ought*. (...) In particular, whereas in science theories are expected to model reality, in technology they are also tools for altering reality – for better or for worse" (Bunge, 1999, pp. 297–298).

3.3 Towards Sociomateriality

This section illustrates the theoretical evolution of STS towards sociomateriality, explains its dissolution of the boundaries between the social and the material, and how this approach impels analysis of technology to include material features and considerations of social practice.

3.3.1 Material features

When STS intersected with organizational studies, a greater appreciation began to emerge for the activities that gave meaning and utility to technological artifacts (Orlikowski et al., 1996) and how their individual configurations allowed for certain interactions (DeSanctis & Poole, 1994; Orlikowski, 2000). Specifically, research began to examine an object's "material features", or "those hardware and software components that make them recognizable as "technological artifacts" (Leonardi, 2007, p. 813). Describing these properties as material grew particularly important with the rise of software-based technologies, as in the digital realm it became "much more difficult to isolate the materials out of which a technology is built", because

> Most information technology artifacts like computer programs and various software applications (…) have no physicality. Such information technological artifacts may be accessible through certain technological artifacts that have physical properties – that are made of identifiable materials (e.g., a computer program is accessible to users through a monitor and keyboard) but the physical properties of the artifacts that serve as "bearers" (Philip Faulkner & Runde, 2011) for the non-physical artifact do not change the composition of that non-physical artifact in any real way (Leonardi, 2012, p. 28).

Simply put, intangible configurations of digital technologies can have very tangible consequences. By deciding to choose certain features over others, technicians may "activate" certain capabilities, and thereby "(transform) the potential that the technology (has) to create, modify, transmit, and store information" (Leonardi, 2007, p. 813). Importantly, materiality in this sense does not equal physicality, but rather "the ways (…) digital materials are arranged into particular forms that endure across difference in place and time and are important to users" (Leonardi, 2012, p. 31).

As Leonardi points out, to be of analytical value, material features have to be those factors that endure in some capacity. But only temporarily, as they constitute properties of a sociotechnical system that can be rearranged. Like Orlikowski writes,

> Technologies are (…) never fully stabilized or "complete", even though we may choose to treat them as fixed, black boxed for a period of time. By temporarily bracketing the dynamic nature of technology, we assign a "stabilized-for-now" status (…) to our technological artifacts. This is an analytical and practical convenience only, because technologies continue to evolve, are tinkered with (e.g., by users, designers, regulators, and hackers), modified, improved, damaged, rebuilt, etc. (Orlikowski, 2000, pp. 411–412).

If materiality, then, highlights those malleable but temporarily enduring features that affect what actions are easily achievable with a technology, sociomateriality emphasizes its reciprocal relation to social processes: Materiality is both made by and affects social context, a point already similarly explored in detail in Section 3.2.2. Just how closely they are theorized to be linked and affect each other is examined in the next section.

3.3.2 Constitutive Entanglement

Inspired by ANT as well as feminist scholarship on technology (Adam, 2006; Hayles, 2008; Kember, 2003), the boundaries between the social and the material influencing each other as two distinct entities has begun to blur. In her groundbreaking work on sociomateriality, Barad, for example, emphasizes that the boundaries between the two sides are neither predetermined nor rigid, but instead exist only in active relation to each other:

> What often appears as separate entities (and separate sets of concerns) with sharp edges does not actually entail a relation of absolute exteriority at all. Like the diffraction patterns illuminating the indefinite nature of boundaries—displaying shadows in "light" regions and bright spots in "dark" regions—the relation of the social and the scientific is a relation of "exteriority within." This is not a static relationality but a doing—the enactment of boundaries—that always entails constitutive exclusions and therefore requisite questions of accountability (…). I offer an elaboration of performativity (…) that allows matter its due as an active participant in the world's becoming, in its ongoing "intra-activity" (Barad, 2003, p. 803).

By drawing on insights from quantum physics and Judith Butler's sem-inal theory of *performativity*, which refers to the social enactment of gender identities through speech and non-verbal communication (Butler, 1997, 2021), Barad outlines her interpretation of the relationship between practices and phenomena, a philosophical account she terms "agential realism" (Barad, 2007). She proposes that no entity precedes an interaction. Rather, only through intra-actions, meanings become determinate, and beings turn material. In essence, Barad argues two things: First, that tech-nological artifacts "become" only when used in social practice. Specific ac-tivities influence the configuration and refiguring of the human-machine relationship. Suchman refers to such practices as "situated actions", mean-ing actions "taken in the context of particular, concrete circumstances" (Suchman, 1987, p. viii). As she puts it: "I take the boundaries between persons and machines to be discursively and materially enacted rather than naturally effected and to be available, for better and worse and with greater and lesser resistance, for refiguring" (Suchman, 2007, p. 12).

It should be noted that practice, in the tradition of social theorists such as Giddens (1984) and Bourdieu (1977) is "not equivalent to individual activity (e.g. doing something); practice is a socially shaped arena in which activities are collectively negotiated" (Leonardi, 2012, p. 35).

Second, scholars following this interpretation of sociomateriality suggest that different aspects of a sociotechnical system cannot be separated from each other, as their existence is integrally intertwined:

> The social and the material are *constitutively entangled* in everyday life.
> A position of constitutive entanglement does not privilege either hu-mans or technology (in one-way interactions), nor does it link them through a form of mutual reciprocation (in two-way interactions). Instead, the social and the material are considered to be inextricably related – there is not social that is not also material, and not material that is not also social (Orlikowski, 2007, p. 1437).

Nonetheless, a sociomaterial approach, too, engages in analysis of these entangled notions of the social and the material. Such moments of obser-vation are called "agential cuts" that enact temporary separability between subject and object, between the social and the material (Barad, 2007, p. 175). This is where some nuance arises between the extent to which proponents of sociomateriality consider the social and the material to be inseparable: In Leonardi's critical realism, as opposed to Barad's agential realism, the social and the material become entangled through human and material agency in a process he terms "imbrication" (Leonardi, 2011).

When these agencies are imbricated with each other through sociomaterial practice, a technology becomes an empirically observable entity.

As the internal debate among the community of sociomaterial theorists shows (Hultin, 2019; Leonardi, 2012; Mutch, 2013), a complete fusion of the two aspects can be difficult to be put into research practice: In interviews as in observation it can prove difficult to entirely separate the social and the material. Adopting a research approach grounded in sociomaterial practice has epistemological implications. First, it assumes that as researcher, one is not just observer but constitutive part of a phenomenon. Second, it assumes that the choice of research practices do not reveal reality, they themselves enact it (Barad, 2003; Hultin, 2019). It means that a relational sociomaterial perspective considers epistemology inseparable from ontology, something Barad has called onto-epistemology (Barad, 2007). A number of researchers have reported practical difficulties in adopting a sociomaterial approach grounded in Barad's agential realism (P. Faulkner & Runde, 2012; B. Mueller et al., 2016; Wagner et al., 2010).

But bringing materiality into the process, for example by asking participants to actively engage with material features while explaining their thoughts and intentions, can sharpen the focus on "materially felt consequences of entangled patterns and how such consequences ripple across circumstances to enact transformation or variation" (Pomerantz & Raby, 2020, p. 6). In effect, this helps the researcher to trace the genealogy (Butler, 1997; Foucault, 1984) meaning "to account for how certain practices and categories, (…) have become enacted as appropriate and legitimate, and ultimately taken for granted over time" (Hultin, 2019, p. 97). Overall, taking a sociomaterial understanding into consideration while doing research means including an appreciation of that enactment of a particular set of activities that meld materiality with institutions, norms, discourses, and all other phenomena we typically define as "social" (Leonardi, 2012, p. 34).

3.4 Discussion

Reviewing the evolving literature of how research has made sense of the genesis and impact of technologies and how the social and the technical relate to each other crystalizes some central disagreements as well as some crucial overlaps. A number of these insights are of great analytical value when considering the role of digital technologies as sociotechnical systems. In this concluding section, I synthesize the main ideas shared by some of these approaches, which I consider crucial for an assessment of AI's implications. They are firmly situated within the Social Study of Technology, as I derive from the more recent literature a clear understanding of the reciprocal effects of the social and the technical. Previous research also clarifies that to understand a system's ramifications requires an examination of how it has been configured. In short, an impact assessment must necessarily include an analysis of how the technology has come to be manifested. The factors that follow are those that contribute to the system and thus constitute its impact.

3.4.1 Relevant actors

One clear similarity among the STS approaches is their focus on pertinent actors that shape the technological artifact. These should include a range of relevant social groups (Pinch & Bijker, 1987), who, through their collective or individual interpretations, define and redefine the apparent problem that the artifact is designed to solve. Rather than focusing just on the system, I consider it important to appreciate users, customers, consumers, and those who do not participate in but are affected by the system, in addition to inventors, engineers, designers, investors, managers, and even opponents to the technology. Specifically, the distinction between those who decide to use the system, those who decide not to use the system, and those who have no choice but to be affected by the system is notably lacking in most of the literature. To fill this gap, my framework includes this consideration. Essentially, all those who give sense to an artifact and those who make sense of it in practice contribute to its trajectory. Part of this analysis includes their scripts (Akrich & Latour, 1992) that are inscribed in artifacts both invisibly through decisions about the technical configurations of a device, and visibly through the narratives and claims about its goals and capabilities. Issues of societal power and economic strength also play a role in the development and potential growth of the system (Pinch & Bijker, 1987). Hence, a discussion of the resources available for the technological innovation and the strings attached to them may crucially inform the analysis of influences on these relevant social groups.

3.4.2 Material features

Given the intangible nature of digital technologies, material features – software design, cloud infrastructure, algorithmic models, data input – are of growing significance. Those configurations, meaning options chosen or excluded, actively or by default, together activate the range of possibilities that an artifact has to offer. These operational choices shape the potential of the technology. In the case of AI, particularly machine learning systems that may evolve based on input, the nature and contours of data are of particular relevance. These characteristics are also a prime example of the relationship between the social and the technical: Human actors, embedded in social context and history, make decisions and default selections about features that provide options to other human actors for their usage. It is due to their choices of interaction that the artifact becomes meaningful because it has been put to a particular use. These relational aspects represent ANT's network complexities (Law, 2001) or, in the sociomaterial interpretation, the notion of entanglement (Orlikowski, 2007).

3.4.3 Sociomaterial practice and structures

Acknowledging the importance of sociomaterial practice means acknowledging just how much human actors and material features produce and affect each other through active enactment. In the study of AI, the interrelatedness of intangible material features and how humans interact with them is particularly relevant: Data, central to any AI system, is contingent as much upon human behavior as upon histories and social norms of what gets measured. This data in turn informs material choices of hardware and software details that drive an AI system in various trajectory directions. Thus, the theoretical grounding in a sociomaterial perspective provides much needed understanding of this intricate entanglement. However, given the practical struggles of researchers adopting a strict agential realist approach, which is likely even more difficult in research involving highly intangible artifacts such as digital technologies, research should experiment as much as possible with methods to include situated material engagement. During the research process this means capturing the practices that have given rise to the particular configuration of the material features and social actions. Still, practice should not be the only focus of analysis lest the structures that condition available actions get overlooked (Leonardi, 2013). I suggest any concept or framework analyzing an AI evaluate how and *why* the system came to be configured. This means grounding the approach in a perspective that appreciates both practice and structure.

3.4.4 External forces

Finally, STS seeks to contextualize an artifact within its surrounding sociopolitical backdrop, including institutions, norms, and values. Given our sociomaterial understanding of entanglement, these already factor into the previous dimensions. However, the previously described approaches differ in their consideration of environmental forces and how they position this environment in their analysis. In contrast to ANT, an LTS approach acknowledges forces external to the system that influence it but are not controlled by it (Hughes, 1986). An analysis of an AI system should indeed acknowledge this environment but focus on how the system is, through conscious and unconscious material configurations, embedded into it. Putting the center of analytical attention on its embedding within the environment again focuses the evaluation on the relations between various components, meaning their constitutive entanglement.

3.5 Conclusion

In this chapter, I surveyed the most prominent manifestations of Technological Determinism and the Social Study of Technology. Specifically, my literature review has demonstrated how analytical understanding of the interplay between social embedding and the technical artifact has evolved. Given that many of these theories were originally developed prior to the widespread diffusion of digital technologies, particularly AI, it is important to acknowledge that appreciation of the social factors infusing the creation and dissemination of these systems has grown increasingly more sophisticated since then. I consider AI systems to be of sociotechnical nature, including the intangible and material entanglements discussed in this chapter. Before I outline my original concept and framework in Chapter 5, I now first turn my attention to a term that, for centuries, has denoted value and leverage: capital. The next chapter examines its history and intersections with digital technologies, including AI. By showing its evolving meaning and application, I demonstrate that, like the development in technology studies, the appreciation of the social aspects of capital has progressed. Its unfolding definition now captures more holistically the ways in which it manifests as impactful. I thereby argue why capital is an apt descriptor for the impact of AI.

4. Related Work: Capital Concepts

"We might even invent laws for series or formulæ in an arbitrary manner, and set the engine to work upon them, and thus deduce numerical results which we might not otherwise have thought of obtaining; but this would hardly perhaps in any instance be productive of any great practical utility, or calculated to rank higher than as a philosophical amusement."
Ada, Countess of Lovelace
Notes on the Analytical Engine, 1842

4.1 Introduction

Capital has had many partners. It has been coupled with stocks, markets, and accumulation, and prefixed with defining adjectives including human, social, symbolic, intellectual, natural, and reputational. The former list reveals its monetary origins, the latter signals its expansive application beyond the economic realm. In all its manifestations, capital represents assets that are of value in a particular context. Those who hold capital can wield its influence with impact.

In my research, I came across the diverse set of implications that an AI system may effectuate, from behavior change to heightened inequality to increasing efficiency. Each of them shows that the potential leverage of AI can be enormous, but together their nature has been difficult to synthesize. Rather than through an inherent, linear logic, the impacts of an AI system unfold through the many individual configurations that helped it emerge. Depending on numerous social and material features, they amount to a repository of leverage in various arenas. Capital aptly captures this valuable repository. Capital, like technology as illustrated in Chapter 3, was once thought to be of intrinsic worth and inherent consequence. It stood for tangible financial value. Over time, its definition grew to include goods, labor, and, eventually, various characteristics that could afford someone authority. It is this broader understanding of capital that my concept builds on.

My goal in this chapter is to show why capital is a fitting descriptor for the impact of AI. I provide a background to the concept of capital and to demonstrate how various digital technologies, including AI, have influenced theories of capitalism. First, I cover a brief history of the economic origins of the term capital and overview its macroeconomic measurement, a trajectory that culminates in the increasing appraisal of intangible[37] assets. Next, I outline the development of a sociological understanding of capital with a variety of examples. These notions significantly expanded the moniker of meanings that the term holds. They deepened our appreciation of social factors that contribute to conditions necessary for influence-wielding and determine its contours and extent.

Moving from the term capital to its structural system of capitalism, I then explain how the large socioeconomic shifts driven by advanced data-centric technologies have spurred various conceptualizations. Some of these notions of capitalism overlap, but they operate on differing levels of analysis, from economic order to business model to moral judgment. While they are each instructive for examining aspects of the economy in the age of digital technologies, they do not directly serve the purpose of this dissertation: It is not my intention to establish a new systemic theory of capitalism. Rather, I focus on concretely capturing the wide-ranging impacts that may flow from an AI system. Thus, I close the chapter by consolidating the insights from this review of capital to show that AI systems increasingly produce value through intangible assets, a stockpile of leverage best expressed through a novel capital concept.

4.2 Capital's Economic Origins

In this section, I review the evolving economic interpretations of capital, from monetary and physical assets, to labor and an intangible value.

4.2.1 Money and Goods

Historical accounts such as British economist Edwin Cannan's *Early History of the Term Capital* trace the first use of the Romans' *capitalis* to its Latin root 'caput', meaning head or top. At its outset, the term was used as an adjective to denote major importance, like its modern equivalent "chief", or concepts having to do with life, as in crime or punishment (Cannan, 1921, p. 469). Merchants then began to use it as a noun to describe monetary

---

37 The terms intangible, immaterial, and non-physical are used interchangeably throughout

assets. In the 12th century, as Fernand Braudel showed, Italians employed *capitale* to mean "money capital of a firm or of a merchant", a meaning that spread through Western Europe (Hodgson, 2014, p. 1063). In 16th century England, accountants kept track of this financial sense of capital as "the holdings of the individual members of a company, when thought of as amounts of money" and their aggregates were "the capital of the company (...), the most important or chief stock of the company" (Cannan, 1921, p. 473). This medieval definition of capital as the financial value of an investment, or "money advanced by owners or shareholders to establish a business," holds in business circles today (Hodgson, 2014, p. 1065).

A second though much less common meaning foreshadowed the complexity of defining capital. In 1611, Randle Cotgrave's *Dictionaire* seemed to imply that the word was synonymous with the worth of wealth, goods, and stock more generally. As Fisher put it, capital is

> a quantity of wealth existing at an instant of time. (...) Such a collection of wealth is, however, heterogenous; it cannot be expressed in a single sum. We can inventory the separate items, but we cannot add them together. They may, however, be reduced to a homogenous mass by considering not their kinds and quantities, but their values. And this *value* of any stock of wealth is also called "capital" (Fisher, 1906, p. 66).

Even this twofold meaning stoked critique. Frank Fetter summarized this dual interpretation as "superfluous and confusing," because

> these two types of capital concepts arc so distinctive in essential thought and practical application that confusion inevitably resulted from the use of one word to designate both. (...) The idea of 'worth', implying valuation, is thoroughly mixed with that of substance, no doubt in the sense of material things in possession (Fetter, 1937, pp. 187–190).

It was Adam Smith who firmly lodged capital's multidimensionality into common usage. In 1776, his seminal work of classical economics, *An Inquiry into the Nature and Causes of the Wealth of Nations*, significantly expanded the notion of capital so that "henceforth among economists the word changed its meaning" (Hodgson, 2014, p. 1065). As one overarching theme, Smith describes the accumulation of capital in addition to the division of labor as the driving force of a nation's productive capacity. In Book 2, *Of the Nature, Accumulation, and Employment of Stock*, he bifurcates an individual's or community's stock into two parts: the one reserved for immediate consumption and the one which is expected to afford revenue – called capital (Adam Smith, 1804, p. 218). This division had notable consequences as it signaled "a very serious departure from the conception of capital which had hitherto prevailed. Instead of making the capital a sum of money which is to be invested, or which has been invested in certain things, Smith makes it *the things themselves*" [emphasis added] (Cannan, 1921, p. 480).

4.2.2 People and Labor

In addition to its application to money and goods themselves, Smith extends the notion of capital to people and their labor. He divides capital stock into "circulating" and "fixed" to distinguish whether the capital generates revenue with or without "changing masters" (Adam Smith, 1804, p. 218). Notably, fixed capital according to Smith includes machines, instruments, profitable buildings, improvements of lands, but also "the acquired and useful abilities" of individuals that "may be considered in the same light as a machine or instrument of trade which facilitates and abridges labor, and which, though it costs a certain expense, repays that expense with a profit" (Adam Smith, 1804, p. 221). Capital then no longer applies merely to finances and physical goods:

> This is a major source of the idea that the term capital applies to people as well as things. By extending the notion of capital to people and their labor, Smith changed its meaning to a productive resource, rather than money or money values. (…) For economics, this shift of meaning was seminal. The term capital acquired the twin and often mutually confused meanings of money and productive goods, but often with the accent on the latter (Hodgson, 2014, pp. 1065–1066).

A century later, Karl Marx' 1867 treatise on the exploitative nature of a capitalist society did not confine the term to a pecuniary interpretation, either. Instead, *Das Kapital* emphasized the role of social relations and power dynamics inherent in an economic system focused on profit maximization (K. Marx, 2010a, 2010b, 2015). Capital according to Marx was the value of money and commodities, including human labor. He states clearly that "the existence of commodities as values is purely social (…) and consequently (…) the form of their value must be a socially recognized form" (K. Marx, 2015, p. 44). A Marxist understanding of capitalist structures asserts that "capital is not a thing, but a social relation between persons, established by the instrumentality of things" (K. Marx, 2015, p. 543). But despite his inclusion of social forces, Marx stuck to the tangible conception of production in terms of physical entities (Hodgson, 2014, p. 1066).

4.2.3 Intangibles and Disputes

It was Thorstein Veblen who most notably added 'intangible assets' to the capital understanding, defining them as

> immaterial items of wealth, immaterial facts owned, valued, and capitalized on an appraisement of the gain to be derived from their possession. These are also assets to the amount of their capitalizable value, which has commonly little, if any, relation to the industrial serviceability of these items of wealth considered as factors of production (1908a, p. 105).

Indeed, Veblen considered immaterial wealth "the substantial core of all capital" and maintained that "the material objects which are formally the subject of the capitalist's ownership are, by comparison, a transient and adventitious matter" (Veblen, 1908b, p. 166).

Numerous other scholars have added to the long-standing dispute about the financial and economic definition of capital as a concept (Böhm-Bawerk, 1890; J. Clark, 1886; Fisher, 1904, 1906; M. Weber, 1968). In the 1950s until the 1970s, transatlantic debate between two camps of British and American scholars about the meaning and measurement of capital became known as the Cambridge Capital Controversy (A. J. Cohen & Harcourt, 2003; Pasinetti et al., 2003). A number of thinkers lament the heterogeneity of interpretations, stating that "since the time of Adam Smith, there has been no established usage whatsoever. On the contrary, the most of what has been written on this vexed subject has consisted in making existing confusion worse confounded" (Fisher, 1904, p. 4). Some have criticized the expansive application of the term both in the economic and, as described in more detail below, the sociological realm, arguing that understanding capital "as a mixture of two types of asset(s): the material and immaterial" obfuscates its meaning to "any relatively durable thing or attribute that leads to the satisfaction of wants" (Hodgson, 2014, pp. 1068–1070). Joseph Schumpeter, too, favored a simpler definition, deploring: "What a mass of confused, futile, and downright silly controversies it would have saved us, if economists had had the sense to stick to those monetary and accounting meanings of the term instead of trying to 'deepen' them!" (Schumpeter,

1954, pp. 306–307). Others see the disagreement over capital's connotations as a signal of the notion's widespread importance as "it simply indicates that capital is one of the most far-reaching conceptions" (Nicholson quoted in Fisher, 1904, p. 386).

An exact interpretation of capital is of particular sociopolitical consequence when its meaning dictates macroeconomic measurement. In his 2014 work *Capital in the Twenty-First Century,* Thomas Piketty employs capital interchangeably with wealth (2014), an interpretive choice which has been criticized for its impact on his measuring methods (Solow, 2017). Like the balancing sheets of companies, calculations of national economic growth have long focused on the accounting of physical assets with lasting value. Mirroring early applications of capital, such measurement conventions largely ignored all non-physical goods. (Haskel & Westlake, 2018). However, a number of theorists have proposed that immaterial capital like knowledge, rather than technological invention by itself, serves as a driver of growth and productivity and should thus be measured (Romer, 1990). While the impact of the Information Technology revolution has been evident in the market since the New Economy of the 1980s (Alexander, 1983), official macroeconomic data failed to capture its manifestation in growth statistics because it excluded intangibles (Corrado et al., 2006). Only at the turn of the millennium did analysts begin to seriously assess intangible assets that yield considerable economic return (Corrado et al., 2006; Young, 1998), such as investments in databases and software, or "knowledge written down in lines of code" (Haskel & Westlake, 2018, p. 40). The market value of intangibles has been steadily rising and in some cases outgrown that of physicals (Corrado et al., 2006; Haskel & Westlake, 2018). Yet still today, traditional GDP-based measurements of productivity and well-being do not reflect the complex value created by a range of popular digital goods (Brynjolfsson et al., 2018). In his work on the nature and value of intangible assets, Baruch Lev argues that they now "generate most of corporate growth and shareholder value" (2004, p. 109) and ignoring them leads to over- or undervaluation:

> A skilled workforce, patents and know-how, software, strong customer relationships, brands, unique organizational design and processes, and the like - (...) they account for well over half the market capitalization of public companies. They absorb a trillion dollars of corporate investment funds every year. In fact, these "soft" assets are what give today's companies their hard competitive edge. (...) Companies need to generate better information about (...) investments in intangibles and the

benefits that flow from them (...) to improve managerial decisions and give investors a sharper picture (2004, pp. 109–110).

This section demonstrated that immaterial goods have become an increasingly central part of appraising capital and that examining its non-physical forms is of vital importance to understand what is driving the economy. To complement the picture, I will outline the sociological understanding of capital next.

4.3 Capital as Social Leverage

Evolving definitions of capital in the economic realm and the inclusion of intangible assets into macroeconomic valuation represent a wider recognition that immaterial forces may engender social rewards that can translate into financial gain. This section looks at the various sociological interpretations of capital.

4.3.1 Interpersonal Phenomena

As early as 1870, German economist Wilhelm Roscher referred to "invisible intellectual capital" (1870, p. 82), and Friedrich Nietzsche mentioned "intellectual and volitional capital" (1910, p. 347), then "intellectual and emotional capital" (1910, p. 354) in his 1878 work *Human, all too human*. In both cases the term labels immaterial resources with implied societal value. Similarly, in his appraisal of labor, Marx evoked that human capacities are of relevant value, in his case to a capitalist market. Even though Marx never used the term explicitly, the theory of human capital, most notably put forward by Theodore Schultz (1961) and Gary Becker (1962), established that "useful skills and knowledge (...) are a form of capital. (...) This capital is in substantial part a product of deliberate investment (...) and its growth may well be the most distinctive feature of the economic system" (Schultz, 1961, p. 1). It was this increasing accounting of human capital that launched a "minor sociological industry (...) to construct sociological parallels to human capital" and has resulted in "a plethora of capitals" (Baron & Hannan, 1994, pp. 1122–1123).

An additional catalyst for the proliferation of capital's social applications was the work of French sociologist Pierre Bourdieu. Rather than measuring the value of human resources through an economic lens, Bourdieu advocates for a distinctively sociological appraisal of social power dynamics. He proposes that it is "impossible to account for the structure and functioning of the social world unless one establishes capital in all its iterations, not just the one known from economic theory" as the latter "reduces the universe of societal exchange dynamics to a mercantile exchange" (Bourdieu, 1983, p. 184). Thus,

> to avoid such reduction, it is important to reintroduce the term of capital and the concept of capital accumulation with all its implications. Capital is accumulated work, either in material form or in internalized, "incorporated" form. (...) The structure of the distribution of the different types and subtypes of capital at a given moment in time represents the immanent structure of the social world, i.e., the set of constraints, inscribed in the very reality of that world (Bourdieu, 1983, pp. 183–184).

Employing the term capital for interpersonal phenomena illustrates Bourdieu's analysis that "social energies" are such impactful assets that they "govern (the social world)'s functioning in a durable way, *determining the chances of success*" [emphasis added] (Bourdieu, 1983, p. 184). His early work distinguishes between economic versus social, cultural, and symbolic capital (Bourdieu, 1983). He argues that their unequal distribution and reproduction have a perpetual, invisible stronghold on societal power relations (Bourdieu, 1983, p. 183). Social capital, one of the most influential manifestations of Bourdieu's sociological analysis of capital, delineates the value of belonging to a group or network (1983, p. 191). First described though not coined by Alexis de Tocqueville in 1838, social capital was subsequently popularized by accounts of rural communities (Hanifan, 1916), class mobility (Bourdieu, 1986), rational action (Coleman, 1988), civic engagement and economic development (Putnam, 1993), trust (Fukuyama, 1995), organizational management (Nahaphiet & Ghoshal, 1998), democratic participation (Putnam, 2000), and cooperation in a free-market (Fukuyama, 2000).

Intellectual, human, and social capital are early examples that inspired a range of future sociological interpretations. Many try to explicitly parallel the economic conception of the term. For example, in his exploration of political capital, Edward Banfield observes that in the arena of politics, "an actor has a limited stock of power which he gives up piecemeal, or 'spends', by trading (influence) for other bits that he particularly needs" (1961, p. 179), "he may have a sizable 'inventory' and many 'accounts receivable' but if his 'accounts payable' are large, his net position is not good" (1961, p. 242), and that "his power is like capital: he can either "consume" it or "invest" it." (1961, p. 312). In *The Economy of Attention*, Georg Franck utilizes economic vernacular to detail the accumulation of attention income and the formation of mental capital (Franck, 1998). Corry Azzi and Ronald Ehrenberg investigate the investment in religious capital assuming the possibility of "afterlife consumption" (1975, p. 28). Luthans, Youssef, & Avolio argue that psychological capital can provide "substantial return" and a "competitive edge" (Luthans et al., 2007). And Grossmann analyzes health as "a durable capital stock" that can produce "an output of healthy time" and has "a shadow price" (1972, p. 223). Some accounts of capital tend to employ more Bourdieuan vocabulary. Sandberg & Pedersen use street capital to denote the embodied culture of drug dealers in a lower-class social space (2011). Others yet, like Catherine Hakim in her theory of erotic capital, explicitly mention both economic and social implications (2010).

4.3.2 Debate

The proliferation of capitals has stoked a number of objections (Baron & Hannan, 1994; Bowles & Gintis, 2002; DiMaggio, 1979; Hodgson, 2014). Common criticisms of applications beyond the strictly monetary sense include measurability, ownership, and transferability into financial collateral. Hodgson advocates a return to its narrow economic use as "the promiscuous associations of 'capital' can give the impression that all political, cultural, social, cognitive and ecological phenomena can be valued and traded in monetary terms and invested like finance capital" (Hodgson, 2014, p. 1081). Some specifically agree with the formulation of the more recent concepts but disagree with their label. As Bowles & Gintis comment on social capital: "It may even be a good idea. A good term it is not. Capital refers to a thing that can be owned" (2002, p. 429). Others contend that the broad use of the term trivializes it because "as the number of capitals increases, the metaphorical currency undergoes inflation and its value declines accordingly" (DiMaggio, 1979, p. 1469).

I maintain, however, that the shared term across disciplines is of significant analytical benefit. It represents one fundamental meaning that the aforementioned types of capital hold: Each respective concept describes assets, configurations of some form, that transform into value, metaphorical or actualized, in their defined realm. In their "power theory of value", Nitzan & Bichler argue that "capital is a mode of power" (2009, p. 3). "a symbolic crystallization of power exercised over large-scale human organizations" (2009, p. 270). While it is beyond the scope of this research to engage in the long history of power itself, the conceptualization of capital as power helps to understand it as a symbolic architecture of influence in various arenas (Nitzan & Bichler, 2009, p. 271). AI systems, too, hold a repository of leverage that can result in various impacts. This is why their potential power can so aptly be described as a form of capital.

In the next section, I examine notions of capitalism driven by digital technologies. While I do not intent to establish a novel structural form of capitalism in this dissertation, it is important to appreciate how other scholars have linked the particular dynamics of digital systems with the economic system as some of these insights inform our understanding of AI.

4.4 Digital Technology and its Capitalisms

A number of concepts have captured the growing interconnectedness of digital technology and capitalism. Two phenomena are central to them: First, the increasingly networked nature of the global economy; second, the rise of knowledge in the form of data used for products whose value increases because of it. In the following section, I review the central tenets of the most relevant concepts and show how they build on each other. Broadly speaking, I purview changes in the *what*, the *how*, and the *why* implied in these evolutions of capitalism: What is of value in this economic system? How are valuable assets being enacted or exercised? And why or to what end does this form of capitalism operate this way? While they relate to aspects of my account of Code Capital, I demonstrate that they, as abstract system definitions, have insufficient explanatory power and analytical precision for the implications spurred by particular manifestations of AI.

4.4.1 The What: Commodifying Knowledge

In his 1996 book *The Rise of the Network Society*, the first in his seminal trilogy *The Information Age*, Manuel Castells coined the term "information economy" to describe the novel market dynamics emerging from a major societal trend of the 1970s: the revolution in information and communication technology (ICT) that transformed the production and distribution of knowledge (Castells, 2011). Castells argues that because the economy had become increasingly organized through large, global networks, information and knowledge had turned into the central source and driving force of productivity and competitiveness.

Contemporaneous concepts sought to describe this underlying societal transformation, too, most notably those of the post-industrial and information society (D. Bell, 1976; Webster, 2014) and the knowledge society (Drucker, 1992). While all three approaches address the emergence of knowledge and information as the basis for value creation, nuances can be found in their differing execution and emphases on certain aspects: Drucker postulates from a practical management perspective, Bell is theoretically and analytically complex, and Castells is led by a more empirical-diagnostic description and most focuses on the role of ICT (Steinbicker, 2001). Still, these prominent examples are only an excerpt of the overarching argument that society in the age of rapid technological development has become increasingly steered by the leverage of knowledge and information instead of raw materials and labor power. As Fuchs summarizes:

> Computerized society, digital society, information society, knowledge society, knowledge-based society, network society, ICT society, Internet society, communication society, cybersociety, media society, post-industrial society, postmodern society, virtual society – we can find many names for and claims about the present structure of Western societies in political discussions, the media, everyday life and academic discourse. Most of these concepts and claims have in common that they stress the importance of knowledge, the production, generation, diffusion and use of information, the rise of the computer and digital network technologies such as the Internet or the mobile phone (Fuchs, 2013, p. 2).

These accounts share the assessment of *what* is increasingly at the core of the economy, arguing that this socioeconomic transformation is "replacing the reproduction of capital as the most important function of society with the reproduction of knowledge" (Suarez-Villa, 2000, p. 4). This development notably emphasizes the rising power of intangible forces as previously described.

4.4.2 The How: Elevating Digital Technologies

This fundamental insight about the commodification of knowledge and information in society has resulted in multiple new labels for aspects of the capitalist system. A review of the plethora of capitalisms in the digital world reveals a diversity of terms for similar developments, such as "virtual capitalism" (Dawson & Foster, 1996; Thrift, 1998), "technocapitalism" (Suarez-Villa, 2000), "digital capitalism" (Schiller, 2000), "cybercapitalism" (Schiller & Mosco, 2001), and "information capitalism" (Fuchs, 2010). These theories have in common the economic logic that the main transformation of the global market system grew out of the emergence of digital technologies, including the Internet. While on the surface, these terms refer to similar socioeconomic developments, their multitude also reveals their imprecision. Different authors have repurposed the same descriptors for various scopes of purview, from large-scale structural transformations to particular cultural manifestations and historical changes in accumulation, production types, or management styles.

For example, Suarez-Villa explains technocapitalism as "an evolution of market capitalism that is rooted in technological invention and innovation. It can be considered an emerging era, now in its early stage" (Suarez-Villa, 2013). He wants to provide a "macro-panoramic" view of technocapitalism, "a conceptual framework that is flexible and open-ended, to which discussions can be added, debated or documented with evidence" (Suarez-Villa, 2013). Meanwhile, instead of referring to a fundamental transformation of capitalist structures, D'Souza uses the same term to describe specifically Silicon Valley's high-tech, entrepreneurial culture, the "pioneers" who "have a vision for the world, (…) are making it happen, and (…) are being rewarded for it", a group who "champions new companies and products, welcomes the rapid pace of change, sees ahead a cornucopia of pleasures and possibilities" (D'Souza, 2002, p. 28) Due to this kind of technocapitalism, he argues, the U.S. is "probably the best society that now exists or has ever existed" (D'Souza, 2002, p. 187).

Similarly, Pace outlines how the notions of digital capitalism described by Schiller as nominalist historical development (2000) and by Fuchs as structural evolution (2013) diverge widely. He laments that "the concept is effectively working overtime, generating more confusion than clarity" (Pace, 2018, p. 254) and, instead, argues for an understanding of digital capitalism as an abstract system as well as concrete history through his own account:

> Digital capitalism is the collection of processes, sites, and moments in which digital technology mediates the structural tendencies of capitalism. Digital capitalism is neither a structural totality nor a historical period. It is capitalism's complex actualization in digital processes (…). Digital capitalism is the modus operandi by which the structural needs of capital are tailored to digital conditions (2018, pp. 262–263).

Notably, as Pace writes about digital capitalism, these varying accounts most often represent the modus operandi, or the way *how* capitalism operates in the digital age.

One of the key aspects of how the digital economy functions is the sensing, collecting, and processing of an unprecedented volume of digital information: Big Data. This central role of data in the economy, particularly because of the rise of AI applications fueled by them, has led to descriptions of "data capitalism" (Fuchs, 2019; Segura & Waisbord, 2019; West, 2019). Indeed, the concept links the *what* – knowledge and information – with the *how* – in the form of digital data – within the structures of capitalism. As The Economist emphasized in its 2017 cover story,

> … Computers (…) extract value – patterns, predictions and other insights – from raw digital information. (…) Data are to this century what oil was to the last one: a driver of growth and change. Flows of data have created new infrastructure, new businesses, new monopolies, new politics and—crucially—new economics. Digital information is unlike any previous resource; it is extracted, refined, valued, bought and sold in different ways. It changes the rules for markets and it demands new approaches from regulators. Many a battle will be fought over who should own, and benefit from, data (Economist, 2017).

Some researchers critical of the free-services-for-data dynamic of myriad technology companies today have suggested data be considered labor, which "as user possessions [...] should primarily benefit their owners" (Arrieta-Ibarra et al., 2018, p. 2). Another approach argues against data as a commodity and for framing it as capital, for "without data, many of these technologies and organizations would not be able to operate, let alone be able to generate value" (Sadowski, 2019, p. 2). Explicitly, this thinking interprets data as capital to be rooted in its economic origins but going beyond them to include sociopolitical manifestations.

In addition to the valuation and monetization of data, another aspect of how the digital economy largely operates relates to the role of companies as platforms. In what some scholars have termed "platform capitalism" (Pasquale, 2016b; Srnicek, 2017; Vallas, 2019), corporations such as Amazon, Google, Facebook, Airbnb, and Uber provide the technological infrastructure to facilitate transactions between third-party entities. Essentially, they become intermediaries for economic exchanges (Kenney & Zysman, 2016). The notion of platform capitalism thereby describes *how* companies are transforming and repositioning themselves to reap the largest profits:

The platform has emerged as a new business model, capable of extracting and controlling immense amounts of data, and with this shift we have seen the rise of large monopolistic firms. Today the capitalism of the high- and middle income economies is increasingly dominated by these firms (…) and the trend is only going to continue (Srnicek, 2017, p. 6).

Related to the evolution of platforms as collective marketplaces are the terms "sharing economy" (Puschmann & Alt, 2016; Richardson, 2015; J. Schor, 2016) and "gig economy" (Healy et al., 2017; Manyika et al., 2016; Prassl, 2018; A. J. Wood et al., 2019). Together, they rearrange relations between workers, buyers, and corporations, and raise questions of inequalities and labor rights (Leong & Belzer, 2016; Rogers, 2016; J. B. Schor & Attwood-Charles, 2017), ownership, and accountability (J. E. Cohen, 2017; Scassa, 2018).

While they represent disparate levels of analysis – historical developments, systemic changes, and new business models – the notions of capitalism examined in Section 4.4.2 mainly describe how the rise of networked technologies, widespread data collection, AI-driven companies, and platform monopolies have shifted market dynamics. The next section goes one step further to examine one heavily discussed notion, surveillance capitalism, in detail, as its conception implies not just method but intent as well as sociopolitical impact.

4.4.3 The Why: Surveilling Others

While the previously described expressions of capitalism focused on its modus operandi, one recently much-cited concept captures not just an "emergent logic of accumulation in the networked sphere" but also "its implications for 'information civilization'" (Zuboff, 2015, p. 75). Simply put, this theory explicitly states the ostensible objective of this emerging form of capitalism and goes so far as to morally assess it. To contextualize the accruement and analysis of extensive digital information and the automation of decisions about citizens, in this section I first review the theoretical origins of surveillance as a form of power. Next, I highlight how the underlying logic of Zuboff's surveillance capitalism expands on this school of thought.

With "surveillance capitalism", Zuboff has introduced a term which she defines, in the preface of her seminal book *The Age of Surveillance Capital-*

ism, with no less than eight interpretations, which are worth quoting in their entirety:

> 1. A new economic order that claims human experience as free raw material for hidden commercial practices of extraction, prediction, and sales;
> 2. A parasitic economic logic in which the production of goods and services is subordinated to a new global architecture of behavioral modification;
> 3. A rogue mutation of capitalism marked by concentrations of wealth, knowledge, and power unprecedented in human history;
> 4. The foundational framework of a surveillance economy;
> 5. As significant a threat to human nature in the twenty-first century as industrial capitalism was to the natural world in the nineteenth and twentieth;
> 6. The origin of a new instrumentarian power that asserts dominance over society and presents startling challenges to market democracy;
> 7. A movement that aims to impose a new collective order based on total certainty;
> 8. An expropriation of critical human rights that is best understood as a coup from above: an overthrow of the people's sovereignty (Zuboff, 2019).

The significant scope of Zuboff's interpretative lenses spans an economic order and logic, new types of power challenging society and democracy, as well as threats to the natural world and human rights. Notably, she explicitly calls this novel system "deeply intentional and highly consequential" (Zuboff, 2015, p. 75). This fusion of intent and consequences implies that her notion encompasses the *why* of this emerging capitalism.

Surveillance as a form of citizen control dates back to the theory of Panopticism. Michel Foucault's interpretation of Jeremy Bentham's Panopticon architecture denotes a society that controls its population through disciplinary mechanisms of constant observation and internalized coercion (Foucault, 1977). Authority in this design is omnipresent and unverifiable, which is

> an important mechanism, for it automizes and disindividualizes power. (...) (It) could be used as a machine to carry out experiments, to alter behavior, to train or correct individuals. (...) (It) functions as a kind of laboratory of power. Thanks to its mechanisms of observation, it gains in efficiency and in the ability to penetrate into men's behavior; knowledge follows the advances of power, discovering new

objects of knowledge over all the surfaces on which power is exercised (Foucault, 1977, pp. 202–203).

Observing people's behavior creates knowledge which translates into power which in turn begets more knowledge. According to Foucault, this system of 'soul training' - or conditioning people to be compliant - operates whenever there is "a multiplicity of individuals on whom a task or a particular form of behavior must be imposed" because "it makes it possible to perfect the exercise of power" (1977, pp. 205–206).

Panopticism has been referred to as a standard metaphor for the advancing modern surveillance market. Its theory spans applications from mental health nursing (Holmes, 2001), to crime prevention (Yong, 2013), to widespread public data collection (McMullan, 2015), to surveillance in professional firm settings (Brivot & Gendron, 2011), and to management studies more generally (McKinlay & Starkey, 1997). Two important points have since been added to the discourse surrounding it. First, in "The Viewer Society", Thomas Mathiesen contested the one-way nature of power relations that Foucauldian Panopticism seemed to imply (Mathiesen, 1997). "Something of crucial importance is missing," he wrote, "a highly significant counterpart" to the idea, that only the few see the many: "The development of a unique and enormously extensive system enabling *the many to see and contemplate the few* (through) the total system of the modern mass media" (1997, p. 219). This phenomenon, which he coined Synopticism, described the ability of groups to focus on the common experience of watching individuals, for example on television, a powerful viewpoint and insight unprecedented in the exposure it afforded at the time. Mathiesen's central point emphasized that the power mechanisms of the Viewer Society run both ways, top-down and bottom-up.[38] Given the temporal context of his writing before the turn of the millennium, Mathiesen referred mostly to the rise of television, while his argument was built for "the total pattern or Gestalt" of the mass-mediated world (1997, p. 230). Indeed, more recent scholars have taken Synopticism to apply to the wider technological notion of the networked age of the internet and argued that Panopticism and Synopticism interact and fuel each other (Doyle, 2011).

---

38 Similarly, Niklas Luhmann wrote about the power of employees to counter the surveillance of their superiors with what he called 'subveillance' (*Unterwachung*) (Luhmann, 2018).

Second, the nature and scope of the instruments of Foucault's notion of disciplinary surveillance have been greatly expanded given more recent technological developments. Haggerty and Ericson underline that "we are witnessing a convergence of what were once discrete surveillance systems to the point that we can now speak of an emerging 'surveillant assemblage'" (Haggerty & Ericson, 2000, p. 606). It is constituted by a mix of sensors, cameras, phone data, social network analyses, geographic tracking, and many more aspects that combine to observe and monitor people:

> This assemblage operates by abstracting human bodies from their territorial settings and separating them into a series of discrete flows. These flows are then reassembled into distinct 'data doubles' which can be scrutinized and targeted for intervention. In the process, we are witnessing a rhizomatic leveling of the hierarchy of surveillance, such that groups which were previously exempt from routine surveillance are now increasingly being monitored (Haggerty & Ericson, 2000, p. 606).

These two elaborations render Foucault's concept more relevant to the connected technological world of today: While Panopticism has a counterpart in Synoptocism that offers an alternative layer of power to the many, the surveillant assemblage "marks the progressive 'disappearance of disappearance' – a process whereby it is increasingly difficult for individuals to maintain their anonymity, or to escape the monitoring of social institutions" (Haggerty & Ericson, 2000, p. 619)

One rebuke of Foucault's relevance today ties to his conception of surveillance as a centrally managed form of organizational social control over unwilling participants for mere discipline. First, it appears more dispersed and integrated today, as the aforementioned surveillant assemblage signals already: "While the panoptic model suggests surveillance is centrally organized, in fact surveillance proliferates often without much centralized control" (Doyle, 2011, p. 289). Second, participants are no longer necessarily as unwilling as the incarcerated cell inmates of an institution. In what she termed the 'Information Panopticon', Zuboff outlined early on how information and communication technology services now provide an infrastructure that facilitates far-reaching surveillance but also offers benefits to willing participants in the form of access, knowledge, and power (Zuboff, 1988). While the system seeks to produce vulnerable users to monitor still, they are not defenseless and without means. Nonetheless, others argued that under surveillance capitalism, some users can be "coerced" into digital participation (Barassi, 2019). Third, and relatedly, modern surveillance systems have surpassed their once single purpose of observation for organizational discipline as they operate in service of an evolving capitalist infrastructure (Haggerty & Ericson, 2000; Zuboff, 2016). Foucault, too, contended that capitalist forces and industrial management needs were the fertile ground that ushered in widespread measures of discipline to begin with:

> If the economic take-off of the West began with the techniques that made possible the accumulation of capital, it might perhaps be said that the methods for administering the accumulation of men made possible a political take-off in relation to the traditional, ritual, costly, violent forms of power (...), which soon fell into disuse and were superseded by a subtle, calculated technology of subjection. (...) The growth of the capitalist economy gave rise to the specific modality of disciplinary power, whose general formulas, techniques of submitting forces and bodies, in short, 'political anatomy', could be operated in the most diverse political régimes, apparatuses or institutions (Foucault, 1977, pp. 220–221).

Since then, some have interpreted capitalism not merely as a condition that gave rise to the phenomenon of surveillance, but rather the motivating system that sustains itself, advances, and significantly transforms through it. Specifically, monitoring people to gain knowledge about the detailed parameters of their lives serves social control for profitable ends:

> Instead of being subject to disciplinary surveillance or simple repression, the population is increasingly constituted as consumers and seduced into the market economy. While surveillance is used to construct and monitor consumption patterns, such efforts usually lack the normalized soul training which is so characteristic of panopticism. Instead, monitoring for market consumption is more concerned with attempts to limit access to places and information, or to allow for the production of consumer profiles through the ex post facto reconstructions of a person's behaviour, habits and actions (Haggerty & Ericson, 2000, p. 615).

Zuboff and others argue that this seduction into the market economy is potentiated by AI systems: Machine learning models function and improve by feeding large volumes of human data into preconceived models to be able to predict future behavior. While Haggerty and Ericson assume that the notion of panoptic 'soul training' used to be more repressive in Foucauldian terms, others maintain that it still exists today in a profit-driven surveillance system where the designs of many widespread services nudge the user into participation and become 'habit-forming products' that nurture the surveillance apparatus (Eyal, 2014). Specifically, Zuboff proffers that surveillance technology creates what she calls *behavioral futures markets*, because it "aims to predict and modify human behavior as a means to produce revenue and market control" (Zuboff, 2015, p. 75). The data includes input from all kinds of different sensors and platform interactions present in society, which represents a self-reinforcing economic logic: "The competitive dynamics of these new markets drive surveillance capitalists to acquire ever-more-predictive sources of behavioral surplus: our voices, personalities, and emotions" (Zuboff, 2019, p. 8) This, she argues, has corrupted the overall capitalist system in the digital economy:

> Capitalism has been hijacked by a lucrative surveillance project that subverts the "normal" evolutionary mechanisms associated with its historical success and corrupts the unity of supply and demand that has for centuries, however imperfectly, tethered capitalism to the genuine needs of its populations and societies, thus enabling the fruitful expansion of market democracy. Surveillance capitalism is a novel economic mutation bred from the clandestine coupling of the vast powers of the digital with the *radical indifference and intrinsic narcissism* [emphasis added] of the financial capitalism and its neoliberal vision that have dominated commerce for at least three decades (Zuboff, 2016).

In addition to attributing explicit human causes to this new economic order she also presents clear sociopolitical consequences. Though she contends that the technologies and available data could be employed in different ways, Zuboff associates the AI-driven world as one essentially inspired by deeply capitalist purposes:

> Surveillance capitalism has gradually constituted itself during the last decade, embodying a new social relations and politics that have not yet been well delineated or theorized. While 'big data' may be set to other uses, those do not erase its origins in an extractive project founded on formal indifference to the populations that comprise both its data sources and its ultimate targets (Zuboff, 2015, pp. 75–76).

As users become the data points that help train and improve profitable systems, they turn into both recipients of products (consumers) and part of their production (producers), rendering them a modern-day version of Alvin Toffler's 'prosumers' (Kotler, 2010; Ritzer, 2015; Ritzer et al., 2012). Their contribution, proponents of surveillance capitalism contend, directly feeds into the maintenance and promotion of the digital economy that affords them certain privileges – connection, convenience, choices – which motivates them to participate and agree to be monitored in the first place (Gibson, 2010). Others may choose to exercise self-restraint and self-censorship in the face of modern technology and perceive their abstention as their own form of capital (Manokha, 2018). All are thereby "involved in efforts to maintain or augment various social perks" (Haggerty & Ericson, 2000, p. 615), while their behavior is transformed into capital.

This in-depth examination of the underlying theories and arguments of surveillance capitalism has revealed a framework of economic logic and social dimensions, including intents and consequences. Surveillance capitalism represents one interpretation of the digital economy's evolution, but it is normatively inflexible. As the name suggests, each system or platform operating within this form of capitalism appears to be associated with the objective of behavioral forecasting and the desired societal effect of widespread surveillance. While Zuboff's concept is of strong analytical value when it comes to understanding the dynamics of predictive power, social control, and the role of monopolistic platforms, it does not account for AI systems created outside of or with safeguards against these particular intents and consequences. The range of use cases for AI is varied and heterogenous, as demonstrated in Chapters 1 and 2. In addition to overarching emerging logics of capitalism, we need concepts and frameworks to grasp the contours of impact that individual AI systems exert. Otherwise, we risk losing nuance, context, and a precise understanding of how AI transforms capitalism in myriad, specific ways. Because "when we encounter something unprecedented, we automatically interpret it through the lenses of familiar categories, thereby rendering invisible precisely that which is unprecedented" (Zuboff, 2019, p. 12).

4.5 Discussion

A few lessons flow from the previous explorations of the evolution of capital from its economic roots to its sociological interpretation and the various capitalisms related to the digital economy.

The first insight is that our interpretation of capital and the kinds we choose to take into account matters. It is of consequence when its meaning influences how thoroughly we understand an economy driven by AI. In *Capitalism without Capital*, Haskel & Westlake argue that the development towards a more intangible-heavy economy is significant in two ways: First, intangible assets fly under the radar of most statistics which means "we are now trying to measure capitalism without counting all the capital" (2018, p. 7). Second, intangibles tend to exhibit at least four attributes with a distinct impact on the economy: Investment in immaterial assets is often irrevocable, meaning the cost is sunk (Haskel & Westlake, 2018, p. 68). Their benefits tend to be non-rival which means they can easily spillover to be of advantage to other businesses (Haskel & Westlake, 2018, p. 72). Combining different intangible increases their value because they have synergies with each other as well as with tangible assets (Haskel & Westlake, 2018, p. 81). Finally, particularly due to the "network effects" of the digital age, both physical and non-physical capital can produce "supercharged scalability" (Haskel & Westlake, 2018, p. 66). Sunkenness, spillovers, synergies, and scalability are defining features of the intangible assets fueling the modern market.

The second insight is that an AI-driven economy will become increasingly intangible-intensive not only in the economic sense but in the form of immaterial capital forces overall. AI systems boost these underappreciated socioeconomic dynamics

> in part because software and data are intangibles, and the growing power of computers (...) is increasing the scope of things that software can achieve. But ...(it's) not just about software. (...) It involves other intangibles in abundance (Haskel & Westlake, 2018, p. 23).

Specifically, in addition to amassing economic value, AI systems have become arbiters of distributing and reproducing a range of previously identified socialized forms of capital, like the currencies of networks, influence, attention, and behaviors. Together, these spheres of impact constitute the potential social leverage of a particular AI system. Currently, we lack a concrete analytical understanding of how this clout is accumulated and leveraged.

Finally, the third insight is that while much valuable work has developed different forms of capitalism that contribute to the digital economy, these terms vary widely in interpretive scope, at times overlap or contradict each other. None individually holds the explanatory force or analytical precision needed to account for the intangible power of AI. It is not the goal of my research to define a new kind of capitalism as an abstract structure, historical development, or business model framework alone. Rather, I argue we need a definition of capital to accurately describe the actual and potential societal impacts through human-made assets of an AI system. With the introduction of my original concept in Chapter 5, I employ the term capital as a symbolic representation of power and offer an analytical framework to assess a particular AI system.

4.6 Conclusion

In this chapter, I have shown that capital has undergone a transformation spanning multiple centuries. Its meaning and ways to measure it have morphed, but all its manifestations represent assets that are of value and can be exercised as influence in a particular context. This symbolic representation of capital as socially embedded power is what makes it a particularly apt descriptor for the impact of AI. As the explorations of digitally driven capitalisms has shown, too, these systems encompass a stockpile of leverage that may affect what is of value, how it is exchanged, and why new objectives have given rise to novel business models. They have altered means of production and dissemination, collective institutions, and individual behaviors. While the nature of AI implications has been difficult to summarize, it is evident that many configurations, social, technical, material, contribute to them. Similar to the changing understanding of technology's genesis and impact, the term capital began as a concept that seemed to imply inevitability and linearity. Over time, its meaning transformed into an expansive but clear expression for a symbol of influence. It is this understanding of capital as socially enacted and socially acting that my original concept of Code Capital builds on, which I will outline next, in Chapter 5.

5. Code Capital

5.1 Introduction

AI can generate substantial economic, social, and political power. As the previous chapters have shown, current academic notions discussing AI are insufficiently accessible, holistic, and concrete to express their impact. While the varied implications of these systems have proven difficult to synthesize, it is evident that many configurations - social, technical, material - constitute them.

Chapter 3 demonstrated that the understanding of technological systems has evolved to include the contribution of their social environments and of less tangible material features entangled with the technical artifact. Creation and consequences continuously constitute each other. To understand the latter, we must examine the former. Common descriptions of AI systems fail to contextualize how their construction by and effects on society interact. Chapter 4 showed that, like analytical approaches of technology's genesis and impact, the term capital has expanded from its financial origins to comprise intangible factors, including sociological dimensions.

In all its iterations, capital characterizes assets that are of value and can be exercised as power in a specific context. I argue that this interpretation of capital as socially embedded influence is an apt conceptual basis to account for the impact of AI.

In this chapter, I continue my argument by outlining an original concept called **Code Capital** and its analytical framework. Conceptualizing the impact of AI as this new form of capital offers a nuanced and comparative ontology, and an analytical assessment and design tool for such systems. While my *concept* describes the overall meaning I intend to infer, the *framework* is a guide for analysis in each individual case. It requires an examination of how a particular system emerges along four dimensions, how it siphons benefits of the technology and unleashes its risks through human configurations and social interaction. Code Capital thereby acknowledges that each AI system manifests as valuable in individual ways, and its value is enacted in distinct forms of influence.

My framework for practical analysis provides four dimensions that comprise the eponymous acronym of CODE: **Conception, Operations, Data,** and **Environment.** In tandem with arguing the rationale for these foci, I offer a plethora of potential sub-categories for each as well as guiding questions. Rather than judge the influence of a particular AI system, Code Capital should be introduced as standard practice to enable a shared and comparative understanding of its current and potential impact and to bring its normative forces to the fore. At its core, my approach is a sociotechnical one, assuming that the multidimensional relationship between people, an AI system's formation, and its effects are entangled. The resulting model that I propose is instructive, not directive. It is a flexible guide to help identify the individual societal manifestations of AI systems through the lens of capital. It can be used in two ways: As an analysis of a deployed system and as a guide for the design of a novel system. Not all characteristics are necessarily present in every system. More work is needed: Refining and applying the framework to case studies is critical to assess its validity and fit for broader application. Appreciating AI systems' value should serve as a starting point to more accurately anticipate and modulate both intended and unintended interaction effects between the technology and humans.

5.2 Code Capital: The Concept

In order to introduce Code Capital, I will first define it as a concept before detailing the practical framework behind it. While the concept describes my underlying idea, the framework operationalizes the analytical dimensions.

Throughout its development process and life cycle, an AI system's power manifests through the interaction of humans with each of its configurations. It can be turned into impact in a range of arenas: economic, social, political, environmental, and others. These socially embedded forms of influence together represent the source of the system's value. I propose to call this account of an AI system's potential impact its **Code Capital**. *Code* does not refer to its software code, the specific technical program instructions, as such a purely computational notion would be too narrowly construed. Rather, it is *the capital encoded* within the system's unique social, technical, and material configurations overall. Besides, the framework will later illustrate the four analytical dimensions that comprise the eponymous acronym of CODE.

Four considerations are important to note. First, as I have previously defined, an AI system represents the deployment of an application in a particular context. As the case studies in Chapters 6 & 7 will demonstrate, the more nuanced the definition of the system to be analyzed, the more refined the Code Capital analysis. For example, applying my framework to assess conversational agents in general would lack in contextual focus. An examination of the Code Capital of Google's Duplex AI used for restaurant reservations in the United States, however, could yield a much more holistic picture of its socially embedded impact.

Second, as the above point clarifies, every AI system is embedded in its context, which significantly affects the system but is largely out of its authority. As described in Chapter 3, this parallels the notion of the LTS approach, suggesting that systems are comprised of "different but interlocking elements" (Bijker et al., 1987, p. 5) but have a remaining outside "made up of influences and forces that affect, and are affected by, the system, but are not controlled by it" (Hughes, 1986, p. 290). This means that Code Capital can be altered by external forces. But this alteration is mainly driven by how a system is embedded within an evolving environment. For example, one material feature of a system may be ruled illegal due to a change in regulation, changing prospects for its business model. However, modifying the system in accordance with regulatory developments may preserve and even strengthen its Code Capital. The focus of the concept of Code Capital and its analytical dimensions are thus the dynamic factors that directly contribute to how system is embedded, while taking into account external environments. In short: Humans have immense agency in shaping Code Capital.

Third, Code Capital does not express an inherent judgement or preference. It is guided by a premise aptly formulated by historian Melvin Kranzberg in 1986:

> Technology is neither good nor bad; nor is it neutral. (…) Technology's interaction with the social ecology is such that technical developments frequently have environmental, social, and human consequences that go far beyond the immediate purposes of the technical devices and practices themselves, and technology can have quite different results when introduced into different contexts or under different circumstances. Many of our technology-related problems arise because of the unforeseen consequences when apparently benign technologies are employed on a massive scale (1986, pp. 545–546).

Like technology itself, the Code Capital of sociotechnical products and services is neither intrinsically good nor bad. But it is Kranzberg's addendum that is central to my concept: Nor is it neutral. Code Capital, too, represents value that, when enacted, is never neutral. A system can have an enormous Code Capital with the potential to be used for either beneficial or nefarious purposes or even unintentionally to dangerous effect. Incidentally, Kranzberg explains his non-neutrality interpretation by alluding to the various factors that are reflected in each analytical dimension of the CODE framework, as I will elaborate below. First, all the configurations of an AI system occur in relation to their social ecology with immediate purposes of technical devices and practices. The configurations result, intentionally and unintentionally, in environmental, social, and human consequences, at times beyond their own defined scope. When employed at massive scale, these can occur in problematic proportions. Finally, when introduced into different contexts or under different circumstances, these effects can vary widely. I offer my concept of Code Capital to capture the multidimensional dynamics and ramifications Kranzberg refers to. It expresses impact that is neither good, nor bad, nor neutral. Code Capital brings to the fore these normative forces inherent in AI systems.

Fourth, the framework I will outline in Section 5.3 can be employed in two different circumstances. First, it serves as an *impact assessment tool* of an AI system already employed (see Chapter 6). In this case, a Code Capital analysis is based on established facts, external insights, and observable behaviors. Its main objectives are to assess and trace back the various impacts. The analysis will concentrate on the *explanatory power* of Code Capital. Second, the CODE framework can be used to *guide the design* of an AI system before it is deployed to better anticipate and manage its effects (see Chapter 7). In this case, the examination is based on processual investigation and insights, but also includes speculations about potential behaviors of users and other environmental aspects. Its main objectives are to *project potential effects* and to *offer trajectories* of adjusting the system with regards to prospective outcomes. Like much scholarly work in the realm of ethics by design, anticipatory technology ethics, and values in design has previously shown (L. D. Introna & Nissenbaum, 2000; Shilton, 2015, 2018), various sociopolitical forces are embedded into every step of the technological design process. At any point in a system's life cycle, a CODE analysis should empower those in control of affecting the system by incorporating considerations of Code Capital to make responsible decisions.

I have outlined my concept of Code Capital as the symbolic representation of the implications that may flow from an AI system. Code Capital is descriptive and instructive rather than normative and directive. It emphasizes that social actors have agency in manifesting and changing the impact of AI. In the next section, I will detail the four dimensions of the analytical process, their associated categories, and the range of questions they serve to prompt.

5.3 The CODE Framework

To establish a particular AI system's Code Capital, in this section I offer a framework for practical analysis. Through my research I have distilled four dimensions that comprise the eponymous acronym of CODE: **Conception**, **Operations**, **Data**, and **Environment**. To arrive at these, I synthesized my insights from three realms: First, as I illustrated in Chapter 3, my review of the literature on technology studies underlined the evolving understanding of the social, technical, and material factors that comprise a machine as deeply entangled. They beget each other. Their relation, enacted in practice, should factor prominently in an impact assessment. Second, as I showed in Chapter 4's study of capital, I derived that economies and societies driven by AI rely increasingly on intangible forces, most of which are difficult to quantify. In particular, configurations of software and data have become a strong currency. Third, I connected these theoretical insights with observations of the actual wide-ranging effects of common AI systems and their emergence, examples of which I outlined in Chapter 2. By consolidating the theoretical fields and aligning the results with empirical data, I crystallized the four categories described below as the key components that affect a system's manifested impact. In tandem with arguing the rationale for these foci, I provide a plethora of potential subcategories as well as guiding questions for each. Finally, I consider the question of metrics. A summary of the framework's ontology can be found in Figure 5.1. This framework is a flexible guide. While I consider the four dimensions integral, inalienable parts of any case study of Code Capital, certain subcategories might be more relevant for an individual AI system's analysis than others. Different case studies might require different anchors of analysis within the four CODE dimensions.

Figure 5.1 shows the CODE framework

Conception
Sensegiving actors
Narratives
Investment & expected returns
...

Operations
Model infrastructure
User interface
Device
...

CODE

Environment
Sensemaking actors
Social acceptance
Regulatory boundaries
...

Data
Collection
Pre-processing
Ethical concerns
...

5.3.1 Conception

A Code Capital analysis seeks to address various configurations of how the system has been conceived. **Conception** can refer to the original creation if a system is examined prior to deployment, or to the evolving conceptualization of the system at any point in time. The C-dimension of a Code Capital analysis examines the factors that contribute to the core beliefs, perspectives, priorities, and competencies that give rise to the system, the histories that precede and stories that shape the vision for it, and the incentives that drive decisions in a significant way. It should aim to uncover the imagined outcomes for the AI system, as well as the resources and constraints due to which it emerged. This element begins to map the foreseeable and *intended* consequences. Simultaneously, tracking them is the first step in signaling potential areas of oversight that can lead to *unintended* consequences because of heedless goals, perverse incentives, dereliction of responsibility, or perspectives that are lacking. Consider, for example, that an assessment of Facebook notes that this leading global social network platform might have "reconfigured society without *apparent intent* to deceive" [emphasis added] (Groth et al., 2019). A system's conception configurations can be gauged through various subcategories. I will outline three that can be particularly salient before suggesting potential others.

5.3.1.1 Sensegiving Actors

First, it is vital to understand the relevant social groups (Pinch & Bijker, 1987) who shape the seamless web (Hughes, 1986) of an AI system. This category should investigate how *sense is given* to the AI system more broadly. *Sensegiving* includes the definition, framing and dissemination of a desired future image (Fiss & Zajac, 2006; Gioia & Chittipeddi, 1991), a vision that is inscribed in the technological object (Akrich, 1992). As can be seen in many instances of AI systems in use today, priorities and preferences of those who give sense to the system can flow into defining the problem it seeks to solve. For example, in his analysis of the culture of coders, Clive Thompson observes that a pronounced affinity with notions of efficiency and optimization is pervasive among software developers which affects how they approach the conceptualization process. Thompson calls the tendency "so compelling, it's almost like an aesthetic (...). When optimization is your hammer, everything looks like a nail" (Chen, 2019)[39]. As a case in point, Thompson recalls the focus on engagement optimization in the case of many large social networks, which turned them

---

39 Thompson goes on to say: "Software engineers find it so compelling to improve and solve this one small aspect of code that it can be hard to look up and see the whole picture. Engineers like to make things and they like to make things used

"into these unbelievably high-throughput engines of everyday expression. (Coders) want people to click and stare all the time and so they create algorithms constantly trying to find the most outrageous and extreme expressions to push to the top because that's what compels and mesmerizes" (Chen, 2019). Sensegiving practices attempt to influence how those who use the system *make sense* and construct their meaning of it. Therefore, the notion of sensegiving implies "an element of power and politics involved in the design of technology" as "the prerogatives of sensegiving at the design stage may have an important effect on the sensemaking and sensegiving that are subsequently granted to others" (Ramiller & Chiasson, 2008, p. 124). This analysis considers who participates and who explicitly does not partake in the sensegiving of a system because "power is expressed in acts that shape what people accept, take for granted, and reject" (Weick et al., 2005, p. 418). More specifically, it examines the beliefs, values, and perceptions of these sensegiving actors and how their practices shape the conception of the system.

Questions about sensegiving actors should include: Who are those who give sense to the system, including those who invent, engineer, finance, facilitate, manage, and promote it? Which influences act upon them? How do professional lenses affect their logic and practices? What circumstances led them to conceiving of the system's purpose? To answer these prompts, interviews with sensegiving actors as well as supplementary material and empirical insights about circumstantial factors can serve as an input source.

5.3.1.2 Narratives

In addition to examining sensegiving actors and the influences acting upon them, a Code Capital analysis includes the stories they devise to give sense to the system internally and externally. Analyzing these *narratives* clarifies the problem the sensegiving actors consider the system to solve and identifies their goals for it. These may significantly diverge from the eventual system outcomes, but signal possible motivations for other operational choices (see subsequent sections). For example, the founders of the trading app Robinhood put their narrative focus for the system on the democratization of investing. While this is part of the offering, their un-

---

by people and it's very easy to get swept up in technical challenges and ignore the larger economic and social impact" (Chen, 2019).

derlying business model approached customers quite differently, as Forbes put it: "The perfect stock trading app for the videogame generation was supposed to 'democratize finance' with zero-commission trades. But the primary plan was to get rich by selling customer trades to the market's most notorious operators" (Kauflin et al., 2020). Overall, narrative analysis can serve as a rhetorical mirror of the intentions behind the AI system and the desired potential pathways. The objective should be to gauge how the formulated logics might reasonably or have already observably manifested.

Questions about narratives should include: What would a successful deployment of the system look like? What explicit stories shape the perception of the system? How much thorough consideration has been given feasibility of these logics? To what extent does empirical evidence support them? Input for this analysis can include documentation of the system's vision, its functions, and desired outcomes. In addition to direct descriptions by the sensegiving actors, internal memos, workshop records, marketing materials, or explainers can be a particularly relevant source.

5.3.1.3 Investments and Expected Returns

An examination of the system's conception requires an analysis of the financial dynamics and incentives involved. Specifically, the *invested resources and expected returns* give an indication of the funds that allow the system to emerge as well as the potential business model that might motivate its development. Financial assets can be decisive in matters of scaling a system, for example when infrastructure expansion is necessary, or data collection is costly. More specifically, the aspect of investment is relevant due to the fact that monetary interests can influence priorities and "(deform) decisions," for example "what code gets written and why" (Thompson, 2019, p. 57). Additionally, a system may introduce an entirely new business model that serves as an industry disruptor. For example, a number of platform companies have disrupted the way technology firms act as intermediaries who match on-demand labor from third parties to demand by its customers, facilitating peer-to-peer economic transactions. While eBay and Craigslist revolutionized the recirculation of goods, companies like Airbnb did the same for the utilization of durable goods, TaskRabbit for the exchange of services, and co-working spaces for the sharing of productive assets (J. Schor, 2016). Implications are likely not just individual and collective but systemic changes to the economic ecosystem. In short, this sub-category may influence choices on operational matters and issues of embedding the system in its environment. Facebook, for example, employs certain operational features to ensure the continuation of its business model and thereby, some argue, "creates all this civic harm because of the infernal synchronization of their advertising needs and ability to encourage and seduce people" (Chen, 2019).

Questions about incentives should address: What types of resources contributed to conceiving the system? How does financial gain factor into the purpose of the system? Are commodification mechanisms tied to the system objectives? If yes, do the expected returns align with the explicitly stated goals or could they produce underlying, perverse incentives? If the commodification mechanisms involve users' behavior and personal data, are they communicated clearly? These questions can be answered through interviews with sensegiving actors, financial documents and contracts, and independent investigation of funding sources.

While these are three significant aspects of the C-dimension, others can add context when relevant: They might include *historical background* and how the trajectory of past systems employing similar AI technology has influenced conception; *current competition* and how it shapes the objectives, narratives, and incentives for the system; and *active opposition* from distinct stakeholders to the emergence of the system.

5.3.2 Operations

Next, Code Capital comprises an examination of how the intentions of those who conceive the system have been operationalized. **Operations** comprise the translation of objectives into material features and the specifically constructed infrastructure of the AI agent. While previously mentioned aspects investigate the socioeconomic influences on the system, this dimension focuses on the practices and decisions of implementing the system; it thus involves what Star termed an "ethnography of infrastructure" (Star, 1999). The material contours of the AI system such as its algorithmic models, optimization priorities, user interface design, and hardware specifications together make up the possibilities and constraints for using the system. Articulating the conscious and default choices made by the sensegiving actors, why and how they were configured, underlines them as "decisions about what should be delegated to a machine and what should be left to the initiative of human actors" (Akrich, 1992, p. 216). Modeled after Russell & Norvig's "principles for building successful agents (...) that can reasonably be called intelligent" (2010, p. 34), the O-dimension concerns itself with the constitution of the AI agent itself. However, the analytical approach should focus on the relational process between the social and material, and on how their entanglement has led to particular selections of operational infrastructure. The objective of this dimension is, broadly speaking, to assess how factors of Conception are expressed through material features. Depending on their extent of alignment, this element can further signal potential areas of oversight.

5.3.2.1 Model Infrastructure

One central subcategory addresses the details of the chosen model(s) performing the system task. It includes considerations of the algorithms used to train the model, the performance measures that determine criteria for the agent's success, and an understanding of the type of task environment the agent acts in (Russell & Norvig, 2010, p. 37). Understanding the type of algorithmic goal - for example classification, prediction, or clustering – and the algorithms chosen to create a representation of the input data, means grasping the key building blocks of the AI system. It can also identify possible system implications beyond the intended outcomes: A chosen algorithm might fulfil the stated objective, but, driven by socially embedded data (see Section 5.3.3) and embedded itself in a human context (see Section 5.3.4), could also lead to unintended interaction effects. For instance, Google's PageRank, the algorithm first used to weight websites to determine their importance, relevance, and authority (Page et al., 1998) optimizes for numerous confidential factors (Evans, 2007). Consider that the optimization priorities encoded in this large model direct the search results that sort and rank information for billions of users every day. Suggestion networks triggered by the engine's auto-complete function may perpetuate stereotypes (P. Baker & Potts, 2013; Karapapa & Borghi, 2015; Robertson et al., 2019). Moreover, given that the outcome is also tied to individual search histories to improve user relevance, the same query may generate different outcomes for two people (Bai et al., 2017; Tan et al., 2006). As this dynamic is not intrinsically apparent, users, however, may perceive the system to offer equivalent results with the veneer of objectivity. As this example shows, the opacity of the algorithmic infrastructure lacks transparency and has created some unintended consequences. Especially in an AI system with billions of users, these impacts can be exponential: "(Coders') instinctive desire to optimize – and scale – is what has led to many collisions between software firms and civic life. (...) Code makes efficiency and scale easy, seductive, almost inevitable" (Thompson, 2019, p. 20). Thus, a Code Capital analysis must investigate the main functions and material features of the model architecture to deduce implications for how the task is carried out.

Questions about the model infrastructure should address: What is the prioritized task? What are the most significant characteristics of the task environment? What influenced the choice of algorithms employed? Which variables most affect the outcome of the model? Do the defined performance measures correspond to the overall objective of the system? This is best documented through interaction with those responsible for the development of the actual model or a direct investigation of the written code.

5.3.2.2 User Interface

Decisions about the user interface design significantly guide the experience of people with the system in practice (D. Stone et al., 2005). For example, user interface design can impact affective states, such as a sensation of flow (D. Johnson & Wiles, 2003). While international standards of usability center around effectiveness, efficiency, and satisfaction (Oppermann, 2002), this sub-category is concerned with the bridge between the intended objective of the system, the model infrastructure in its backend, and the final material features that users interact with. Interface configurations can have significant implications, such as infinite newsfeeds radically changing user habits through intermittent rewards (Neyman, 2017; Pettman, 2016), or the autoplay feature for videos leading to increasingly extreme content recommendations (Stöcker & Preuss, 2020). Design and functionalities that comprise the "choice architecture" of the user interface can nudge people's behavior to both positive and negative effects (Thaler et al., 2013). More generally, the particular configurations can contribute to sensemaking of the system.

Questions about the user interface might include: What concerns and considerations influenced the choice architecture? Does the interface correspond to the overall objective of the system? What target user group characteristics were used as a basis for design and for testing? To what extent does the interface communicate the purpose and functionality of the system clearly and accessibly? An independent analysis and test of the user interface can add context and insights to information given by the sensegiving actors.

5.3.2.2 Device

In tandem to the material features of the user interface, configurations concerning the physical features of the system device can have wide-ranging implications. For example, a facial recognition system integrated into a smartphone might have very different implications than a clandestine public camera set-up. The device components, such as the agent's perception sensors and actuators for execution, as well as their design in relation to user experience should be taken into account.

Questions could address: How do the physical features align with the stated objectives of the system? What target user group characteristics were used as a basis for design and for testing? To what extent does the artifact clarify or obfuscate the AI system's goals and functionalities? Again, an independent examination and test of the technical artifact can add insights to information given by the sensegiving actors.

These three, model architecture, user interface, and device, are significant sub-categories of examining the O-dimension. For more context, a Code Capital analysis might include an examination of the *hardware* components and how they determine the system's performance and user experience; the *evaluation* of performance measures and how the system's success is defined. Crucially, the agent neither functions nor learns without data input. As the next section shows, due their centrality in an AI system, data merit their own dimension.

5.3.3 Data

The D-dimension analyzes the **Data** fueling the AI system in more detail. More specifically, it examines how data are conceptualized, produced, and used within a social context. As the constitution of data has direct ramifications for agent behavior and outcomes, numerous choices along the way are of interest. Data are not only vital for training the initial computational models, they continue to drive the system as the model learns (Russell & Norvig, 2010, p. 39). Processes to collate, clean, analyze and leverage digital information are decisive because the quality and nature of the data directly impacts the outcomes of the AI system. Importantly, "as a result of its social situatedness, information has an intrinsic ethical dimension" (Goguen, 1997, p. 1). Real life data reflects a reality that is heavily biased - because humans are. For example, the dataset used to train Google image search included so few people of color, that users found that in response to queries for the term 'gorilla' the algorithm included photos of non-white persons, thereby reinforcing racist tropes (Barr, 2015). Moreover, in its in-depth analysis of the risk assessment algorithm that purports to forecast criminal recidivism rates, ProPublica found substantial racial differences in the predictions. Specifically, people of color were almost twice as likely as whites to be wrongly tagged as future criminals. Meanwhile, whites are much more likely to be misidentified by the algorithm as low risk (Angwin et al., 2016). As the type of affected groups illustrate, these reproductions based on biased data exacerbate existing inequalities. Previous biases can accumulate in code to be encrypted as rules for the future. Rather than being a mere representation of information, data and the way it is constructed affects how humans derive meaning from it. Factors such as the logic for data choices, the sources, means of collection, inclusion and exclusion criteria, processing protocols, as well as other social considerations during each step directly contribute to the contours of the system's impact and must be investigated.

5.3.3.1 Collection

Collating the data for the system's model involves many choices. Both the data for training the model as well as the data later fed as input are analytically relevant. While the former kind originally steers the model of the system and is the basis for the initial pattern recognition, the latter is its engine in practice. This sub-category seeks to examine the means of collection and how choices about the sources of data influence outcomes. It should consider the accessibility and static or dynamic nature of these data, as access to troves of dynamic data, for instance, offers trajectories of large scale. Questions should address: How were the sources for and methods of data collection chosen? What socially embedded factors impact the datasets used for training? Is the nature of the data static or dynamic? How large is the potential to scale the data collection process? Are those most affected by the AI system meaningfully represented in the data?

5.3.3.2 Pre-Processing

Next, techniques to prepare the collected data as a quality gate for processing govern which pieces of information are deemed relevant and of sufficient condition for inclusion. They can comprise quantitative and logical cleaning methods to detect and repair errors as well as lapses of necessary standards (Chu et al., 2016; Prokoshyna et al., 2015). As these exercises involve the sifting through raw data, which may be restricted in aggregation for some domains or for privacy reasons, protocols for how to prepare the data can impact the overall outcome of the system. Questions should thus include: What techniques are used for identifying and repairing quality failures? What criteria determine relevance for inclusion and exclusion of data? How does the resulting data impact the training of the model or the regular operating of the trained system?

5.3.3.3 Ethical Concerns

Given the volume and often personal nature of the data used in AI systems, their handling raises a host of ethical questions. Particularly when employed in sensitive domains, issues of privacy and bias are of central concern. For example, the data collected and processed by widespread facial analysis technologies can lead to consequential privacy violations. Moreover, biased data can result in system outcomes with life-changing consequences like in the case of health care delivery (Char et al., 2018) or felony verdicts (Angwin et al., 2016). As data can reflect the discriminatory societal practices of the past and present, models trained to learn and incorporate these patterns may continue and even exacerbate inequities by generating self-fulfilling prophecies (Eubanks, 2018; O'Neil, 2017). A lack of consideration for the ethical dimensions of data in AI systems may lead to outcomes that range from controversial and unethical to illegal. Several recent data protection laws dictate the purposes for and the conditions under which personal data may be collected, processed, and stored. Generally, these include stipulations about transparent communication, consent, and accountability mechanisms. This sub-category thus considers how various ethical logics manifest in the handling of data for the AI system under analysis. Questions should address among others: How is the detection of disproportionate bias enabled? How are privacy, security, and consent requirements ensured? Do the available data enable efficacy and integrity in performing the agent's stated task responsibly?

In addition to the three sub-categories mentioned above, the D-dimension might take into account techniques for *processing* the data and configurations of *storage*; in addition, *quality gate management* in terms of continuous batch learning might factor into consideration. This part of the analysis necessitates external insights about the ethical standards and state-of-the art protocols in addition to interviews and documentation.

5.3.4 Environment

The final dimension examines how the system is embedded in its overall social ecology. While its surroundings are not governed by the system, they play a crucial role as "not only environment becomes organism, but background merges into foreground. (...) The so-called social and political background are embodied in the technology" (Hughes, 1986, p. 290). That is to say, the Environment refers to how the system is positioned and entangled within its surroundings. It includes consideration of the people who make sense of the system within their social and cultural context, the regulatory boundaries that directly affect the implementation of the system, and the potential social interaction effects prompted by and fed back into the system. As technology acceptance models and their empirical evaluations demonstrate, the successful dissemination and integration of an innovation significantly depend on factors of social context, prior experience, and community norms among others (Venkatesh et al., 2003, 2012). Institutional frameworks can further constrain disruptive systems. For instance, Uber's AI driven ride-sharing service experienced vastly different societal and industry receptions in the United States versus Germany and other worldwide settings (Thelen, 2018). Moreover, the introduction in recent years of the General Data Protection Regulation (GDPR) as well as the EU Guidelines for Trustworthy AI have introduced markedly distinct legal frameworks for AI systems in the European Union compared to many other contexts on the international stage. Thus, the E-dimension's objective is to capture how those in control of affecting the system choose to embed it within these environmental factors.

5.3.4.1 Sensemaking Actors

To gauge an AI system's impact in a particular community, those who make sense of the system in practice have enormous influence on its implications. As the outcomes are largely enacted in relation to those who are affected by the system, their background for sensemaking in terms of potential historical precedents, recent events, societal values and cohesion, trust in institutions and technology, as well as needs and habits, are of interest. Crucially, there are three distinct types of sensemaking actors. First, there are those actors who actively decide to participate in the system by using it. Second, there are those actors who actively decide not to participate or use the system. Third, there are those actors who have no choice of participation but are still affected by the system. This can then be distinguished into those who are aware of their involvement and those who are ignorant of it. For example, in considering the Code Capital of a search engine one might examine those who make sense of the platform by using, those who decide to actively disengage by not using it, and those who might be featured as a data point in the results of the search engine, either knowingly or unknowingly. Thus, this sub-category investigates whose actions, narratives, and logics willingly or unwillingly contribute to the sensemaking of the system.

Questions that cover the sensemaking actors should include: Who gets the option to participate and why? How does the system represent or reject the conventions and values of the local community? Does the cultural context of the sensegiving actors come into conflict with those of the sensemaking actors? To answer these, betatests of prototypes in the case of system in development or empirical observations and research of actual user demographics, behaviors and reactions to the system can serve as evidence.

5.3.4.2 Social Acceptance

To holistically assess the potential impact of an AI system, one of the most central factors lies in the anticipated *social acceptance* of the system. Without it, the system will fail. While an AI has the potential to change fundamental social dynamics, human agency must be acknowledged not just on the part of the sensegiving but also the sensemaking actors as they choose to accept and integrate, reject or demand change of the system. As many models and studies have shown, a range of social, political, economic, cultural, and psychological factors influence human-machine interaction, including the acceptance of the technology. For example, research has demonstrated the human tendency to be influenced by the perceived impression of what opinions or behaviors are common or considered desirable by one's societal reference group (Cialdini & Goldstein, 2004; Paluck & Shepherd, 2012; Sherif, 1936; Tankard & Paluck, 2017). Through interaction with family members, friends, peers, and important social leaders, individuals gather information and adjust their behavior according to expectations of what is accepted and what is rejected (Bandura, 1986). People may infer such social norms through the observation or reports of others' behavior, through distributed summary information about a group, or institutional signals such as the introduction of new innovations, public rules, or systems of rewards and punishments (Tankard & Paluck, 2016). Both the impressions of current status quo norms and directional norms about what may be desirable in the future may alter a person's conduct in the present (Tankard & Paluck, 2017). In interviews as part of their study of the acceptability of face biometrics, Krol et al (2016) found that a number of people mentioned their concern for what others would think and stated that they would use the technology if a critical mass of others would. Some work has shown that shifting perceived social norms can influence actual behavior even when one's personal beliefs do not change (Paluck, 2009; Paluck & Green, 2009). Even when individuals misinterpret others' feelings and beliefs about a particular topic these flawed estimates may influence the receivers' expression of their opinions and behavior in a way that perpetuates the erroneous norms (Hines et al., 2002; Lambert et al., 2003; Prentice & Miller, 1996). Thus, examining the perception individuals have of social norms around an AI system is crucial for understanding what may affect differing acceptance levels across countries. A Code Capital analysis attempts to gauge how the sensemaking actors' reaction to and behavior towards the system fundamentally contributes to and can even change its impact. Questions that address this human-machine interaction should include: What social factors determine people's acceptance of the system? To what extent does the system impact a diversity of human lives, individually and collectively? Empirical data and observations about these factors should complement interviews to answer these questions.

5.3.4.3 Regulatory Boundaries

Crucially, the legal landscape of rules that directly or tangentially apply to the deployment of the system, as well as those regulation proposals currently in development and potentially relevant in the future, should be taken into account. Specifically, given that the E-dimension focuses on the embedding within an environment, this subcategory investigates how the system's configurations adhere to regulatory boundaries, how they have influenced the previous three dimensions, and how it might be in conflict or even newly challenge legal conventions. Given that regulation tends to lag in time behind technological innovation, particularly in the realm of

AI, emerging systems often confront the lack of standards or laws in a given industry. Particularly with regards to the processing of personal data and in the case of unprecedented, disruptive business models, these regulatory boundaries form an important backdrop to the system's manifestation of impact. Questions should include: Does successful implementation of the system adhere to or challenge existing laws or ethical standards? How do choices of its embedding affect its legality? Does the system affect or upend current institutions? Qualitative data should be complemented by the study of necessary legal frameworks.

In addition to these key aspects, the E-dimension could consider a range of sub-categories. For example, one could examine aspects of *Sustainability* and how the system's constitution and deployment might impact the natural ecology. As Kate Crawford details in *Atlas of AI*, several environmental resources contribute to the development and maintenance of many large AI systems (Crawford, 2021). This sub-category would investigate how processes and practices in the creation of AI could be designed in a more sustainable manner to mitigate ecologically harmful impacts. Next, considering *Psychological Dynamics* would entail an examination of how bi-directional human machine interaction might change such neurological processes as cognition. For example, theories of Distributed Cognition posit that rather than considering only the human individual as the unit of analysis, functional relationships between various elements that can include external technical artifacts are what delimits a cognitive process (Hollan et al., 2000). This implies that using a technological tool may become embodied into what is considered our cognitive process, with both influencing and shaping the other, a phenomenon discussed as Extended Mind (A. Clark & Chalmers, 1998).

5.4 Discussion

In the previous section, I elaborated on the concept of Code Capital and the CODE framework. While the concept of Code Capital defines the central idea that AI systems hold intangible assets that can be turned into valuable impact, the CODE framework provides the ontology for a common approach to identify and evaluate this impact. It is designed to be customized for an individual AI system throughout its life cycle and is therefore not specific to any industry or sector. To complement both, in this section I reflect on further steps for operationalization and potential theoretical implications.

To apply the framework as described above and derive meaningful insight from its results, a range of measurement techniques may be considered. While it is not in the scope of this work to establish firm benchmarks of methods for each of the CODE dimensions, I expect to develop them in future research. Three sets of standards from different disciplines may serve as examples to inspire such benchmarks. First, my framework should help focus impact considerations and serve as a useful guide for decision-making. Similarly, the Balanced Scorecard (BSC) provides four dimensions for assessing strategy performance (Kaplan, 2009; Kaplan & Norton, 1998). To begin with, two insights resemble the premise of Code Capital. First, again, an evolution from a sole focus on the economic to the inclusion of sociological factors can be seen: The BSC was considered particularly innovative because it combined financial as well as non-financial objectives and measures (Chavan, 2009). Second, the framework marries not only external with internal influences, but insights about past performance with predictions for drivers of the future. Code Capital, too, seeks to evaluate how configurations of the past and present may influence impact in the future. Moreover, the BSC can be customized to determine and illustrate evolving priorities. In tandem to the CODE framework, it integrates the insights from four distinct arenas to offer a more holistic analysis. Within each dimension, managers choose a limited number of indicators which are then translated into clear, quantifiable metrics. In contrast to the focus of the BSC, however, Code Capital does not function in a purely quantitative way, a point which the next example addresses.

A second instance for inspiration is the major international standard of multi-dimensional impact ratings on Environmental, Social, and Governance (ESG) performance indicators to guide investment decisions. Examples of ESG factors are pollution (E), working conditions (S), and executive pay (G). Relative to each industry, third-party providers weight averages on key issues in these three crucial areas to rate a company based on its impact in comparison to their relevant peers. In 2006, the United Nations additionally established the Principles for Responsible Investment (PRI) to support signatory organizations in integrating ESG considerations into their decision-making (United Nations Environment Programme, 2020). While many third-party providers have sprung up to analyze numerous data sources and to issue verdicts, the methodology, rating scales, and scope vary widely. Some use an AAA-CCC or AAA-D scale, others rank out of 100, or in the 1st to 10th decile (Huber & Comstock, 2017). Attributes that are included differ from one ratings agency to another, as do their measurements and the aggregation of certain indicators into one score (Berg et al., 2019). Finally, some factors necessitate subjective decisions which might lead to reasonable dispute. And yet, given the intersectoral approach of ESG ratings, challenges in comparability are currently unavoidable. Similarly, Code Capital is not easily comparable as a single score – nor should it be. The specifics of the framework must be individually tailored to each AI system for maximum relevance. This involves choosing certain subcategories within each of the four dimensions over others. Rather than a guide merely for financial investment decisions, Code Capital should serve as an internal framework for making informed decisions that directly control the system to responsibly manage impact and as an external one for holding the system accountable.

Third, the International Standards Organization (ISO), a global body for developing widely applicable norm specifications on a range of topics, has issued guidelines on integrating *risk management* into institutional practices. In their introduction, the definition of risk is the "effect of uncertainty on objectives" with a further explanation that it comprises the "external and internal factors and influences that make it uncertain whether they will achieve their objectives" (International Standards Organization, 2018)[40]. Code Capital, too, evaluates how the configurations of an AI system make some consequences more or less likely, and whether they align with or contradict the objectives. Importantly, these particular ISO recommendations advise to collate information on *consequences* with their respective *likelihoods*. They express no preference for qualitative or quantitative approaches to identify, analyze, and evaluate risks in order to treat them, instead explicitly stating that both types of techniques can be combined to reach useful conclusions (Purdy, 2010). Similarly, the range of factors within the C, O, D, and E dimension of my framework require a mixed methods approach.

As stated above, my future research will narrow in on the formulation of these processes, including methods for predictions, recommendations, and accountability mechanisms. At this stage, I stipulate that an ideal practice for a deployed system would be to make Code Capital analyses available to interested outside parties, including, crucially, users, so that anyone can appraise motivations and conscious decision-making practices to understand how the AI system is configured and manifests desired

---

40 Similarly relevant ISO recommendations to consider might be No. 22317 on Business Impact Analysis (International Standards Organization, 2015) and the upcoming No. 37000 on Governance in Organizations (International Standards Organization, 2020).

effects. This could occur in the form of explicit Code Capital impact predictions that express how each of the four CODE dimensions might lead to likely outcomes. Evidence should include quantitative as well as qualitative research. In the case of a Code Capital analysis at the design stage of a system, recommendations should be issued for the case that predictions diverge from the stated objectives or indicate unintended ramifications. My two case studies (Chapters 6 and 7) shed further light on the actual applicability of the framework to real-world AI systems, which I will reflect upon in Chapter 8.

Finally, another consideration concerns the theoretical implications of Code Capital, as this is a novel approach to contextualize AI systems through the lens of an interdisciplinary repository of various capitals. Previous notions of capital were defined by the similarity to their economic roots, for example, by their ways of accumulation, reproduction, and conversion. For instance, financial capital can be obtained by economic transactions, cultural capital by increasing one's social resources. Capital can thus be acquired and expanded. At this stage, I consider Code Capital to be acquired by expanding one's command of an AI system's actual and potential assets. Acknowledging that these configurations are entangled and together impact "the social world's functioning in a durable way" (Bourdieu, 1983), one can expand an AI system's Code Capital by consciously leveraging the four dimensions. Through my two case studies, I will further explore whether and how certain choices may serve to reproduce existing power structures and whether Code Capital is convertible into other forms of capital.

5.5 Conclusion

In this chapter, I have introduced my original framework of Code Capital. Its main contribution is the synthesis of relevant interdisciplinary concepts into a framework that considers AI systems through the lens of a novel notion of capital. Against the backdrop of the increasing public relevance of AI systems, Code Capital can serve as a two-fold analytical tool for computer scientists, entrepreneurs,investors, and policy makers. First, it may be used as an instrument for responsibly designing an AI system, anticipating unintended consequences and deliberately shaping outcomes along relevant priorities. Second, it can be used as a model to evaluate an AI system's potential for impact at a particular point in its life cycle and dependent on variouscultural contexts. In the next two chapters, I will demonstrate my own application of the CODE framework to two AI case studies. The first examines a case of facial recognition technology, the second addresses synthetic voice generation.

6. Impact Assessment: Facial analysis

"We've opened Pandora's box. We have unleashed this."
T.C., personal communication, 2021

6.1 Introduction

One of the most successful machine learning applications deployed into the real world involves the automated analysis of human faces. Smartphones, closed-circuit television, and other camera systems capture human behavior in private and public settings at an unprecedented frequency. As major international companies like Apple, Facebook, Google, Alibaba, and Baidu have integrated some type of facial analysis into their platforms, an ever-expanding trove of applications and data is now available. Rules and laws regulating the technology are as sparse as the debate thereof is vigorous, spanning from the halls of the U.S. Congress to the parliament of the European Union. Given the ubiquity and consequential relevance of facial recognition technology (FRT) today, grasping its novel implications is important for researchers, practitioners, and policy makers alike. How can we analyze the actual and potential impacts – the Code Capital – of FRT?

First, this chapter will consider the technical nuances and varying global adoption cases of, concerns raised by, and global public perceptions of FRT. I present empirical data from an original cross-country study on the factors driving social acceptance of public FRT in four nations, which demonstrates how different societal environments and cultural norms affect citizen approaches to the technology. This research also clarifies that, like other AI systems, FRT entails a set of dynamic, entangled sociotechnical relations. Appreciating societal variations that manifest as the context for FRT applications is necessary but not sufficient to grasp the technology's wide-ranging implications. An assessment of potential impact requires a concrete case study to investigate how the system is configured by the complexities of context. Specifically, it must consider how chosen and default configurations form inflection points in the technology's interaction with users of a scope far beyond the technological realm. Thus, for the rest of the chapter, I then apply the CODE framework and closely examine the four dimensions of one particular system, FacesOfTheRiot, a facial analysis tool that emerged in the aftermath of the insurrection of the US capitol on January 6th, 2021. This unit of study is a project to automatically detect faces and make them publicly available for further recognition and identification purposes. Developed anonymously with the purported aim to provide the U.S. federal authorities with material to identify perpetrators, this technology raises and differentiates many of the issues associated with the wider realm of facial analysis, such as rights to and boundaries of privacy, bias in accuracy rates, and the consequences of facial recognition in the hands of law enforcement. To better understand the sensegiving motivations and detailed operational decisions that constitute the system in its current form, I conducted interviews with three key participants in the process, including the anonymous developer of FacesOfTheRiot, and triangulated publicly available information about the project's purpose and functionalities. Finally, I discuss and reflect on the technology's Code Capital and the process of analysis.

6.1.1 Facial Recognition Technology and its Global Use

FRT operates by scanning input captured as a still or moving image to localize critical regions of a face, encoding its features, and matching them to a reference database for comparison to distinguish particular identities (L. D. Introna & Nissenbaum, 2010). Computational goals for such a software comprise face detection (Rowley et al., 1998; Viola & Jones, 2001, 2004), classification (Lyons et al., 1999), verification, and identification (Parkhi et al., 2015). Its applications span a wide variety (Huang et al., 2005): Methods of face detection and classification have been employed to examine identity factors like sex (Abdi et al., 1995; Brunelli & Poggio, 1993) and race (Scheuerman et al., 2020) as well as emotional states associated with facial expressions (Benitez-Quiroz et al., 2017; Picard, 2002) which in turn can be used to support the diagnosis of neuropsychiatric disorders (Hamm et al., 2011) or marketing efforts to predict consumer behavior (Shergill et al., 2008). Identity verification through FRT may guard access to sensitive spaces (Center, 1998) such as airports (Bates, 2009), casinos (Zielke & Wolfer, 2008), border crossings (del Rio et al., 2016), and to restricted resources such as financial transactions (Aru & Gozie, 2013) or personal devices (Tao & Veldhuis, 2010).

In addition to its myriad applications on personal devices, FRT is used by law enforcement agencies around the world to monitor the public space via biometric database. In combination with existing public video surveillance, law enforcement agencies use FRT to complement policing practices through individual identification of suspects or criminals based on face recordings (Gates, 2011). Compared to other biometric measurements such as finger prints, FRT has a clandestine capability as the non-intrusive collection of individual features is possible at a distance when faces are visible in public (Woodward et al., 2003, p. 7).

International adoption rates of FRT by both governments and private companies vary widely. In China, FRTs are particularly common as, fused with other big data collection tools have become central to the government's plan to be the world's leader in AI. Government agencies have begun using FRT for multiple purposes, including pension payments in Shenzhen and social control of Muslim Uighur minorities in Xinjiang (Mozur, 2019). To register the 850 million mobile Chinese internet users, an official decree now mandates an identity-verifying facial scan before obtaining any new phone or internet service (Li, 2019). Meanwhile, widespread commercial applications have firmly embedded the technology in the daily lives of citizens through offerings such as smile-to-pay (AFP, 2019), largely popularized by ecommerce platform Alibaba's financial arm Alipay. Local FRT providers have also begun to expand its customer base outside of China: In addition to providing their own government with AI to sift through troves of facial data, FRT firms SenseTime and Megvii have begun supplying foreign clients in over a dozen settings outside of China (Simonite, 2019).

In Germany, by contrast, with the historical backdrop of two precedents for oppressive surveillance states in the recent past, FRT adoption has been lower in terms of speed and scope. In 2016, the Ministry of the Interior announced plans to equip airports and train stations with the technology (J. Baker, 2016). Since then, border crossings at major airports offer the EasyPASS system with integrated FRT for identity verification. Results from a first real-life test of an FRT application at one of Berlin's subway stations in the summer of 2018 were mixed and met with vociferous concerns for privacy by citizens (Delcker, 2018).[41]

In the United Kingdom, a nation long equipped with extensive CCTV particularly in its capital, both law enforcement actors and private companies have employed FRT. Currently not governed by a particular legal

---

41 Legally, the EU's GDPR requires consent to process sensitive data like biometrics, but substantial public interest such as national security or public safety may afford a path for circumvention.

framework, FRT falls under existing UK privacy and data protection laws, while police databases hold an estimated 20 million facial records (Burgess, 2019). At least two major UK police departments utilize live face-tracking, a development condoned by a British High Court in an unprecedented lawsuit about real-time uses of FRT (Satariano, 2019). A London property developer in charge of the city's central hub King's Cross has deployed the technology for monitoring the 67-acre area, which includes shops, offices, and a university, leading to an investigation by the country's information commissioner (Murgia, 2019). According to a UK liberties advocacy group, British shopping malls, museums, and conference centers around the country have installed FRT (Big Brother Watch UK Team, 2019).

In the United States, a country of particular relevance to this chapter, public and commercial use of FRT has become increasingly widespread. While the US Department of Defense has long funded research on a range of biometrics for national security purposes, the 9/11 terror attacks prompted a surge in the implementation of technology-driven public safety measures including FRT (Bowyer, 2004). Researchers estimate that one out of two US adult faces exists in a law enforcement database (Garvie et al., 2016). News reports confirm that myriad police departments, the Federal Bureau of Investigation (FBI) as well as Immigration and Customs Enforcement make use of FRT, in some cases in combination with the driver's license photos of thousands of unknowing US citizens without any legislative authorization (Harwell, 2019a). US cities including San Francisco, Oakland, and Somerville responded to the expansive use of the technology by banning it for its own municipal departments and police forces (Metz, 2019), prompting the state of California to pass a bill to ban biometric surveillance including FRT (Morse, 2019). Rights groups such as the American Civil Liberties Union and the Electronic Frontier Foundation have lobbied Congress to consider a suspension of FRT (Lecher, 2019).

Protest has also erupted over the installation of FRT for security purposes in US schools (St. Vincent, 2019) and residential buildings (Durkin, 2019). Commercial application of FRT through US-based companies reaches particularly large scale because of globally operating technology companies like Facebook and Apple who offer, for example, automatic photo-tagging (Taigman et al., 2014).

While prominent American firms like Microsoft and Amazon have been among the providers of facial analysis software for governmental use in the past, their executives have publicly endorsed regulation, though notably favoring controlled use over outright bans (Fussell, 2019). In 2020,

Microsoft, IBM and Amazon announced a moratorium on police use of their FRT until regulation would be passed (Allyn, 2020; Greene, 2020). However, several smaller providers of the technology moved fast to fill the void in offering FRT to law enforcement (Greig, 2021). Given that citizens face various moments of potential interaction with FRT, some of which do not include their active consent but their imperceptible biometric capture, the processing of citizens' identifying features by both governments and commercial firms continues to significantly affect public and private life.

6.1.2 Issues of Concern: Bias, Accuracy, Privacy, and Abuse

Multiples studies have demonstrated that training data infused with human bias (Bolukbasi et al., 2016; Caliskan et al., 2017) as well as algorithmic mechanisms have led to discrimination through AI systems (Datta et al., 2015; Lambrecht & Tucker, 2019; Sweeney, 2013). Research has specifically illustrated such risk of discriminatory effects in FRT (Braca, 2017; Ngan & Grother, 2015). Studies have demonstrated that bias in performance disproportionately impacts women and people of color (Klare et al., 2012). For example, Buolamwini & Gebru uncovered substantial disparities in the accuracy of gender classification systems applied to facial analysis, showing that the technology disproportionally misidentified the faces of darker females (2018). Another study showed similarly weak performances on transgender individuals and an inability to classify non-binary genders (Scheuerman et al., 2019).

Moreover, given the rise of synthetic "deepfake" media, facial recognition services might also be prone to deception due to impersonations. As a recent study demonstrated, FRT applications from leading companies like Microsoft and Amazon were unable to register the fraudulent imitations as impersonation attacks in a majority of cases (Tariq et al., 2021).

Like with other forms of surveillance technology, increasing applications of FRT by law enforcement have prompted debates about the balancing of privacy rights and security measures (McCoy, 2002; Milligan, 1999). Legal scholars who consider existing privacy law insufficiently suited for FRT that may scan publicly available images without requiring consent of individuals have argued for the need of a user opt-out regime (McClurg, 2007). In combination with live-tracking and body-worn cameras, some posit the use of FRT by law enforcement might also redefine public spaces by erasing anonymity therefore endangering free speech protections (Ringrose, 2019). Concerns about the technology's variations in accuracy are particularly noteworthy when FRT is expected to produce reliable, admissible evidence to be used for law enforcement.

Finally, abuse of FRT may cause disparate implications for already vulnerable groups. Controversial research efforts to demonstrate a correlation between facial features and criminality (Wu & Zhang, 2016) or sexual orientation (Yilun Wang & Kosinski, 2018) signal the potential for misappropriating the technology. Applying FRT for tracking ethnic minorities (Leibold, 2020; Mozur, 2019) and for sensitive personal use cases such as healthcare (Martinez-Martin, 2019) or individual access to government services (Fouquet, 2019) raises particular ethical questions.

With the ubiquity and potentially covert nature of facial capture, discussions of tradeoffs between progress, security, and liberties (Bowyer, 2004; Gray, 2003; L. Introna & Wood, 2004) have spurred numerous calls for greater accountability and oversight of FRT (Mann & Smith, 2017; Naker & Greenbaum, 2017). Therefore, regulatory boundaries to FRT have recently gained much attention, which I discuss in more detail in Section 6.5.

6.1.3 Interaction with the Public

Depending on national and cultural contexts, divergent notions of privacy, security, and discrimination affect the public perception, reaction and thus interaction with FRT in different settings. Thus, approval rates of biometric surveillance technologies vary in international comparison. Previous studies have shown that people are most likely to accept technologies, including facial recognition, that they are most familiar with (Buckley & Nurse, 2019). This suggests prevalence of FRT may affect familiarity and thus acceptance. In one study of Chinese Internet users, 80% of participants either somewhat or strongly approved of the government's social credit surveillance toolbox, which includes FRT, with higher education predicting higher acceptance rates (Kostka, 2019). While studies have assessed public opinion of surveillance technologies by German citizens (van Heek et al., 2016), few so far have concentrated on public opinion of FRT specifically. When a UK research institute surveyed 4,109 adults, 49% support its use in policing practices given appropriate safeguards but 67% oppose it in schools, 61% on public transport, and a majority of 55% want restriction placed on its use by police (L. D. Introna & Nissenbaum, 2010). In the US, a Pew Research Center survey of 4,272 American adults showed that more than half trust law enforcement actors to employ FRT responsibly, but only 36 % think the same of technology companies, and 18 % of advertisers (Aaron Smith, 2019).

As evidenced by this brief review, research of FRT acceptance by the public has largely focused on one national setting at a time. Samatas (2005) emphasizes that a nation's political context and history with surveillance may shape the framing of studying such practices significantly, which can render direct cross-country comparisons among disparate surveys difficult. To gauge international differences in interaction with FRT, a major part of the CODE framework's **Environment** dimension, I co-developed a cross-country study on factors driving its social acceptance in four nations. Partial results and parts of this chapter have previously been presented at the 2020 International Conference on Machine Learning's Workshop "Law and Machine Learning" (Steinacker, Meckel, et al., 2020). Additional results and insights from the same survey have been presented at the 2020 International Communication Association (Steinacker, Kostka, et al., 2020) and have been published elsewhere (Kostka et al., 2021a). As part of the study, we ran an online survey during August and September 2019 in China, Germany, the UK, and the US. Executed by a Berlin-based firm that cooperates with providers in each of the four countries, the survey employed a river sampling method, drawing both first-time and regular survey participants from a base of 1-3 million unique online users through mobile applications. Our survey reached respondents through more than 100 apps out of a network of over 40,000 participating partners.[42] Our sample comprised 6,633 respondents from all four countries in total, sampled based on age (18-65), gender, and region. Given the nature of conducting the survey online, this sample resembles the Internet-connected population: likely slightly younger and more technology-savvy than the overall population. [43] For the purposes of the analysis, we sought to understand,

---

42 Formats and genres of the applications vary, including e-commerce, photo-sharing, and messaging. Within each application, offer walls provided participants options to receive small financial and non-monetary rewards, such as premium content, extra features, vouchers, and PayPal cash in exchange for taking part in the survey without knowing the topic before opting in. After an initial pre-screening that matched participants with a survey, the conversion rate of users who fully finished ours was 70 % (China), 73 % (Germany), 69 %(UK), and 67 %(US) respectively. Consecutive identical answer choices or disproportionately short periods of time for completion of a questionnaire were reasons for invalidation.

43 Collected data was weighted by each aforementioned variable with a maximum weight of 1.8. Given an estimated design effect of 1.03 for China, 1 for Germany, 1.06 for the UK, and 1.04 for the US, the overall margin of error for estimates

first, participants' stance on FRT deployment in the public sphere (*"Do you accept or oppose the use of facial recognition technology in public?"*) and, second, how they interpreted related issues. We ran ordered logit regressions with the dependent variable of interest being "social acceptance" (for full results see the Appendix).

As Table 6.1 shows, in the Chinese sample, considerably more participants accept than oppose FRT use in public, while in the UK, only slightly more do so. On the contrary, among the German and U.S. respondents, slightly more oppose than accept it.

Table 6.1 "Do you accept or oppose the use of FRT in public?"

Response	CHINA	GER	UK	US
Strongly oppose	4 %	18 %	14 %	16 %
Somewhat oppose	18 %	21 %	19 %	22 %
Neither oppose nor accept	28 %	24 %	25 %	27 %
Somewhat accept	39 %	29 %	30 %	24 %
Strongly accept	11 %	8 %	12 %	11 %
	100 %	100 %	100 %	100 %

To understand contributing factors of participants' acceptance levels, we examined their impressions of relevant dimensions related to FRT. First, we gauged perception of FRT's consequences, such as *privacy violations*, *discrimination*, and *surveillance*, as well as *convenience, efficiency*, and *security*. As Table 6.2 shows, almost half of all German and US respondents (49 % and 45 % respectively) expect FRT to increase privacy violations, while only 31 % of Chinese and 41 % of UK participants do. A clear majority of Germans (63 %) and more than half of UK and US respondents believe that FRT increases surveillance, yet only 27 % of Chinese agree.

---

is 2.4 % for China, 2.4 % for Germany, 2.5 % for the UK, and 2.5 % for the US. Of the 6,633 respondents in our sample, 8.1 % (N = 534) had *never heard about FRT* prior to taking the survey. As their attitudes are nonetheless relevant for understanding overall public opinion on the matter, we did not exclude their further responses. After the initial gauge of awareness, a short prompt summarized for participants: *"Facial recognition technology is used to automatically identify people by scanning their face from an image or video."*

Table 6.2 "Do you think FRT increases any of the following?"

Response	CHINA	GER	UK	US
Privacy violations	31 %	49 %	41 %	45 %
Surveillance	27 %	63 %	57 %	56 %
Discrimination	3 %	15 %	17 %	17 %
Convenience	65 %	23 %	21 %	33 %
Efficiency	56 %	21 %	26 %	33 %
Security	62 %	55 %	64 %	67 %
None of the above	3 %	5 %	8 %	6 %

Given the extensive research demonstrating various discriminatory effects of FRT due to accuracy discrepancies, it is notable that, in all four countries, very few participants, less than 1 in 5, consider FRT to be an exacerbating factor in discrimination. A majority of the participants from China (65 %) yet only 23 % in Germany, 21 % in the UK and 33 % in the US think that FRT increases convenience. More than half of Chinese respondents expect FRT to advance efficiency (56 %), while 1 in 5 of German, 1 in 4 of UK, and 1 in 3 of American respondents do. Strikingly, a majority in all four countries (62 %, 55 %, 64 %, and 67 % respectively) expect FRT to increase security.

Second, the study examined participants' impressions of the technology's *reliability* in comparison to previous methods. As Table 6.3 illustrates, in all countries, fewer than 1 in 5 respondents rate FRT's reliability lower than other forms of identification.

Table 6.3 "Do you think that facial recognition technology is more reliable or less reliable than other identification methods (e.g.: fingerprints, identity cards)?"

Response	CHINA	GER	UK	US
More reliable	43.1 %	30.7 %	32.5 %	34.0 %
Neither more nor less	40.1 %	37.6 %	38.1 %	37.3 %
Less reliable	6.7 %	18.9 %	17.2 %	15.3 %
Don't know	10.1 %	12.8 %	12.2 %	13.4 %
	100 %	100 %	100 %	100 %

For further examination, we analyzed various dimensions relevant to policy-making for FRT: *issue concerns* involving law enforcement, levels of governmental *trust*, and perceptions and support of *surveillance* more generally. Across all four countries, a majority of participants is worried about crime (59 %, 67 %, 74 %, 74 %) and, except for China, about terrorist threats (47%, 56%, 66%, 67%). As Table 6.4 shows, the UK and the US stand out with over 40% of their participants respectively indicating that they are concerned about the control of their nations' borders, while less than 30% in both China and Germany do. Around half of Chinese respondents are concerned about violations of rules & regulations, while around 38% of Germans, 36% of UK and 41% of US participants are. Finally, a majority in both China (51%) and the UK (54%) find socially unacceptable behavior concerning.

With regards to the question of trust in governmental institutions, as can be seen in Table 6.5, we observe that only in China, a majority of participants (61%), reports having *a lot* of confidence. Meanwhile, only 23% in Germany and merely 10% in both the UK and the US do.

Table 6.4 "Are you concerned about any of the following issues in your country?"

Response	CHINA	GER	UK	US
Crime	59%	67%	74%	74%
Terrorist threats	47%	56%	66%	67%
Border control	29%	28%	42%	43%
Violations of rules & regulations	49%	38%	36%	41%
Socially unacceptable behavior	51%	42%	54%	36%
None of the above	14%	14%	9%	10%

Additionally, we investigated participants' judgment of their government's domestic surveillance history and their current support of governmental surveillance. While 46% of respondents in Germany, 41% in the UK, and 54% in the US believe their country's government has employed domestic surveillance negatively in the past, only 13% of Chinese do (Table 6.6).

Table 6.5 "How much do you trust governmental institutions in your country?"

Response	CHINA	GER	UK	US
Not at all	1.2%	14.5%	17.4%	11.8%
Very little	5.6%	23.0%	30.7%	28.3%
Somewhat	24.4%	32.1%	36.7%	42.1%
A lot	61.5%	22.9%	9.7%	10.1%
Prefer not to answer	7.3%	7.55%	5.4%	7.7%
	100%	100%	100%	100%

Table 6.6 "Do you think that the government in your country has used surveillance against its own citizens in a negative way in the past?"

Response	CHINA	GER	UK	US
Yes	13.5%	46.3%	40.6%	53.5%
No	36.9%	23.4%	18.6%	14.8%
Don't know	49.6%	30.3%	40.8%	31.7%
	100%	100%	100%	100%

While in China and the UK, considerably more people somewhat or strongly support (52 % and 44 %) surveillance than somewhat or strongly oppose it (16 % and 24 %), in Germany (34 % vs 40 %) and the US (31 % vs 37 %) the two sides appear roughly equal. About a third of all respondents in each country neither oppose nor support surveillance in their country (Table 6.7).

Table 6.7 "Do you generally support or oppose the use of surveillance by your government in your country?"

Response	CHINA	GER	UK	US
Strongly oppose	3.9 %	14.6 %	9.4 %	12.3 %
Somewhat oppose	11.9 %	18.8 %	14.6 %	19.2 %
Neither oppose nor support	31.9 %	26.8 %	31.5 %	31.9 %
Somewhat support	34.2 %	32.1 %	31.1 %	26.0 %
Strongly support	18.1 %	7.6 %	13.4 %	10.6 %
	100 %	100 %	100 %	100 %

Finally, to gauge the effects of a number of these factors on public approval we ran an ordered logit regression with social acceptance of FRT use in public as our dependent variable and privacy threat perception, consequences of FRT, and national issue concerns as independent variables (see Table A, Appendix). Our analysis shows that the interpretation of privacy threat is a strong and significant negative predictor of acceptance. In other words, the more a participant perceives the technology as a risk to their privacy, the less likely they are to accept FRT use in public. This finding is statistically significant across all four countries and in each setting individually. Convenience has a significantly positive effect on acceptance overall, and in each country individually, with the exception of Germany, where the sign turns. That is to say, the more likely German participants perceive FRT to increase convenience, the less likely they are to accept it, pointing perhaps to cultural scepticism towards a hyped comfort of technology. Across all countries, overall and individually, impressions of increased efficiency as well as security raise the likelihood of acceptance as the corresponding coefficients are significant and positive. Discrimination is a significantly negative predictor overall as well as in Germany and the UK specifically while in China and the US, the coefficients are not statistically significant. Strikingly, in international comparison, the more a participant perceives FRT to increase surveillance, the more likely they are to accept it, with the exception of China, where the effect is negative, and the US, where the result is not significant. Considering that backlash to surveillance practices is generally strong in the three Western countries studied, we assume this results could be due to participants associating surveillance with increased security.

Our analysis shows that the perception of terrorist threats is a significant positive predictor across all four countries. As such concerns are influenced by media coverage and framing on the one hand, and the system narrative – its raison d'être – on the other, this insight is a point of relevance for the case study discussed in more detail later. When perceived as a national concern, socially unacceptable behavior has a significant, positive relationship to approval of FRT in public overall and in Germany. On the other hand, neither concerns about violations of rules and regulations, nor about crime or border control are significantly linked with higher rates of acceptance.

In conclusion, first, there appears to be no consensus on the public use of FRT across the four countries studied. Varying international acceptance levels signal that there might not be a feasible unified approach to governing FRT. Respondents from China and the UK express more acceptance than disavowal, compared to the opposite in Germany and the US. Similarly distributed are the frequencies of who perceives FRT to increase privacy violations. When they do perceive the technology as a privacy threat, though, people across all countries are more likely to oppose its use in public. This finding suggests that a rise in reports and investigations of privacy violations related to FR might contribute to a decline in global acceptance in the future. Second, a majority of respondents in all four countries expect FRT to increase security. This emphasizes that in the nations studied, the perceived main trade-off of FRT appears to be between security and privacy. Third, awareness of the discriminatory effects of applied FRT is very low across all four countries and our findings imply greater awareness would lead to lower acceptance. Fourth, across all countries studied a concern about terrorist threats affected acceptance rates more significantly than perceptions of crime or border control. This suggests that respondents have distinct thresholds of justification for FRT used by law enforcement.

Our study emphasized how different national environments affect the social acceptance of FRT in various ways. It demonstrates how the environment sets the social, cultural, and regulatory stage for human-machine interaction and thus underlines the importance of analyzing these dimensions to gauge the Code Capital of a particular AI system. However, FRT entails a set of dynamic, entangled sociotechnical relations. Assessing societal variations that manifest as the context for FRT application is necessary

Figure 6.1 shows the CODE framework as applied to FacesOfTheRiot

Conception	
Sensegiving Actors	Whose actions give purpose to the AI system?
Narratives	What narratives shape the vision for the system?
Investment & Expected Return	What types of resources factor into the system and its potential business model?
Operations	
Model Architecture	What process constituted the chosen models and algorithms?
Concerns	What societal considerations influenced the overall design of the system?
Data	
Collection	How was the data collated and chosen?
Processing	What criterion determine relevance for inclusion and exclusion of data?
Embedding	
Sensemaking Actors	How does the system interact with cultural and social norms and relate to a diversity of lives, individually and collectively?
Regulatory Boundaries	How do relevant legal and ethical standards pertain to the system's potential uses?

but not sufficient to grasp the technology's wide-ranging implications. Thus, for the rest of the chapter, I will now closely examine the Code Capital of one particular case of facial analysis, the project FacesOfTheRiot[44], by applying the CODE framework as shown in Figure 6.1.

6.2 Conception

In this section, I examine those actors who shape the purpose of the system through sensegiving practice, the narratives that inscribe a vision into it, and the investment and expected returns that influence design choices

---

44 https://facesoftheriot.com/

6. Impact Assessment: Facial analysis

and material configurations. In sum, I analyze how the system is being conceived.

6.2.1 Sensegiving Actors

On January 6th, 2021, a mob of rioters marched to the U.S. Capitol and turned their protest against the formal certification of the federal election count into a failed attempt to overthrow the government. Breaching metal barricades and police perimeters, the insurrectionists vandalized and trespassed the Capitol building and assaulted dozens of law enforcement officers while high-ranking officials in the Senate chamber were escorted to safety. In total, five people died and 140 police officers were injured in addition to an unknown number of rioters (Evelyn, 2021; Jackman, 2021). Many of the rioters posted videos of their actions on the conservative-leaning microblogging and social networking platform Parler[45].

Nine days later, on January 15th, 2021, a newly launched website featured a grid of 6,000 images, depicting the faces of people present at the foiled insurrection. Entitled FacesOfTheRiot, the project was created by a senior Computer Science student at the Virginia Polytechnic Institute and State University, who is currently enrolled in a machine learning course. In my interview, he described himself as being politically on the left side of the political spectrum and has requested to remain anonymous.[46] In the aftermath of the events of January 6th, the creator took notice of the public leak of more than 50 terabytes of videos showing people engaged in the riot, anonymously scraped from the network Parler's servers. Specifically, on January 13th, a Twitter user by the name of Tommy Carstensen (@carstensenpol) posted a since deleted tweet: "Twitter, would it be useful for anyone, if I populate a page with Parler videos from the Capitol from the 6th?". On his personal website linked to in the Tweet, entitled "Capitol Terrorist Attack", Carstensen then began hosting the Parler videos. On the bottom of the page, Carstensen thanks another user, a media artist named Kyle McDonald, for processing the metadata of the leaked Parler videos which were initially collected by a researcher with the Twitter handle @donk_enby and another anonymous collaborator (Carstensen, 2021a). For the purpose of this case study, I have conducted personal interviews with the creator, Carstensen and McDonald.

---

45 https://parler.com/
46 In quoting him, I shorten "anonymous creator" to A.C. for all citations.

Given the raw material from Carstensen, who FacesOfTheRiot credits on the page for providing the videos, the creator first conceived of the idea as "a great little side project," which he "would love to experiment with" as he is "very interested in machine learning." Surprised by the high quality of the emerging data, his initial interest soon morphed into a larger concept, as he told me:

> When the (videos) from the riot became public and I started working with this, I thought I would be dealing with really crappy cell phone footage that was compressed beyond recognition and we would maybe find one or two faces. And then I realized some of these videos are just straight up 4k 60 fps completely raw footage from people's cell phones. And Parler didn't care about transcoding and just stored them all at max resolution. Within 10 minutes, I was getting much better results than I thought I would. So, I went: 'Instead of just making this all about just a personal project, I'm going *to make a website to help everyone identify these people*' [emphasis added]. And it quickly went from just a personal interest to 'this is a way that I can *really help the community that's working on generating FBI reports work a lot faster*' (A.C., personal communication, February 23, 2021).

This chain of events involving multiple actors demonstrates the configurations that contributed directly or indirectly to the conception of the project: Parler stored high resolution videos of the riot with evident security vulnerabilities; the hacker scraped these videos prior to the platform being suspended from Amazon Web Services' servers on January 10th for failing to moderate violent content; numerous engineers then processed the metadata and hosted the videos to make them accessible for further use; and finally, the creator sought to make sense of the available data by using open source machine learning methods for facial detection. This, in turn, allowed him to develop a structured presentation of faces extracted from each video to be seen by the public with the explicit aim of aiding the submission of FBI reports. His conception gave sense to the project as a tool for users to sift through the database of faces and, in the case of personally recognizing someone or spotting resemblance to FBI wanted posters, to send identifying information straight to law enforcement.

6.2.2 Narratives

Contextualizing information about the genesis or goals of the project cannot be found directly on the site. However, atop the grid of faces, the creator begins the page with the following disclaimer:

> DO NOT ATTEMPT YOUR OWN INVESTIGATION INTO ANY-ONE SHOWN ON THIS WEBSITE. REPORT THEM TO THE FBI USING THIS LINK INSTEAD. THANK YOU. See an incorrect image (not a face, not a rioter, etc)? Send a message to @RiotFace on twitter. Please include a screenshot of the image as well as the text under the image (*Faces of the Riot*, 2021).

To understand the creator's narrative for FacesOfTheRiot, this early prompt points to two concerns he holds: The possibility of vigilante justice and misidentification, both of which he seeks to avoid. As he explained: "It would be terrible, really, if people were to just say: I recognize this person. I'm going to go out and badmouth them and maybe try to hunt them down myself. That's caused disasters in the past" (A.C., personal communication, February 23, 2021). Instead of spurring citizen investigations, two main driving motivations for the project became apparent: public accountability and the potential of crowdsourcing identifying information for law enforcement. As the creator puts it in his own words:

> The purpose behind this was: You tried to overthrow the United States government and killed a bunch of police officers and got some of your own supporters killed and the FBI is investigating you and I don't really care what side you're on. (…) Everyone should know that you decided to attack the Capitol. (…) The only people who are being held accountable prior to me and other people doing these projects were (…) some famous people, the people who made a good news headline shot. (…) But 5.000 other people just slipped by and nothing happened to them. And they didn't get in trouble for it. And that's not really right. That's not *justice*. (…) So it's not just crowdsourcing the identification, but that's part of it. The more people who see this website, the better, because the higher chance that someone's going to see someone they know. (…) It's about *holding everyone who is there accountable*. (…) It only feels right that *everyone who is involved faces justice* for it (A.C., personal communication, February 23, 2021).

Notably, the public nature of posting people's facial close-ups automatically extracted from videos associated with a crime scene, which they might have assumed to only appear on Parler, stands in contrast to the narrative of wanting to prevent vigilante justice and signals wider concerns of privacy. This point will be discussed in more depth in section 6.3, as it relates to the creator's operational choice not to enable direct facial recognition on the site. Meanwhile, in sections 6.3. and 6.5, the question of misidentification and potential wrongful accusations will be examined.

While the creator repeatedly emphasized the issue of accountability, he framed this as a focus on the violence committed and, more generally, the explicit aim of overthrowing governmental institutions, instead of the particular political ideology behind it. Specifically, he explained that he was committed "to do this, regardless of what political affiliation the violent organization has (…) you can't just do something like this for people you don't like. It's not right." He gave a further example:

> If in 2024, God forbid, Trump wins the election somehow, and (Antifa) stormed the capital and tried to kill the senators when they were certifying the votes, I would bring this back up for that, too. (…) I would never do this for a peaceful protest, that's not the point. That's where you really turn into 1984. I'm doing this because they got people killed. They almost breached into the room where (Vice President Mike) Pence and the senators were being sheltered. They stormed the Senate floor and tried to kill the people in Congress. It was a disaster. They built gallows and chanted 'Hang Mike Pence'. That's not OK in the slightest (A.C., personal communication, February 23, 2021).

His reference to George Orwell's seminal social science-fiction novel *Nineteen Eighty-Four*, published in 1949, in relation to using his project at "peaceful protests" raises the widely cited concern of surveillance through ubiquitous video footage (Gray, 2003). This will be discussed in more detail in section 6.5. The creator also noted that he did report the entire video repository to the FBI but assumed that without additional identifying information about specific faces it would be of little help.

In summary, the narrative for the AI system's conception is framed by its creator with a focus on the sense of justice, ostensibly fulfilled in part by creating public awareness about those individuals who participated in the riots of January 6th, and in part by aiding the process of law enforcement that follows them. This conception narrative still raises ethical considerations about privacy, wrongful inclusion in the database, and implications of surveillance as the rest of the chapter will examine. It also remains to be seen if the operational choices reflect some of the ethical concerns the creator himself noted.

6.2.3 Investment and Expected Return

Resource configurations, both investment into and revenue expected from an AI system, can significantly influence its conception and thereby range of impacts. In the case of FacesOfTheRiot, financial input has been kept to a minimum, while the potential of a business model has been ruled out by the creator. Specifically, when his first choice of provider to host the site, Bluehost, became too costly given the attention it was attracting, the creator switched to an anonymous personal provider for free:

> That's part of the reason why we're able to keep this with never going to be asking for donations or putting ads on it because there's zero hosting cost. And I would have only been able to keep this up for a few months otherwise because we got a lot of traffic and we got kicked off of Bluehost. (…) Now we're able to keep this up and keep it the way I want it, because I don't want to make money off of this. It just seems wrong. So we're able to keep to that principle (A.C., personal communication, February 23, 2021).

Given the high attention in its early days, the creator used a Google Analytics calculator to estimate that advertisements would have yielded 3-4000 USD in the first few weeks – but he decided against them. He reported having invested "around 30-40 hours" of his time to develop the project from start to finish. Still, his expected return, in addition to his expressed objectives for building the project in the first place, appears to be focused merely on the added value of learning to use the particular machine learning methods. Notably, the creator referenced a similar project with the title "US Capitol Attack Facial Recognition", CapitolMap in short, which includes not just one key operational difference in the facial analysis features it offers – which will be discussed further in the next section 6.3 – but also a note prompting users to "Help us pay our expensive server bill" with a donation button underneath (Anonymous, 2021). The creator of FacesOfTheRiot mentioned the site's crowdfunding aspect specifically as a factor he seeks to avoid. When prompted if he were ever willing to sell his site for a substantial amount of money, he doubled down on his principle and narrative:

> No, I don't really care about getting money off of that. (…) This was an insurrection. There was violence. People died. *I don't want to make money off something like that. It just feels wrong* [emphasis added] (A.C., personal communication, February 23, 2021).

His rationalization with regards to financial gain again appear to be framed through a lens of justice. Given that the creator does not know the identity of the anonymous host, this aspect introduces a level of uncertainty because the host's motivations are unclear.

6.3 Operations

In this section, I focus on the material configurations of the system, including its model architecture and the various concerns that impacted its design. These parts make up the system's operational set-up.

6.3.1 Model Architecture

Two aspects of the system's set-up are particularly noteworthy: First, it was created by open-source machine learning tools available to anyone with the appropriate skill set. Second, the creator explicitly considers the main task of the project to be the *detection* of faces but decided against including a retrieval feature on the site, a search tool that would allow users to upload and match individual photos with his database. Essentially, while the algorithms used are capable of facial *recognition*, they were only used to cluster and remove duplicates of images of the same person after faces were detected and extracted from the videos. The following section will consider both facets more closely.

6.3.1.1 Open-source Set-up

Face detection can be achieved by a wide variety of algorithmic techniques (Hjelmaas & Low, 2001). Based on his knowledge of available open-source software options, the creator decided to use a detector based on the MobileNetV2 architecture (Sandler et al., 2018). This is a family of computer vision neural networks released by Google's AI research arm (Sandler & Howard, 2018), which runs on TensorFlow, the company's end-to-end platform for machine learning models. Next, he sought to extract the feature points from each face to cluster and then deduplicate faces from the database of about 136,000 pictures from 827 videos to around 6000 faces. He used the facial recognition software and self-contained library Dlib for this task. According to the creator, about 80 % of these clusters, stored on his personal computer, have now been manually reviewed and cleaned. When it first launched on January 15th, FacesOfTheRiot simply featured a grid of more than 6,000 images of faces (see Figure 6.2 left), including an ID tag below each face for the associated Parler video source.

Figure 6.2 shows screenshots of facesoftheriot.com on January 16 and February 25, 2021

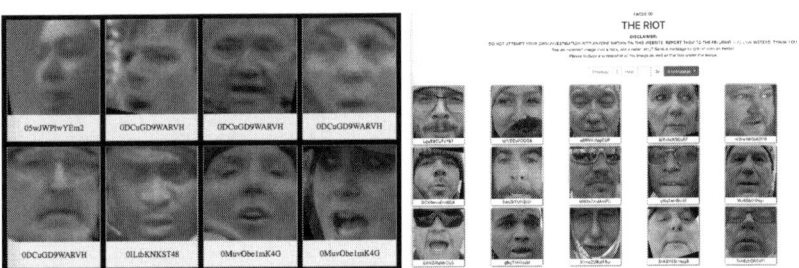

There were no other features available and no contextualizing information about the scene in the video or the actions of the people involved. To give this context, the creator soon added not just the disclaimer but hyperlinks, too, so that users can watch the source video by clicking on an image and thereby differentiate between violent rioters, peaceful protesters, and individuals who happened to be bystanders (see Figure 6.2, right).

The backend of this system was developed neither by a private company nor a governmental institution. Instead, it was created by an individual developer with access to open-source tools. To make adjustments to the frontend, he received help from a friend with website design experience. Given that he was able to construct this system within a few hours with the help of open-source software, the creator himself stressed the improvised nature of the process as well as the implications of the possibilities of facial analysis ML tools coupled with the large troves of image data available:

> Everyone who has CS experience can learn this. And it's becoming a lot more widespread. It's a lot more widespread than people either recognize or are willing to admit to themselves. This is becoming bigger and bigger as we go on (A.C., personal communication, February 23, 2021).

However, the ad-hoc nature can lead to gaps in control of the system. When the video hyperlinks at some point no longer led to a functioning source URL, the creator was left trying to find a solution, as he reported:

> Our videos are currently hosted by Tommy Carstensen. And the way our system works, with his permission, is that we are we have a content delivery network that pulls from Tommy Carstensen's website and cashes for 72 hours any video that someone requests. (…) But it seems like his site is not hosting these videos anymore. When I look at them, they're all just like "source not found" (A.C., personal communication, February 23, 2021).

This lack of full control significantly influences the configuration of the system: Given that adding the sources of each image was an important step in contextualizing what the individuals in the videos were engaged in, non-functioning links temporarily change the nature of project back to an indiscriminate amalgamation of still facial photos.

6.3.1.2 Detection vs Recognition

Some configurations are central to an AI system because of the decision *not* to include a feature. In the case of FacesOfTheRiot, the creator underlined the important distinction between facial detection (the automated discovery of a face within an image or video) and facial recognition (the identification or verification of a particular human by matching their face against a database). While the first allows a speedy extraction process from raw video footage to obtain faces, the second would enable correlating the data with real-life identities. Having employed recognition tools in the backend process for clustering, the creator decided against the functionality on the user-facing website in the form of a frontend retrieval option and stressed this point multiple times:

> There's a reason I did not implement any customer or consumer facing ability to perform facial recognition. I personally don't really agree with how that technology gets used by law enforcement. And this could then be abused by law enforcement. I don't want to be making them a database of people – of any people really – that they can easily search. My biggest thing is I don't want to really normalize the use of facial recognition for any situation (A.C., personal communication, February 23, 2021).

Evidently, his explicit concerns relate to current use cases by the police but also to the technology's inaccuracy which would complicate a recognition feature used by citizens, too:

> I've always had the stance that at least in its current state, facial recognition is terribly inaccurate, at least in the implementation that I would be able to produce and the implementation that most people without a significantly larger budget would be able to produce. (…) I'm sure the government has something much better, but the technology isn't really public for consumers. (…) The technology is not at the point yet where you don't need someone who's trained in forensic analysis to be operating it. Because as it stands (…) given a database of 6000 faces, if you were to say: 'Computer, is this face in the database?' you would get maybe 10, 20, or even 30 results back. And your average person who just goes to the website and plugs in their neighbor's face isn't necessarily going to read all of the instructions and understand that these are the *closest matches* in the database and not a *confirmed match*. (…) I'm very concerned about that. Also leading to vigilante justice, false positives, a bunch of reports that don't need to be made. (…) Humans are still better than machines at matching two faces. And humans are really not that good at matching two faces (A.C., personal communication, February 23, 2021).

Indeed, there have been a number of wrongful arrests due to false facial recognition matches when the technology was used by law enforcement (Hill, 2020c, 2020d). As mentioned in the introductory review, many studies have demonstrated that the technology works less accurately on women and minorities and have raised privacy concerns. This body of research contributed to the decisions by major companies to either suspend their development of facial recognition tools overall or their cooperation with law enforcement to avoid discriminatory practices and violations in the as of yet unregulated realm of facial data (Greene, 2020). While his decision of not including the facial recognition tool in the system is aligned with the creator's explicit objection to users' access to these technologies, the remaining configurations of his project do not rule out that it does, in fact, contribute to its further spread: It is likely that law enforcement is able to utilize the extensive database with their own facial recognition tools to specifically identify individual people. Furthermore, the display of faces on a public platform might not allow users the direct feature of automated identification, but it nonetheless creates awareness of people's participation in the riots on a scale that could indeed lead to vigilante investigations and real-life repercussions.

However, other notable sources published the videos for reasons of public awareness given the political stakes of the scenes on the ground. For example, the non-profit investigative journalism outlet ProPublica argued that their decision to release the videos in their entirety – which essentially amounts to displaying the faces present as well – offered "a unique experience of the historic event through hundreds of participants' eyes" (Klein & Kao, 2021). Moreover, excerpts of the data were shown in a compilation video as part of the impeachment trial following the events of January 6th, arguably providing a platform of awareness on a much bigger scale (NBC News, 2021).

6.3.2 Concerns

Given the contentious context of FRT today, several ethical concerns played into the development of the system.

6.3.2.1 Accuracy

Prompted about the technology's accuracy biases and potential discriminatory effects for those more often misidentified, the creator noted that his particular set-up, focused on detection, might actually favor those individuals because they might be less likely to be spotted and included in his database. He fails to acknowledge, however, that given the higher rates of misidentification for women and minorities, the clustering of images in the backend might work less precisely and thus mismatch individuals from more vulnerable populations (Buolamwini & Gebru, 2018).

6.3.2.2 User privacy

Privacy concerns influenced decisions about the analytics configurations of the site. According to the creator, when it first gained attention, the site attracted between 30,000 - 40,000 unique visitors a day, and still counts between 8,000 - 10,000 now. Assuming that "a lot of the people who are going to access this probably don't want to be tracked by Google and every other ad network," he decided against the inclusion of the Google

Analytics API. Instead, a server script filters through the NGINX Access Logs to count visitors.

6.3.2.3 Abuse

Given that the creator does not know the identity of the anonymous collaborator who hosts the site, this aspect introduces a level of uncertainty as the host's motivations and commitments are unclear. Indeed, the creator hypothesized:

> Who knows who it is. Maybe they'll keep it up. Maybe they'd be like, you know what, I'm going to make this domain point to somewhere completely different because I was at the riot and I want my face not here (A.C., personal communication, February 23, 2021).

This configuration signals a lack of consideration for the sensitive nature of the project, the personal facial data involved, and the potential implications for individuals displayed. The creator conceded that "someone could scrape all of the images, make their own facial recognition database," but also acknowledged that projects like "CapitolMap" had already done so without his system as a basis. He concluded: "No matter what, this was going to happen, whether or not I had made this website. It makes me feel better that someone did this without using my website for it" (A.C., personal communication, February 23, 2021).

6.4 Data

In this section, I examine the particular configurations that influenced the collection and processing of data related to the system.

6.4.1 Collection

As described in 5.2., FacesOfTheRiot obtained the video material due to their processing and release by media artist Kyle McDonald who in turn had received the raw data after a researcher-turned-hacker had scraped them from Parler's server. As one journalist who interviewed the hacker identified by her Twitter handle @donk_enby summarized:

(She) began with the goal of archiving every post from January 6 ... what she called a bevy of "very incriminating" evidence ... hoping to create a lasting public record for future researchers to sift through. ... The scope of the project quickly broadened, (...) (she) began the work of archiving all of Parler's posts, ultimately capturing around 99.9 percent of its content. (...) The copious data may also serve as a fertile hunting ground for law enforcement (Cameron, 2021).

6.4.2 Processing

In total, the leak amounted to roughly 42 Gigabytes of videos (Greenberg, 2021). Each video came with a metadata file, approximately a million in total. Kyle McDonald then compiled the metadata of all videos in one single CSV file that he shared, including, inter alia, the latitude and longitude information for each. Other actors in the chain, like Tommy Carstensen, later added attributes such as individual phone model types and resolution to their own files. These compilations enriched the facial analysis process. The creator of FacesOfTheRiot confirmed that he does not plan to add any additional videos because the Parler leak constituted

> the ones that are confirmed with GPS metadata and time stamped to be at the riots. We're being careful to not include other videos that might not be from the riot. (...) This is the way we're doing it safely (A.C., personal communication, February 23, 2021).

Collaborator Kyle McDonald has publicly praised this safe approach of FacesOfTheRiot in addition to the exclusion of user-facing recognition features (Greenberg, 2021). To reduce the risk of displaying people unassociated with the criminal acts of insurrectionists, the creator decided to remove from the data all faces he assumed belonged to police officers and representatives of the press. In addition, the creator reported two instances of contact with people after the site was launched who proactively sought to be deleted from his database: One, who could provide evidence for being at the crime scene as an undercover journalist, another as a police officer. According to the creator, these professional groups were generally easily identified because they were by and large wearing masks or face shields due to concerns about the coronavirus pandemic. As many rioters failed to wear such health safety measures, this added a circumstantial sorting layer in the data, because

Obviously, when you wear a mask, it makes it a lot harder for an algorithm to even tell that there's a face there. (...) If everyone had worn masks...this wouldn't have existed. I wouldn't have been able to do anything (A.C., personal communication, February 23, 2021).

6.5 Environment

In this section, I analyze how the system is embedded in its environment. This includes interactions with its sensemaking actors, related issues of surveillance and public acceptance of FRT use by law enforcement, as well as regulatory boundaries.

6.5.1 Sensemaking Actors

FacesOfTheRiot was created by an individual at a U.S. university, employs an open-source ML platform by an American technology company, utilizes video data scraped from a U.S. app, and its conception appears singularly focused on its relation to the attack on the U.S. Capitol and helping U.S. law enforcement prosecute predominately U.S. citizens. While these sensegiving factors are all heavily centered on the United States, the fact that it is a globally available website means the system and its functionalities have a potentially international audience of sensemaking actors in practice. Moreover, the hacker who initially collected the video data from Parler was identified in one article as "an Austrian lover of free speech" (Jennings, 2021), while video host Tommy Carstensen is a Danish citizen according to his Twitter profile (Carstensen, 2021b). These two details indicate the international dynamics that together configure the final AI system. To understand the range of actors who make sense of FacesOfTheRiot in practice through usage, this next section examines how this AI system interacts with cultural and social norms of surveillance, what factors might influence people's acceptance, and how regulatory boundaries affect its relation to a diversity of lives, individually and collectively.

6.5.1.1 Surveillance

As elaborated upon in Chapter 4, Mathiesen expanded the Foucauldian perspective on Panoptic surveillance with the concept of Synopticism which denotes "the development of a unique and enormously extensive system enabling *the many to see and contemplate the few* (through) the total system of the modern mass media" (Mathiesen, 1997, p. 219). Recent research has applied Synopticism to the wider technological assemblage of the networked age, arguing that Panopticism and Synopticism interact and contribute to each other (Doyle, 2011).

Applied to surveillance by FRT, Panoptic power is bestowed upon actors with the facial analysis algorithms, computing power, and, crucially, the necessary volumes of data to indiscriminately process and identify individuals, often without their knowledge or consent. One example for this level of authority is Clearview A.I., a U.S. private company that supplies its FRT systems to law enforcement across the country. Its tool uses a database of three billion images the firm purports to have scraped off platforms like Facebook and YouTube which "goes far beyond anything ever constructed by the United States government or Silicon Valley giants" (Hill, 2020a). Underlining its power as an instrument for the few to surveil the masses, before it was employed by police forces, Clearview A.I. is reported to have been used by wealthy individuals to "spy on the public" (Hill, 2020b). By 2021, the software was reportedly used by 3,100 U.S. law enforcement agencies including the Army, the Air Force and Immigration and Customs Enforcement (Hill, 2021d), while it was ruled illegal in Canada (Hill, 2021a). Officially, the company has declined to offer its services to the public, but similar applications such as the Russian FindFace have, and Facebook has announced such plans (Hill, 2021c).

In the case of FacesOfTheRiot, on the other hand, the Synoptic notion of a "system enabling the many to see and contemplate the few" might aptly describe the surveillance concerns related to the automated processing and public display of people's facial data. The FBI's official most wanted list associated with the events of January 6th, too, provides hundreds of publicly available images of individuals who "made unlawful entry into the U.S. Capitol building and committed various other alleged criminal violations, such as destruction of property, assaulting law enforcement personnel, targeting members of the media for assault, and other unlawful conduct" (Federal Buerau of Investigation, 2021). These images are, however, posted because they show suspects wanted for known crimes. FacesOfTheRiot, on the other hand, currently indiscriminately displays people present at the riots with no individual context or specific accusation, it therefore "doesn't distinguish between lawbreakers and people who merely attended the protests outside" (Greenberg, 2021). When the creator of FacesOfTheRiot noticed that another Twitter account by the handle @SeditionHunters similarly collected individual still frame images of the various faces with the prompt "Do you know this person?", he began to use the hashtag #seditionhunters in his own posts. According to him, he saw the initiative as a movement to get greater reach and exposure for the images. Indeed, on April 21, 2021, an affidavit filed by the FBI detailed that a post on @SeditionHunters helped the law enforcement agency identify and arrest an individual rioter who had assaulted police officers (Vincent, 2021b).

An examination of Twitter references to the site since its launch demonstrates both the Orwellian potential on the one hand – which the creator himself alluded to with the mention of *Nineteen Eighty-Four* – as well as the possibilities for abuse on the other: One Twitter user with the handle @TradeCNBC commented "This #FacesOfTheRiot show is scary, like a McCarthy hearing, or Russian dissenter hunt" (TradeCNBC, 2021). Another with the handle @hologram_stan asked: "Any #facesoftheriot bounty hunters out there? We're looking for a guy that owes us some money ...." (UBI Hologram, 2021). A third posted: "Their faces should be published. Every last one of them should be charged, tried and convicted of sedition" (Bonham, 2021). Another actor in the chain of conceiving the project, video provider Tommy Carstensen, acknowledged what he called his own "intense" consideration of the possibility that these projects legitimate similar uses and abuses of FRT, saying: "Now we have opened Pandora's box. We have unleashed this. Now the other side is definitely going to use this" (T.C., personal communication, March 5, 2021).

Notably, the decision to apply facial *recognition* only in the backend of the system materializes as a marked difference in the functionalities directly available to those who make sense of FacesOfTheRiot in practice. Nonetheless, the combination of secretly obtaining the video material with the accompanying metadata from Parler with applying the facial analysis tools to achieve such a structured, easily searchable grid of public faces is what renders the final system that emerged as FacesOfTheRiot a privacy concern: Even if the protests, riots and acts of insurrection occurred in the public realm, most people affected might have not been aware of the privacy implications of participation nor consented to the processing of their personal data.

Still, media artist Kyle McDonald points out the fine line between featuring someone's visual appearance in such a public online way and revealing their specific identity:

> There is a big difference in my mind between presenting a set of tips or hints and making some statement about identify. We see people

throughout our lives all day. We see people on the bus, on the street, wherever, but we don't know who they are. We couldn't shame them for anything because we don't have any idea what their name is or where they live or anything that is personally identifying information. Once you make that connection between someone's appearance and their identity that's where you have problems. I think just showing someone's photo *can* kick that off (…). But I don't see this site itself as being that problem. It could be *used to cause that problem* [emphasis added] (K. M., personal communication, March 25, 2021).

When it comes to judging responsibility, McDonald appears to place the blame on the abusers of the system.[47] Simultaneously, he considers it to be the obligation of the sensegiving creators to reflect on a system's future trajectories, particularly when it comes to issues of technology employed for acts of surveillance:

My two guide lights that I keep in mind are about community accountability and its scale on the one hand, and impact on the other hand. (…) The potential impact (I have as an artist) is much different, (…) than if I built a startup to sell face recognition to the cops. If I sell the exact same technology to the cops, there is much more potential for abuse and for the legitimization by the objective veneer. As an artist I can only do so much damage. (…) When I am building these kinds of tools, I talk with everybody I care about a lot – people who are experts, people who are non-experts, I talk with my relatives who don't know how this tech works but have feelings about how they want to be seen by the state or by me, I talk with friends who have very different life experiences than me (…). I try and figure out whether I can really release this kind of work in a way that does right by all of them. (…) I try to remember the potential impacts that I can have and to stay accountable to everyone that I know. There are projects that I haven't done because the impact would be potentially outsized (K.M., personal communication, March 25, 2021).

---

47 Indeed, another site developed after January 6th, which features not just still frames of people's faces, but first names, last names, and home states associated with each individual, which had previously been crowd-sourced and collected via a Google form: https://airtable.com/shruhNrLika1CtFno/tbl1HUS10AwlqY9NV, accessed on March 25, 2021

6.5.1.2 Public acceptance

Given that most research on the acceptance of such surveillance systems has been conducted in single-country settings, international comparisons across surveys are difficult. Thus, to gauge what factors influence the acceptance of FRT – and might thus affect the interaction with a platform like FacesOfTheRiot – this section examines the partial results of a cross-country study developed to support this analysis.

As detailed in our study on international acceptance levels, (Section 6.1.3.), the narrative for using FRT has a significant impact on acceptance levels. When citizens perceive the technology as a privacy threat, people across all countries, including in the U.S., are more likely to oppose its use in public. At the same time, a majority of respondents in all four countries assumed that FRT would increase security, again emphasizing the perceived main trade-off of FRT between security and privacy. A further insight is relevant: Across all countries studied a concern about terrorist threats affected acceptance rates more significantly than perceptions of crime or border control. Considering these two effects, the narratives for FacesOfTheRiot as well as for similar projects are of particular note as they focus on the concept of justice and accountability in the face of extraordinary, politically motivated violence. Referring to the insurrection attempt of January 6th, the Federal Bureau of Investigation's chief Christopher Wray called the attack "domestic terrorism" (Greve, 2021). Framing the system as a means to deliver punishment for terrorism, then, is a configuration that might specifically bolster a more favorable reception by some users. However, it opens the possibility for individuals to define thresholds of rightful intents, if the sensegiving or sensemaking actors perceive a great enough threat or urgent enough need for accountability.

Finally, the very low awareness of the discriminatory effects of applied FRT across all four countries is particularly relevant as varied research has shown their disproportionate impacts on vulnerable populations, particularly when used by law enforcement. Additionally, our research shows that greater awareness would lead to lower acceptance.

Given the relevant question of protections against privacy violations and discriminatory practices, the next section will examine how regulatory boundaries interact with FRT and specifically a system like FacesOfTheRiot.

6.5.2 Regulatory Boundaries

Regulation on surveillance technologies such as FRT confronts the major trade-off between security and privacy. As some analysts of the events of September 11th, 2001, predicted beforehand that facial analysis could help foil such an attack, discussion of law enforcement's use of the technology received renewed attention following that particular terrorist strike (McCormack, 2003). Until today, FRT has been used by US law enforcement in an unfettered way for over two decades. Across the United States, regulation that governs it has been sparse and, if at all existent, binary in its application, meaning mostly "all-or-nothing" bans (Hill, 2021b). In the summer of 2020, US Congress members introduced a bill entitled The Facial Recognition and Biometric Technology Moratorium Act to interdict the use of federal funds for purchasing FRT and other biometric surveillance systems as well as state and local funding for it (*H.R. 7356: Facial Recognition and Biometric Technology Moratorium Act of 2020*, 2020). Champions of the bill particularly drew on evidence by Georgetown University's research group The Perpetual Lineup, which monitors local and federal law enforcement's application of FRT and calls the technology "a uniquely dangerous form of surveillance" due to its racial bias (Johnson, 2020). Nonetheless, the Act did not receive the necessary vote.

While individual city councils were the first to prohibit their police force to use FRT, in late 2020, the state of Massachusetts passed a police reform bill that struck a balance between harness the advantages of the technology while developing safeguards against potential misidentifications and false arrests. These guardrails include the obligation to get a judge's permission before running a facial recognition search as well as specifications on who is allowed to run the search (Massachusetts State Government, 2020). However, a special commission mandated by the law to meet by early February 2021 to discuss racial bias perpetuated by the technology failed to adhere to its first deadline for issuing recommendations (Tiernan, 2021).

Meanwhile, in 2020, the European Commission briefly considered a five-year moratorium of FRT use in public places as was set out in an 18-page white paper (Chee, 2020). These initial considerations spurred concerns of stifling innovation and missing out on security benefits of the technology (Espinoza & Murgia, 2020). Nonetheless, in April 2021, in its proposed AI regulation, the Commission then issued a clear announcement for FRT systems: Real-time and post remote biometric identification of natural persons would qualify as a 'high-risk' system according to the proposal and require ex-ante and ex-post evaluation by the technology provider (European Commission, 2021b). Indeed, the use by law enforcement would be prohibited except for limited exceptions. Thus, if this regulation comes to pass in the future, it would have significant consequences for the application of FRT in European Member States that enact it.

Considering the example of one EU member state showcases the delicate line between harnessing the technology's capabilities and securing privacy protections: In its first case of applying the GDPR, the Swedish Data Protection Authority (DPA) fined a municipality for using FRT to monitor school attendance as the practice violated the purpose limitation of the GDPR and significantly intruded students' privacy (*Art. 5 GDPR – Principles Relating to Processing of Personal Data*, 2016). Shortly after, however, the DPA ruled in favor of certain uses by the Swedish Police Authority based on the claim that FRT can be a more effective method than traditional analysis (International Network of Privacy Law Professionals, 2020). It did, however, fine its police force for the unlawful use of Clearview A.I.'s software without prior authorization (Lomas, 2021).

In the case of FRT intersecting with law enforcement, two regulatory dynamics are particularly noteworthy. First, as evidenced through cases involving Clearview A.I., private companies have been used by police officials in the past, thereby at times circumventing certain rules by using a third-party contractor. The creator of FacesOfTheRiot, shared this concern, noting:

> We've seen the government go against their own regulations. We've seen the government go against civilian oversight bodies. We've seen the government get around the fact that...legally they can't make these databases themselves. We've seen them get around that by using a company like Clearview A.I. because technically it's a private companies database. It's going to take a lot more than legal regulation, a lot of social pressure (A.C., personal communication, February 23, 2021).

Second, as demonstrated by the case of FacesOfTheRiot itself and others like CapitolMap, individuals are now able to develop and utilize this powerful technology on other citizens, either performing the analysis themselves or aiding law enforcement in the identification process. Given the currently wide-ranging technical vulnerabilities and privacy loopholes it can harness, this Synoptic surveillance with the help of a "system enabling the many to see and contemplate the few" poses a particularly complex challenge for regulation. Indeed, the creator of FacesOfTheRiot reflected on this as follows:

> Here's the big problem. (...)You can't regulate what someone prints on a 3D printer. You can't regulate what pictures someone feeds to a neural network to train it. And you can't regulate what code someone writes on their personal computer. You can say it's illegal, but that's not going to stop anything. (...) Eventually, if (facial recognition) was properly regulated, I still don't think I'd be OK with it, but I think it's going to happen. (...) I feel like the world is going to eventually move towards it as a new normal (A.C., personal communication, February 23, 2021).

6.6 Discussion

Examining the implications of a technology as far-reaching as FRT illuminates the magnitude of its Code Capital. Its wide range of applications shows the breadth of potential functionality and impact: It may be used to manage security access or conduct clandestine surveillance; it may bolster targeted advertising or support the search for missing persons. To accurately capture its implications, then, necessitates, first, a clear distinction of the specific technical task and the intended purpose of the system at hand: The preceding case study exemplified the fine line between, on the one hand, the *detection* of a human face in a visual input combined with what I call *backend recognition* used to cluster these faces in groups of individuals and, on the other hand, a *frontend retrieval option* that allows user confirmation of a unique person due to an identity database match. FacesOfTheRiot employs a system whose interface purposefully offers only the former, but is technically capable of the latter, as similar projects like CapitolMap show. Both the prospect of such an identification tool in the hands of a civilian individual as well as his conscious decision not to employ the feature significantly contribute to the configuration of the system. It bears acknowledging that other possible technical trajectories include intents like classification by gender, race, and sexual orientation, or affective analysis that seeks to ascertain emotional states by investigating facial regions, though this branch of research has been contested. These entanglements between technical possibility and socialized decision-making crucially configure an AI system's trajectory and manifest as the nuances of its Code Capital.

Such nuance must be reflected in regulation for various FRT applications. Without a comprehensive rulebook, the Code Capital of FRT will be wielded by the exploitation of legal grey zones and loopholes that largely affect already vulnerable groups. Public funding and investments by tech companies are currently under pressure because of the uncertainty of what defines an acceptable use of FRT. Such uncertainty can be resolved by guidelines from regulatory or legal entities. Debate must focus on safeguarding protections of privacy and non-discrimination, the scope of which must match technological advances and distinct implementation purposes.

As a system created with the help of open-source tools and based on a dataset anonymously scraped and leaked, FacesOfTheRiot illustrates the democratization of AI applications and its societal consequences. One of these effects resembles a concern more often cited in relation to FRT used by law enforcement: Systems like FacesOfTheRiot could be a precursor for the cumulative ripple effect of eroding privacy in the age of ubiquitous visual data capture and facial analysis in the hands of citizens. One key participant in the chain of events described his process of eliminating certain videos from the leaked dataset that seemed "private" as wanting to "have a human touch, you know, where I decide whether this is something that should be shared with everyone." This epitomizes how an individual's technical might intersects with consequential judgments over privacy.

In addition to a general right to privacy, the wide-ranging research showing FRT's disproportionate impacts on vulnerable and minority populations, including women, people of color, and members of the LGBTQ community, underlines the responsibility of developers to improve accuracy and unbiased performance. Research in particular is facing uncertainty with regard to the technology's vulnerability, adversarial attacks, or lack of interpretability or explainability. This is exacerbated in the context of aiding law enforcement, as is the case with FacesOfTheRiot. When applied with such consequential social ramifications, mitigating FRT's current discriminatory effects must be a focus of both the scientific and legislative communities. Moreover, as the empirical survey data in this chapter demonstrates, the public and those debating FRT's merits must be properly informed about the state of research.

Finally, it is important to acknowledge the limitations of the CODE framework. As the case study of FacesOfTheRiot examined a system with a static dataset of videos with no further dynamic user input nor notable monitorable interactions with the interface – it is essentially a website whose contents had been processed by AI but not offering a user-facing

AI tool – the E-dimension in this case is restricted to publicly available information and my own analytical interpretation. This might miss some sociotechnical relations that contribute to the environment and trajectory of the system's Code Capital but are inaccessible to the researcher.

6.7 Conclusion

In this chapter, I applied the notion of Code Capital to examine an AI system that has already been deployed. To contextualize the study, I first surveyed technical variations of applications that automate facial analysis, including the specific case of recognition. Integrating empirical data from an original cross-country survey on social acceptance of FRT, I demonstrated how factors like societal expectations around technology, trust in governmental institutions, and national history of surveillance affect citizens' stance on its use in public. These results reinforced that several sociotechnical influences shape how FRT is perceived and might manifest impact. To concretize this point, I applied the CODE framework to one specific project that employed FRT to create the website FacesOfTheRiot. My analysis showed that the Code Capital of this system relies significantly on various interdependent configurations. Choices such as the exclusion of a frontend retrieval option, for example, determined the nature of the overall system, distinguishing a product that used FRT in its own development from a service that offers users the possibility to use FRT on others. FacesOfTheRiot is a particularly noteworthy case because it was designed and deployed neither by a company nor a state, but by a young, individual citizen with the help of similarly motivated individuals, though with the explicit aim to support law enforcement. It illustrates how open-source AI models can blur power structures and severely challenge social norms of privacy, surveillance, and accountability. As the law to regulate and oversee FRT is significantly evolving, decisions on who is allowed to employ these systems for which purposes bear far-reaching implications for citizens worldwide. As shown in this chapter, a rigorous understanding of a particular system's Code Capital in a bespoke setting can begin to grasp these effects and how they emerge.

7. Systems Design: Text-to-Speech Synthesis

"To invent a speaking machine and to execute it according to a well thought out plan would be one of the most audacious designs that ever arose in a human's soul."
Wolfgang von Kempelen,
Mechanics of the Human Language, 1791

"My voice is my passport. Please verify me."
Sneakers, 1992

7.1 Introduction

Humans have sought to produce synthetic speech with mechanical contraptions for centuries. Developments in machine learning processes have rapidly advanced the artificial computer-aided production of speech based on written text. Such text-to-speech (TTS) systems have long been employed as an assistive technology tool for people with various disabilities. In more recent years, AI-generated speech has been applied in voice interactions with smart devices, such as Apple's Siri or the Google Assistant, and other user engagement chatbots. But with increasingly natural-sounding synthetic output, TTS has also been employed to imitate individual human voices, such as in the case of deepfake media (see Section 2.3.3). Given the rising challenge of verifying media and identities online, and the state of vague regulations on the use of such personal data, understanding the manifestations of TTS technology is important for researchers, practitioners, policymakers, and users alike. This is especially relevant in the design process of such an application. How can we anticipate and better manage the potential implications, the Code Capital, of a TTS system in the making?

First, this chapter will contextualize the different use cases and concerns raised by TTS systems more generally. Forecasting future impact trajectories, however, necessitates a closer examination of a specific case study. For the rest of the chapter, I thus apply the CODE framework to a TTS system during its design process. The project in question, now called VocallyYours, employs natural language processing and text-to-speech (TTS) technology to imitate the specific tonality and conversational style of an individual in the form of synthetic audio output. This case study investigation into the system occurred two years into the project's development, but prior to its deployment. It includes an examination of central documents, workshop materials and notes, as well as interviews with three key participants in the process.[48] The analysis accounts for all CODE dimensions as summarized in Table 7.1. I conclude with reflections on the technology's Code Capital and the process of analysis. This chapter shows how the system's initial configurations, both chosen and default, could influence its future impact in divergent ways and with vast socio-technological scope. Notably, it also demonstrates that as a design instrument instead of a reality check like in the previous chapter, the CODE framework is an exercise in early transparency and contingency planning to assess whether the execution of the AI system combined with its context will likely produce the intended outcomes. In addition to its analytical value such an impact forecast includes recommendations to mitigate unwanted consequences.

7.1.1 Text-to-Speech Synthesis

As early as the 18th century, humans ventured their first attempts at speech synthesis. In Vienna in 1791, Hungarian inventor Wolfgang von Kempelen mused "whether language was created by humans, or whether it was created for them" (Von Kempelen, 1791, p. 28). A curious and creative mind though no scientist by training, von Kempelen sought to understand the genesis, functionalities, and natural instruments of human speech in order to transfer these powers to a machine.[49] "To invent a speaking machine and to execute it according to a well-thought-out plan," von Kempelen wrote, "would be one of the most audacious designs that ever arose in a human's soul" (Von Kempelen, 1791, p. 388). In his *Mechanics of the Human Language*, he laid out the foundations for The Speaking Machine: Imitating the human anatomy for vocal production, the wooden apparatus was designed to produce a range of complete words as separate syllables (Dudley & Tarnoczy, 1950). Instead of pre-programming an automaton,

---

48 To ensure interviewees' anonymity, I abbreviate the three key participants to K.P.1, K.P.2, and K.P.3.

49 Twenty years earlier, in 1770, von Kempelen had invented the infamous chess-playing automaton hoax "The Mechanical Turk" that serves as a namesake for the eponymous crowdsourcing website.

operating it resembled playing a musical instrument. Today, the German Museum in Munich exhibits *Der Sprechapparat*, the first manually operated speaking machine in history,[50] and a team of researchers were able to produce a replica that can successfully generate, among others, the most human of words: "Mama" and "Papa" (Berdux, 2015).

Modern-day automated speech synthesis builds on more than 60 years of speech processing research which integrates linguistics, phonetics, speech signals and signal processing (P. Taylor, 2009, p. xix). In practice, various TTS systems have been widely deployed eg. in call-centers (Qiu & Benbasat, 2005), linguistic instruction (Liakin et al., 2017), and disability assistance (S. G. Wood et al., 2018). Publicly available descriptions of commercial TTS technologies focus on the benefits of vocal personalization and speech assistance, such as the start-up Speak:Unique's claim to offer "personalized synthetic voices for use in communication aids by individuals who have lost or will lose the ability to speak using the individual's own voice or blended recordings matching characteristics" (*Similar Companies to VocaliD*, 2021). Similarly, Voiceitt is described as "an app for people with non-standard speech" (*Voiceitt: Home*, 2021). Lyrebird particularly emphasizes its affective modulation capacity, promising "a new generation of speech synthesis technologies, (...) the very first of this kind to allow copying voices in a matter of minutes and control the emotion of the generation" (*Similar Companies to VocaliD*, 2021). Even more explicitly, the latter stresses that its system will soon become a central technology in the evolution of human-machine interaction: "We believe that vocal human-computer interfaces will become more and more widespread in the future and we want to lead the race" (*Similar Companies to VocaliD*, 2021).[51]

7.1.2 Issues of Concern

A number of issues have arisen in relation to TTS-systems. In what follows, I discuss questions of automating human communication, authenticity expectations, as well as potential shifts in participation and intimacy.

---

50 https://www.deutsches-museum.de/forschung/forschungsbereiche/wissenschaftsg esch/sonic-visual-exhibit/sprechapparat/

51 In 2019, Lyrebird.ai was acquired by podcast editing company Descript, which turned it into an in-house AI research division and remodelled the technology into a feature called Overdub (Campbell-Wilson, 2020)

7.1.2.1 Automation

Automation in the realm of communication has repeatedly culturally updated and socially transformed human connections. Around the turn of the 20th century, automated telephone switchboards began to replace manual operators to address the central organizational challenge of scale: Humans could barely keep up the speed needed to initiate the exponential volume of connections between the rising number of callers. As Mueller argued in 1989, they faced a "confrontation with the multiplying possibilities of an expanding network" resulting in increasingly "slower service and higher cost" also known as "exchange diseconomies" (M. Mueller, 1989, p. 535). With the electromechanical switch systems, first invented by Almon Strowger, automated machinery gradually substituted for human-led processes. While a telephone exchange itself "is a radical rearrangement of social space" (M. Mueller, 1989, p. 534) that collapses distances between people and establishes vocal connection, the introduction of an automated mediator presented a similarly radical rearrangement through the boost of "social scale", which implies that

> when it comes to the *relations of communication* that bind the society together, growth not only increases the complexity of communicative relations, but it increases it at a *faster* rate, than the growth in the group's size (M. Mueller, 1989, p. 559) (emphasis in the original).

This early formulation of social scale foreshadows aspects of the network effects particularly salient in later highly networked technologies such as the Internet (Katz & Shapiro, 1985, 1994; B. Metcalfe, 2013; R. Metcalfe, 1995): With intensifying connection comes higher value for users coupled with exponential complexity, impenetrability - and potentially less oversight.

A similar argument can be made about the dynamic of machine learning processes used to automate parts of human communication. In 2020, Brown et al published the latest iteration of the Generative Pre-trained Transformer (GPT-3) architecture, an autoregressive natural language processing model that utilizes 175 billion parameters to produce human-like text (Brown et al., 2020). While the system has successfully produced content ranging from poetry, news articles, and blog posts to computer code (Hao, 2020; Sotala, 2020), commentators criticize GPT-3's results for lack of context or reasoning skills, arguing it "often spews contradictions or nonsense, because its statistical word-stringing is not guided by any intent or a coherent understanding of reality" (Simonite, 2020). GPT-3, too, has the dimension of social scale, despite not being a social network, as more users will mean training the model with more diverse use cases which render it progressively more valuable as its applications expand. Social scale includes added communicative complexity as well: GPT-3's examples signal the shift of an invisible social threshold, a blurring of the distinction lines between machine- and human-generated texts.

Comparable shifts could be expected from the rise of more widespread TTS-systems. Automating the generative process of speech production will become higher in quality the more user data is available to train the machine learning models. But the democratized access to these systems combined with the novel technical possibilities of unique voice imperson-ation mean a wider range of use cases beyond the assistive realm, including for nefarious purposes as the next section discusses. To repeat: With more users, the automated system rises in value but also in complexity, impene-trability and lack of oversight.

7.1.2.2 Authenticity

Advances in synthetic speech generation similarly challenge notions of verifiable human *authenticity* in vocal communication. When Canadian start-up company Lyrebird first published demos of its English-version TTS technology in 2017, a number of experts remarked that systems like it intensify the risk of unwanted vocal impersonation, complicate verifica-tion mechanisms that could be used in court, and might engender unwar-ranted trust in people listening to it (Gholipour, n.d.; Vincent, 2020). Many observers have raised such ethical concerns of TTS systems and other synthetic media known as deepfakes (Ajder, 2019; Jaiman, 2020). Business-related audio deepfake scams have become such a concern that the US Federal Trade Commission held a workshop in January 2020 on the ethics of what they coined "voice cloning technologies" and fraud using "social engineering" (Federal Trade Commission, 2020).

In addition to potential cybercriminality, TTS systems used for the purposes of manipulating information may contribute to the greater con-text of "fake news" (Tandoc et al., 2018; Wardle & Derakhshan, 2017). Specifically when used for political means, such synthetic media may af-fect perceptions of uncertainty and trust in news (Vaccari & Chadwick, 2020). Lyrebird's demo included clips of US Presidents Donald Trump and Barack Obama, as well as US Secretary Hillary Clinton. If such media are maliciously used, they could influence democratic processes such as elections through deception, reputational harm, and the undermining of trust in political candidates (Diakopoulos & Johnson, 2019).

7.1.2.3 Participation

Additionally, TTS systems may broaden the circle of those able to participate in the social norms of spoken communication at all. As with numerous other technological inventions, interest in speech synthesis has roots in the assistance of differently abled people. "Speech in the broadest sense", Wolfgang von Kempelen wrote in 1791, "is the ability to make one's feelings or thoughts known to others through signs" (Von Kempelen, 1791, p. 1). Among his motivations in building The Speaking Machine was its potential for people who had no or restricted ability to use their natural voice to make their feelings or thoughts known (Trouvain & Brackhane, 2011, p. 163). Today, Apple's inbuilt VoiceOver technology allows automated screen-reading to increase basic accessibility for the visually impaired (Leporini et al., 2012; Smaradottir et al., 2018). Various assistive technologies expand the range of communication options for people with disabilities which may help increase independence (Seelman, 1993) and social inclusion (Owuor & Larkan, 2017). Assistive synthetic speech applications have enhanced natural speech production (Buschak, 1999) and boosted positive prejudice towards speech-disabled people (Stern et al., 2007). In turn, studies have demonstrated that synthetic speech systems themselves might be perceived more favorably when employed by people with disabilities (Stern et al., 2002). However, research shows that even assistive technology meant to be "a gateway to opportunity and voice as a metaphor for agency and self-representation" is still subject to biases and inaccessibility that reinforce structural inequalities with regards to gender, race, and class (Alper, 2017a). Some of these power imbalances relate to the limited range of voice data used to train these systems and the generic nature of the speech produced.

7.1.2.4 Intimacy

A sociolinguistic analysis might further raise the question if relegating the production of human-sounding speech to machines could mean a loss of vocal *intimacy* between communicators. While speech of a more generic nature, such as navigation systems, might not suffer equal losses due to TTS technology, the receiver of an artificial imitation of a unique natural voice, depending on the output quality, might be ignorant to its synthetic nature while the system might falsely imitate familiarity and trust. On the contrary, various instances of computer-mediated communication (CMC) have been shown to expand our notions and conventions of connection. Walther's *hyperpersonal communication model* (Walther et al., 2015) states that "there are several instances in which CMC has surpassed the level of affection and emotion of parallel FtF (face-to-face) interaction" (Walther, 1996, p. 17). As Reid argues, CMC "forces users to deconstruct many of the cultural tools that form the basis of more conventional systems of interaction" (Reid, 1991). In their investigation of relational intimacy in CMC compared to FtF interaction, Hian et al found support for Walther's thesis (Hian et al., 2004). Reasons for this intensified intimacy include the opportunity for social cues to be revealed through self-selective performance rather than appearance (Walther, 1996, p. 20), which allows users to "manage impressions and facilitate desired relationships" (Walther, 2007). These effects have led some to question whether simulations of closeness through digital means, such as the fictionalized account of a human-machine romance in Spike Jonze's 2013 movie *Her*, constitute a "substitute for human companionship or a new type of digital intimacy" (Schwartz, 2018). In either case, communicating with a TTS system may enable human listeners to modulate their personal exposure in a way that might lead to increased relational intimacy.

Figure 7.1 shows the CODE framework as applied to VocallyYours

Conception	
Sensegiving Actors	Who gives sense to the AI system?
Narratives	What narratives explicitly shape their vision?
Investment and Expected Returns	What types of resources factor into the system and its potential business model?
Operations	
Model Architecture	What process constituted the chosen algorithms?
Evaluation	How was the success of the system's task optimized and validated?
User Interface	What considerations flow into user design?
Data	
Collection	How large is the potential to scale the data collection process?
Pre-Processing	What criterion determine relevance for inclusion and exclusion of data?
	Are the available training data representative of the people they affect?
Storage	How are privacy, security, and consent requirements ensured?
Embedding	
Sensemaking Actors	How does the system interact with cultural and social norms and relate to a diversity of lives, individually and collectively?
Regulatory Boundaries	How do relevant legal and ethical standards pertain to the system's potential use cases?

Evidently, TTS systems offer a host of potential benefits and bear risks of consequences, intended as well as unintended. Any new TTS system is configured by a set of dynamic, entangled sociotechnical relations. For the rest of the chapter, I will now closely examine the Code Capital of one particular case in its design and development stage, the project VocallyYours, by applying the CODE framework as shown in Figure 7.1.

7.2 Conception

In this section, I focus on the actors who shape the purpose of the system through sensegiving practice, analyze the narratives that inscribe a vision into it, and examine the investment and expected returns that influence design choices and material configurations. In sum, I assess how the system is being conceived.

7.2.1 Sensegiving Actors

To understand the constitutive actors who invent, engineer, finance, and manage the AI system at hand – who give it sense through practice – includes acknowledging the trajectory that backdrops its invention and technical execution to grasp the beliefs inscribed in the technological object (Akrich, 1992). For the purpose of this dissertation, the chosen case is a joint project by the University of St. Gallen's Institute of Computer Science and ada, an education technology start-up, formerly of German business publishing house Handelsblatt Media Group. As the co-founder of ada, I am part of the project's genesis though not its technical development. Together, our teams obtained funding from the 2018 Google Digital News Initiative to develop a German-language text-to-speech system that could generate synthetic spoken word based on written input while mimicking individual voices at a high-quality threshold.

In the case of VocallyYours, the sensegiving actors are researchers and practitioners of media and communication as well as engineers with expertise in machine learning and signal processing. Their objective is to employ technology to automate a part of communication by creating artificial audio with the unique likeness of individual voices. From a media standpoint, the interest in VocallyYours is focused on innovating the creation of personalized, authentic audio output for a variety of communicators and journalists. From a technological standpoint, the project seeks to optimize intelligibility and naturalness of machine-generated German speech. These professional perspectives contribute to the conception of VocallyYours. Through their acts of decision-making as well as unintentional choices, this constellation of actors shapes the system in a significant way, for "the prerogatives of sensegiving at the design stage may have an important effect on the sensemaking and sensegiving that are subsequently granted to others" (Ramiller & Chiasson, 2008, p. 124).

7.2.2 Narratives

Collectively performed narratives about an AI system create shared meaning, frame implied desirable futures and lend them normative force. It is particularly salient in the creation of a vision for the system, internally and publicly, both by its creators and by its users. "Such visions," Jasanoff writes, "have the power to influence technological design" (Jasanoff & Kim, 2009, p. 120). They thereby help to clarify the conception of a system. To give the observations of narratives that shape the examined project empirical weight, discursive elements of its descriptions can underline the logics and framings of the system. For context, the following analysis is embedded into comparatives narratives of similar start-up efforts to offer TTS for individual voice imitation.

As VocallyYours in its unlaunched state has no official publicity documents to date, this analysis concentrates on its formal funding application documents, which contain ample information about the overall vision portrayed by its creators and are partly featured on the website of the DNI. Originally conceived in the context of innovations in journalism, the main use case is a TTS instrument for journalists, as clarified in its brief summary statement:

> "VocallyYours will generate speech from text and be able to *mimic an individual journalist's voice* [emphasis added]. (…) It will transfer written input into audio by automatically imitating the *particular tonality and conversational style of a real-life journalist*" (*Vocally Yours (Round 5)*, 2018).

To derive and justify the necessity for such a solution, the narrative creates a scenario with future challenges of scale and scarce individuality:

> "As conversational interfaces move beyond just smart speakers to all the devices around us, studies show that users increasingly seek out audio content. Text-focused media outlets thus face the *challenge* of transforming their quality journalism into high-quality audio formats *at large scale*. Exacerbating this challenge is the issue that to just automate content with a synthetic voice tends to *drown out distinct voices*" (*Vocally Yours (Round 5)*, 2018).

Subsequently, it offers a vision for a desirable future in which the conceived system represents a solution to these challenges:

> "VocallyYours will scale and promote inclusion by highlighting the actual human voice behind the journalism; it will increase trust by inten-

sifying brand association and advance revenue diversification by allowing the mass production of highly personalised audio content" (*Vocally Yours (Round 5)*, 2018).

Within these narrative formulations lie the following logics and framings: The system's solution for scale is implied through the process of automation, ostensibly leading to more efficient production. Its promise of newly generated diversity is premised both on the current state of ubiquitously generic synthetic speech and on the assumption of effort for individual users, particularly journalists, to create audio content with their natural voices. Finally, the narrative projects both a presumed social effect and a business implication: increased trust and revenue diversification.

7.2.2.1 Trust

Expecting amplified trust through anthropomorphizing (from the Greek *anthropos* for human and *morphe* for form) machines reflects insights of a strain of human-computer interaction research that is based on a human-human trust paradigm: Computers are social actors that people place expectations, norms, and beliefs in. Thus, the more human-like the machine, the more trustworthy it appears (Cassell & Bickmore, 2000; Nass et al., 1994). Empirically, one stream of studies demonstrates that anthropomorphized features such as name, gender and voice can increase trust in autonomous vehicles (Forster et al., 2017; Waytz et al., 2014), strengthen trust resilience in automated agents such as an avatar (De Visser et al., 2016), and elicit more social responses generally from users (Gong, 2008). A contradictory paradigm based on human-to-machine trust presumes automation bias, or the human proclivity to trust highly computerized rather than anthropomorphized systems as more effective and rational expert agents (Dijkstra et al., 1998; Dzindolet et al., 2003; Skitka et al., 1999). As the TTS system behind VocallyYours substitutes a human language task rather than a computational task, conversational design research on the matter does suggest that the human-human trust model applies (Seeger & Heinzl, 2018), thus higher levels of anthropomorphizing the audio output might indeed lead to deeper perception of trustworthiness.

Notably, already during the development process aspects of anthropomorphizing the AI system emerged. As key sensegiving actors listened to early demos of synthetic voice imitations, descriptions tended to frame the artificial machine output through a lens of human decision-making by remarking, for instance, about one particularly long and complex content sample "it's amazing that *she* is inhaling – because *she* knows *she* is about to read a three-sentence long title" (K.P.1, personal communication, January 29, 2021). Similarly, another key participant noted that "the model *decides* the speech mood based on the context (...) It has no way to understand which voice characteristics to use" (K.P.3, personal communication, February 8, 2021). This gives an early indication of the potential inferences and relationship-building that users – sensemaking actors – might engage in with the system even if there are aware of its synthetic nature.

7.2.2.2 Revenue Diversification

Visions of revenue diversification through the system are manifold, as initial documents show. VocallyYours' documentation promises that "increased audio content will allow airtime for more audio ads generally, directly augmenting revenue due to a higher quantity of such commercials." For large newsrooms, "the tool itself can also be used to easily produce ads in the trusted voices of journalists" which could lead to "a subscription to a specific voice avatar i.e. to a particularly favored journalist's voice", thus resulting in an uplift of subscriptions. Underlying these promises are the assumptions that the German market for online audio consumption and its commercialization are on the rise; that the technology leads to cost reduction measured by time and financial resources saved; and that VocallyYours helps individuals overcome barriers to tap into this market through their own production. Official statistics appear to confirm the first premise: In 2020, 50 million (70.8 %) Germans aged 14 years and older reported using online audio offers, compared to 43.9 million (62,2 %) in the previous year (Bayerische Landeszentrale für neue Medien, 2020, p. 4). While all different audio format categories are on the rise, podcasts experienced the highest yearly growth rate at 45.2 %, followed by audiobooks at 35.6 % (Bayerische Landeszentrale für neue Medien, 2020, p. 5). These two categories also experienced the highest increase in frequency of use (52 % and 42 %) (Bayerische Landeszentrale für neue Medien, 2020, p. 15). Target groups once less reached, such as women, people over 50, and those with a less formal educational background similarly saw significant boosts in usage (Bayerische Landeszentrale für neue Medien, 2020, p. 9). Out of those who do consume audio formats, 32.8 % use offers they have to pay for, up from 30.6 % in 2019 (Bayerische Landeszentrale für neue Medien, 2020, p. 46).

According to the German Digital Media Association (*Bundesverband Digitale Wirtschaft*), online audio advertising revenues doubled in just three years since 2017, reaching 70 million EUR, while podcast revenues specifically rose from 9 million in 2019 to 14 million in just one year (Bundesverband Digitale Wirtschaft, 2020). Market predictions forecast the country's digital audio advertising industry to grow to 208 million EUR by 2025 (*Audio Advertising - Germany*, n.d.), with additional 23.2 million EUR from Austria (*Audio Advertising - Austria*, n.d.) and 16.6m from Switzerland (*Audio Advertising - Switzerland*, n.d.), capping off the German-speaking market at roughly 250 million EUR by then. As a point of comparison to underline the stark rise of the industry on a global scale: In 2015, US podcast advertising revenues hovered around 105 million USD, in 2019 it surpassed 700 million USD (*U.S. Podcast Advertising Revenue 2019*, 2020).

These numbers show the potential for commercializing output that VocallyYours produces. A more detailed look at the market still raises one potential caveat about this narrative with a focus on freelance journalists: In addition to streaming leader Spotify and e-commerce giant Amazon's Audible, international media company Bertelsmann and television network ProSieben are vying for the dominant market position in the German digital audio industry (Bialek, 2020). Using VocallyYours to produce personalized audio content at great scale with small marginal cost could in fact put these competitors in even more economically advantageous conditions, widening the gap to freelance journalists trying to break into the audio market. Notwithstanding these potentially increasing inequities, the technology could still serve as a useful instrument for individuals to generate and automate their own work.

A narrative analysis has demonstrated visions of procedural efficiency, personalized content production, boosted trust with listeners, and financial gain. Evidently, the manifestation of each of these rests on assumptions about desirable futures that may socially vary, market behaviors, and psychological responses that will in turn affect the system's trajectory.

7.2.3 Investment and Expected Returns

This section examines what types of resources currently factor into the system and its potential business model.

7.2.3.1 Funding

Funding for VocallyYours came from Google's €150M Digital News Innovation Fund. Public information about the initiative portrays it as financial support "to help journalism thrive in the digital age" (*Digital News Initiative*, n.d.). In its final Impact Report, the initiative describes funding 662 projects in 30 European countries to "kick-start the overdue development of an R&D culture in the European news ecosystem" with foci such as "boosting digital revenue" and "exploring new technologies" (*DNI Final Impact Report*, 2020). In the case of VocallyYours, the Terms and Conditions document clarifies on the one hand that the grant includes no obligations to share parts of the project's software, data, or intellectual property rights with the corporation and "there is no requirement to use Google technology"; on the other it also states "that Google (…) may independently (i) create, develop or purchase products, services, information or materials, or (ii) work on, sponsor or commission projects, related to or similar to the subject matter" of one's proposed project (*DNI Terms and Conditions*, n.d.). Various journalistic reports about the initiative have made claims of veiled lobbying against EU copyright reform (Garrahan & Khan, 2018), quoting the head of the DNI selection council as calling it "also a PR instrument for Google to win over the European publishing industry" and noting that a number of projects do use Google services or technology – just like VocallyYours – thereby contributing to the corporations' collection of data (Fanta, 2018). At its current stage of development, funding of the project has finished, and final milestone reports have been submitted. Given that the project expands on the WaveNet architecture for its generative model (see *7.2.1*), developed by Google affiliate DeepMind, the system remains indirectly linked to the technological infrastructure of the multinational conglomerate behind its funding.

7.2.3.2 Business Model

VocallyYours is an AI solution developed as a licensed service product. While it has not currently launched and thus has neither paying nor non-paying customers, initial documents show that the plan is to "license the full-fledged system to independent journalists, entire newsrooms, advertisement agencies, researchers, and numerous other interested parties in the realm of individualized, mass production of audio in the age of AI." Specifically, the business model for individual users is to charge a fee for a singular voice avatar in combination with packages for audio minutes created. As a software solution for organizations, a tiered model for higher user numbers in addition to audio minutes aims at increasing revenue from the system as usage intensity grows.

As these formulations show, while the business model is made explicit, two less visible factors stand out. First, the target user group clearly extends beyond the realm of journalism. Given market developments as shown previously, it is to be expected that a large share of users and thus revenue might be generated in the advertising industry instead. Second, in addition to the direct payment for the solution, users will reward VocallyYours by contributing to the advancement of the system through their personal data input. Audio snippets recorded and submitted with the concordant text basis will continuously train the AI model itself and diversify its transfer capabilities to multiple voices, thereby enhancing its quality and making it increasingly lucrative. They are in "a deeply relational practice as 'con-duc-ers' – producers and consumers" (Orlikowski & Scott, 2015, p. 22). As to avoid obfuscation, this dynamic of user contribution to the data model should be communicated clearly.

7.3 Operations

In this section, I examine the operational choices. This comprises the specific configurations of the model architecture, its evaluation, and the current planning for the user interface.

7.3.1 Model Architecture

From an operational standpoint, the goal of VocallyYours is twofold: First, it is to transform German text into German spoken language (text-to-speech synthesis). Second, it is to condition the generated spoken audio towards an individual person's voice (style transfer), eventually with as few audio input samples as possible. To achieve these two goals, the engineering team made a number of decisions with regards to the operational architecture.

For the entire TTS model to operate, multiple stages are required. To begin with, the input text must be processed, a task executed by an acoustic model. In this first step, an encoder converts the linguistic content by extracting phoneme embeddings from the individual words of the written input. Next, the encoder embeds speaker characteristics into the 512-dimensional vectors, concatenating them with the phonemes. Subsequently, the encoder translates these collective embeddings into an internal representation by producing mel-spectograms (Shen et al., 2018). Finally, the 'vocoder' module converts the spectrograms back into waveforms, decoding the various embeddings, to generate the synthetic speech output. The entire process is shown in Figure 7.2.

Rather than using large databases of single speaker speech fragments (concatenative TTS) or approaches that combine the content and characteristics in the model but sound less natural (parametric TTS), VocallyYours attempts the task at hand in an end-to-end learning setup using neural networks for each part of the system. To address the specific conditions of the German language, VocallyYours adapts and extends existing architectures to train its generative models. Using Tacotron-2, a sequence-to-sequence attention-based encoder-decoder architecture (Yuxuan Wang et al., 2017), as a basis, the team developed 11 combined architectures.

To account for the specific German pronunciation, the encoder translates complete words into phonemic representations of the International Phoneme Alphabet (IPA). This phonemizer extracts from the individual words of the written input meaningful sequential character representations in the form of the IPA. In the case of the German language, its many nested relative clauses must be specifically conceptualized to render them comprehensible. To this end, the encoder and decoder are connected through an attention module. Various attention methods (Locality Sensitive Hashing (Slaney & Casey, 2008), Gaussian Mixture Model (Reynolds, 2009), Forward Attention (J.-X. Zhang et al., 2018)) were tested to evaluate which decoder performed best in processing particularly long sentences while producing the mel-spectogram representations.

While the original Tacotron-2 uses the Griffin Lim algorithm for the final step, the engineering team decided to substitute it by a neural vocoder based on performance quality. After testing alternative models such as WaveNet and WaveGlow, the final constellation employs WaveRNN and Parallel WaveGAN (Yamamoto et al., 2020) as the vocoder to train 50-60 different models in total. Combining these two vocoder models aims to outperform more traditional approaches and to better enable a multi-speaker speech environment (Paine et al., 2016; Shen et al., 2018).

The project portioned the development of the system into three phases: TTS-basic, TTS-plus, and multi-TTS, the distinctions of which reside largely in the acoustic model. TTS-basic establishes the foundational elements and functionality with decent sound quality but accelerated speed of the

Figure 7.2 shows a visualization of VocallyYours TTS as shown in one of the project's demo presentations

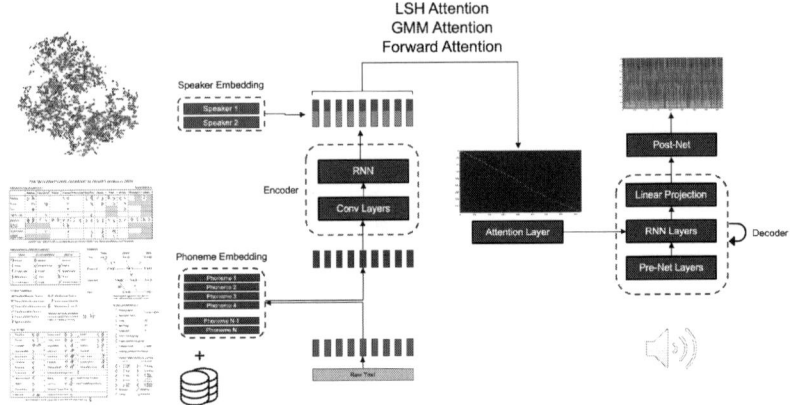

vocal output and faulty pronunciation mainly attributed to the Gaussian Mixture Model originally employed. As one engineer put it, the model "always looks for the future not the past – but it wants to finish, so it's too fast" (K.P.2, personal communication, February 3, 2021). As an advancement, TTS-plus, the current phase of the project, has an improved acoustic model: Based on performance evaluation, the choice to use the Forward attention method led to more natural pronunciation and speed in the final audio output (J.-X. Zhang et al., 2018). Eventually, the multi-TTS model, an as of yet future phase of the project, will employ multiple additional neural network layers to achieve a multi-speaker-environment.

In the current TTS-plus phase of the system, in addition to the neural architecture, a number of pre-processing and post-processing steps were added to standardize the input and output. As one engineer put it,

> to train the neural architecture, you need to make some assumptions – like how the inputs are and how the outputs are supposed to be. For example, if you always assume that the input is a single sentence that ends in punctuation you train the model according to that assumption (K.P.3, personal communication, February 8, 2021).

To fulfill these assumptions, pre-processing is applied to the written input and includes, for example, a database for pronunciation corrections of individual words that the phonemizer has registered falsely (eg. English terms like American brand names such as "Apple" or foreign names such as "New York" or "Khashoggi"). This module formats the pre-processed input into an .xml file, which is readable by the rest of the system. In addition, to train the model on prosody variance, the process of speaker embedding encodes the corresponding individual speech characteristic of each utterance. This becomes particularly relevant the longer the written input becomes. As a very last step, post-processing includes speaker-dependent denoising of the final audio wave file. While the training model has been designed locally, its training employs a fast DGX-2 server in Switzerland to accelerate the deep learning process. Afterwards, the model will be migrated to an Azure Cloud server, which will eventually communicate with users through an API and a graphical user interface (GUI, see Section 7.3.3).

Throughout the process of configuring the model architecture, the engineers trialled different algorithmic constellations to optimize for the given task. While the sub-tasks for each element of the overall system were clear, at times the specific reasons for why certain compositions performed better than others were less so. As one developer put it: "The stage that we're at in deep learning is more like chemistry. We try different combinations and see if it works and all we do is based on our assumptions" (K.P.3, personal communication, February 8, 2021). This experimental dimension points to what scholars have termed AI's "black box" challenge: the fact that the exact mechanisms of a deep learning model are impenetrable and lack transparency (Bathaee, 2017). Various initiatives, including the EU's push that algorithmic decision-making must be made explainable to affected subjects have called for "making techniques like deep learning more understandable to their creators and accountable to their users. Otherwise it will be hard to predict when failures might occur—and it's inevitable they will" (Knight, 2017a).

7.3.2 Evaluation

To evaluate the perceptual quality of the audio output, the Mean Opinion Score (MOS) is a standard measure of subjective sound quality. To test MOS, various synthetic audio samples produced by VocallyYours were played for and then rated by German-speaking study participants on the crowdsourcing platform MechanicalTurk (MTurk). First, 50 sentences were generated for the different models. Evaluators were then asked to grade ten out of the 50 possible sentences of speech samples featuring three different voices on a five-point Likert scale with regards to their naturalness. Each sentence was assessed by at least five different annotators in total to reach a MOS. Thus, each system had at least 250 evaluations and was tested in multiple voices. To ensure that people spoke sufficient German and remained attentive throughout the exercise, the task included ten audio clips plus randomly shuffled test questions involving mathematical prompts. While the human-generated version ('ground truth') of one speaker received a naturalness MOS of 3.98, the best performing models received a MOS between 3.41-3.61. A second speaker's ground truth MOS of 3.96 compares to best performing model MOS of 3.56-3.92. Evidently in the latter case, the model MOS demonstrate that the synthetic outputs perform very similarly to the human version with a difference of just 0.02. Potential additional experiments for evaluation could include MOS tests for *similarity* as well as a *preference test* comparing two audio samples from the same individual voice. Notably, however, MTurk is a crowdsourcing platform that attracts a particular demographic when used for subject recruitment. Studies have shown that MTurk's respondent pool is often more representative than in-person convenience samples, but less representative than Internet-based panels or national probability samples (Berinsky et al., 2012). One comparative study between respondents on MTurk and the US Cooperative Congressional Election Survey (CCES) found differences with regards to representation of minorities and behaviors such as interest in the news (Huff & Tingley, 2015), both of which could be relevant for the evaluation of a synthetic voice generator for journalists. The same review found that MTurk's respondent pool is similarly skewed towards urban representation as the CCES (90 %) which suggests a lack of respondents from rural, less digitally connected areas. While these caveats do not invalidate the MOS judgments from MTurk respondents, they might point to missing beta evaluation subjects that could be informative for the further development of VocallyYours.

7.3.3 User Interface

As it is a software-as-a-service product, users will eventually interact with VocallyYours-TTS via a web-based communication interface that connects the production server with end-use devices. There are multiple options for the manifestation of this interface, such as a Graphic User Interface (GUI). For the journalist users specifically, the user interface will be in the form of a Content Management System (CMS). Since the project is in the final stages of training and evaluation, this interface has not yet been designed and will involve a different front-end developer team. Overall, the initial engineering team is focused mostly on the development of the model architecture and its training. Meanwhile, the software behind the interface is responsible for later data collection and pre-processing. It will thus serve as a mediator between the user and the requirements of the receiving backend. With inputs likely in need of extensive data cleaning due to variations in recording quality, the software must prepare the data and feed all necessary information linking the speaker characteristics to the text input into the backend of the TTS-system in a structured manner.

At this point in the process, the backend engineers reported perceiving very little connection to the final interface, as one admitted: "We make a split between our system and what is supposed to be designed for the GUI" (K.P.3, personal communication, February 8, 2021). Indeed, the journalist members of the group had not yet delivered the interface specifications. During the interface design stage, this 'split' might require bridging certain backend necessities with user preferences, as one example shows: While the backend engineers aim to portion the input text into smallest possible segments to achieve efficient processing – currently in paragraph form at most – the GUI will have to take into account users' needs to process much longer texts, such as journalistic articles and potential podcast scripts. Acknowledging this incongruence in objectives, one engineer remarked about the future input design: "I don't know at what level these decisions are made – or if they are made at all" (K.P.3, personal communication, February 8, 2021). Their comment reveals a level of obfuscation about some design decision-making processes and, further, raises the question of unconscious choices that create unintentional defaults: Early engineering choices based on individual objectives may create operational consequences for later stages of the development process or even human-machine interaction.

7.4 Data

In this section, I take a closer look at the data at the core of the system. It will mainly address the input used to train the model with references and inferences made about the user data to be captured by the system in the future.

7.4.1 Collection

Three main sources of data served as the training basis for the model. One comprised various book manuscripts and audiobook recordings from an author, while a second was a professional speaker's reading of diverse journalistic texts. After the model was trained on the two initial sources, a third source was used to apply the model to a new speaker: The source was publicly available audio with concomitant transcripts of a high-ranking German official, whose position requires the archiving of their speeches. Overall, two of the voices were classified as female, one as male, all native German speakers. It is noteworthy, that while one of the training data subjects has a slight regional dialect, none have accents, which might precondition VocallyYours to perform better for users with native pronunciation. Specifically, as the phonemizer in the acoustic model is optimized for standard German, any deviant pronunciation will likely face a less successful performance. To be more representative of potential users, future training should include a wide variety of speaker inputs.

Once deployed, the audio input to train for a new speaking voice as well as the subsequent text uploads will be collected through the GUI and prepared by the software for pre-processing (see Section 7.4.2.). As more individuals use VocallyYours, adding more speaker characteristics as well as diverse genres of texts, we will continuously train our foundational TTS-model at certain points in time while injecting quality gates, thus the data will be dynamic in nature with enormous potential for scale.

However, as became clear in the early stages of the project, there was a huge lack of properly prepared training data which required a large human effort to produce. Given the particular set-up, the training data had to be prepared in a strictly structured and restricted format: Audio snippets had to be precisely aligned with the written text, which in turn had to be temporally segmented so as to signal the contours of each sentence. Throughout the pre-processing it became evident that such properly cleaned, matching audio and written data was rare. Ideally, the data should have been recorded with the purpose of training this model in mind and including an option for technically registering, for example by clicking a button, at the end of each sentence. This was an important insight with regards to how data will be collected and prepared for processing in the future. A user interface should offer options to record spoken text in the standardized format that is necessary for optimal training of a new voice.

7.4.2 Pre-Processing

Data preparation for processing was key to the training process as stark variance in sound quality, transcript accuracy, and prosody translates into sensitivities of the model. Even variations in recordings, caused eg. by varying equipment conditions, volume variation, or background noise, affect training dynamics and thus the performance of the model. One training source had such deviant prosodies in the different data files that their voice was split into 7 speakers. Similarly, as unclean transcriptions or improper tagging would have resulted in skewing the model, some data was discarded. One major criterion that determined inclusion and exclusion of data was thus prosody stability and speech-to-transcript alignment. This could result in bias for future data recorded in unfavorable settings or with less professional recording equipment.

As section 7.5.1. details, under the European Union's GDPR, the legal boundaries applied to a system processing personal data, such as VocallyYours, are manifold. Privacy, security and consent requirements must be upheld and clearly communicated to users. Particularly with regards to how each individual voice is processed as part of training the larger model and to the consent given to specific uses of the synthetic imitation, such communication must be proactive, readily available, and comprehensible to a wide range of users.

7.4.3 Storage

At the current stage of development, the plan is to host VocallyYours on a service provider server, where the future data will be stored. In parallel to the processing of sensitive user information, GDPR obligations for the protection of such personal data related to security and consent apply to storage conditions, too, and will be central to a successful deployment of the system. As GDPR stipulates, privacy must be built into the core of storage design. Rights of the data subject at the stage of storage include the right to view and correct personal data, as well as the right to be forgotten (see 7.5.2).

7.5 Environment

In this section, I examine how the system is embedded in its environment. This includes making inferences about its interactions with sensemaking actors, and about related issues of participation, intimacy, and, finally, regulatory boundaries.

7.5.1 Sensemaking Actors

As this system has yet to be deployed, we can currently only deduce possible consequences based on, first, what research on human-machine interaction in the field of voice agents has previously shown, and second, on prior use cases and recent developments. To understand how actors make sense of VocallyYours in practice, I will examine how the system might interact with cultural and social norms of communication and how it might relate to a diversity of lives individually and collectively. By anticipating how this particular system and its sensemaking actors might interrelate, I will synthetize recommendations for how to better manage these effects.

In considering how actors will make sense of the automation of a central part of human communication – speech – we must question who gets to participate on which side of the automated dynamic. This issue is two-pronged. First, we might consider the power dynamic of having a machine speak on one's behalf versus having to listen to or interact with a machine as the receiver. As studies of other technology applications such as the neighborhood-based social network Nextdoor have demonstrated, certain systems can exacerbate real-world social inequities leading to what Kurwa termed "digitally gated communities" (2019). In the case of VocallyYours, this might manifest as digitally gated communication if affluent users employ a TTS system as their virtual mouthpiece, while economically disadvantaged actors remain strictly in the position of the human listener. While such inequities already exist in the form of human personal assistants, inserting a machine into the interaction may further emphasize the superiority of one individual's time valued over another's. As Grevatt puts it in his discussion of Google Duplex, an AI-driven voice assistant, using AI to talk to people who do not have a choice in whom they speak to "increases the moral weight of this unequal valuation by challenging the dignity of those Duplex interacts with" (2018, p. 2). In this case, Google reacted to the substantial public backlash by offering Duplex in a manner more useful to diverse users: as a tool to screen calls from unknown numbers. In the feature, named Call Screen, the voice assistant discloses its artificial nature and then empowers the user to have oversight of potentially unwanted phone interaction. This new mediating role "reverses the nature of the power dynamic" (Grevatt, 2018, p. 4). While these power considerations apply particularly to conversational voice agents, it is conceivable that VocallyYours will be used as the voice generator for such agents in the future. Its particular use cases should thus take the impact of communicative power relations into account. For example, previous research has shown, that non-native English speakers derive less satisfaction from dialogue-based interactions with voice assistant that involve multiple levels than native speakers do because of significant misunderstandings (Pal et al., 2019). This leads directly to the second dimension of participation: Who may use VocallyYours to imitate their voice?

In order to create a model as representative of a broad user base as possible, the data fed into it should be intentionally diverse. This includes the vocal idiosyncrasies of people from different linguistic backgrounds, dialects, accents, as well as people with various disabilities. Its planned trajectory should ensure what Alper calls "keeping voices attached to people" as "speech synthesis should be intersectional and polyvocal, and voices should be engineered and designed by more than just able-bodied cisgender white men" (2017b). VocallyYours' multi-TTS feature addresses this point by synthetically generating unique voices. It allows anyone to copy their individual tonality, prosody, and mannerisms. To lower the threshold of participation for those not able to afford costly licensing for their own vocal imitation, an initial training of a user's voice avatar should be free of charge for individuals. The business model could then shift its focus on charging minutes of audio created. This would encourage a large set of people to initially experiment with the AI and experience its reproduction of their audio character. Moreover, it would foster a more diverse dataset for the training of the model behind VocallyYours-TTS.

In addition to anticipating effects on social power relations, considerations of misuse are of high priority. Specifically, as illustrated in Section 7.1.2.3, a number of instances have exemplified the problem of fraudulent voice imitations. VocallyYours, too, is currently susceptible to this type of abuse. A case in point: Early versions of VocallyYours were trained on the voice of a high-ranking European official in unpublished demos for training purposes. This possibility alone, because of the ubiquity of written and vocal output by politicians, and the high quality of this data because of its official uses, clarifies the urgent need for verification mechanisms.

To address this point, VocallyYours must include a digital authentication process, either to signal an output file was generated artificially or alternatively that this creation was, indeed, commissioned by the rightful "owner" of the voice data used. Considerations for verification mechanisms should be central to the ongoing development process of both the backend and frontend user interface. For example, steganography methods would allow encoding an audio watermark to each voice output, which could be uniquely and securely tied to an individual's personal data (Desmedt et al., 1998; Sinha et al., 2015).

Finally, the authentically intimate nature of human communication may be challenged by the type of human-machine interaction VocallyYours allows. For example, one of the criticisms of Google Duplex included that callers "unwittingly interact(ed) with an AI instead of the person with which they would do business" (Grevatt, 2018, p. 3). Legal scholars have called this dynamic "deception by design" (Kuss & Leenes, 2020). After backlash to the demonstration of Google Duplex, which was described as "eerily lifelike" (Hern, 2018), the company, too, announced it would include a disclosure feature to "make sure the system is appropriately identified" as an artificial bot (Statt, 2018). As some regulation, such as the GDPR and the recent EU AI regulation proposal would require, VocallyYours should include a disclosure feature to ensure that the line between automated and human speech, while approaching likeness in quality, is transparently communicated to users.

However, this disclosure might also affect the configurations that have led some technologies to elicit the Uncanny Valley effect. Its theory is grounded in psychoanalytical work that described the mysterious effect of perceiving something as familiar yet strange at the same time. While the Uncanny Valley effect generally applies to visual cues and movement, research has suggested that similar dynamics might exist for sound (Grimshaw, 2009). With its feature to imitate unique human voices, VocallyYours could potentially be influenced by this cognitive dissonance: With increasing indistinguishability from its human vocal counterpart, users' reaction to the technology might shift from affinity to revulsion, particularly when they are aware of its artificiality early on (Mori et al., 2012). Additionally, marketing research has shown that self-identification by a conversational AI agent decreases people's willingness to purchase products, implying the possible existence of a negative disclosure effect (Luo et al., 2019). Thus, to mitigate these effects, an inbuilt default disclosure requirement could be timed to occur after users have experienced the artificial voice, for example as soon as a user decides to stop listening.

Evidently, should VocallyYours be adopted widely, it could significantly rearrange cultural and social dimensions of communication. It will be made sense of through a variety of lenses in practice: Automation of the once human-generated process of vocal production might increase efficiency but will also spur social scale, including communicative complexity. Given the evolution towards individual synthetic voice imitations, challenges of authenticity will reconfigure realms where verified identity is of importance. Emotional relations might evolve to include expanded forms of computer-mediated connection and interpersonal intimacy. Similar to other machine learning models, pitfalls exist with regards to fairness, bias and representation inherent in the AI system. If the experiences of a diversity of users are taken into account, they could be instructive for designing a system that facilitates more inclusive participation in communication overall.

7.5.2 Regulatory Boundaries

In the 1980s, the American artist Bette Midler fought for ownership of her own voice. Ford Motor Company had used her former background singer, adept at imitating her well-known vocals, in a car commercial. Midler sued for misappropriation of her likeness. After the courts first ruled against her favor, she appealed. Finally, in 1988, the Ninth U.S. Circuit Court of Appeals in *Midler v. Ford Motor Co.* asserted that "a voice is as distinctive and personal as a face. The human voice is one of the most palpable ways identity is manifested" (*Midler v. Ford Motor Co. 549 F. 2d 460 (9th Cir.)*, 1988, p. 4). Bette Midler won. And thereby secured the authority over usage of her own voice.

VocallyYours is developed to be used for German content and to be based out of Germany, an EU Member State. Therefore, the EU's 2016 GDPR, the German Federal Data Protection Act (*Bundesdatenschutzgesetz*), German Copyright Law (*Urheberrechtsgesetz*), and the General Right of Personality (*Allgemeines Persönlichkeitsrecht*) apply. Relevant German supervisory authorities can exercise their power with regards to how VocallyYours operates. Given its European focus on privacy, the GDPR places particular significance on the protection of personal data, which is defined as

> *any information* [emphasis added] relating to an identified or identifiable natural person (…) who can be identified, directly or indirectly, in particular by reference to an identifier such as (…) one or more fac-

tors specific to the physical, physiological (...) identity of that natural person (*Art. 4 GDPR – Definitions*, 2016).

The first, crucial part of this definition is widely inclusive: "Any information" comprises voice, because it is related to a natural person, part of their physiological identity and can potentially be used to individually identify them. Any natural vocal input used for a TTS system, which includes automated processing, may qualify as personal data under the GDPR. Throughout, the legislation repeatedly emphasizes the need for accessible and clear information regarding the collection, processing, and storage of such personal data. As the fundamental functionalities of VocallyYours entail all three dimensions, the system will require ample transparency for its users.

A number of principles apply to personal data, as laid out in Article 5, including "lawfulness, fairness and transparency" combined with "appropriate security" in processing, a "purpose limitation" and "data minimization" approach to collection, as well as a "time limitation and accuracy requirements for storage" (*Art. 5 GDPR – Principles Relating to Processing of Personal Data*, 2016). The accountability lies with the controller of the system. Applied to natural voice data, these principles and requirements translate into direct legal obligations to be factored into the operational infrastructure of the TTS system. Article 6 then clarifies the only lawful avenues of processing, which are fulfilled:

"only if and to the extent that at least one of the following applies:
1.the data subject has given consent (...);
2.processing is necessary for the performance of a contract to which the data subject is party (...);
3.processing is necessary for compliance with a legal obligation to which the controller is subject;
4.processing is necessary in order to protect the vital interests of the data subject or of another natural person;
5.processing is necessary for the performance of a task carried out in the public interest or in the exercise of official authority vested in the controller;
6.processing is necessary for the purposes of the legitimate interests pursued by the controller or by a third party, except where such interests are overridden by the interests or fundamental rights and freedoms of the data subject which require protection of personal data, in particular where the data subject is a child" (*Art. 6 GDPR – Lawfulness of Processing*, 2016, p. 6).

This exhaustive list underscores that, when in action in its intended form, where an individual uses the system to synthetically generate an audio file of their own voice based on their self-authored text, VocallyYours must secure the informed consent of the *data subject* themselves. While Articles 12-23 explicate in detail the varied rights of the data subject[52], Article 25.2 clarifies that privacy-friendly data protection should be ensured "by design and default" in products and services (*Art. 25 GDPR – Data Protection by Design and by Default*, 2016). As the German Data Ethics Commission agreed, the "technical framework" of a product or service "must not lead to a situation in which responsibility for the protection of fundamental rights and freedoms is offloaded onto individual users" (Data Ethics Commission, 2019, p. 118). These stipulations underline the sensitivity of the data being collected, processed, and stored by VocallyYours. They also demonstrate the gravity of responsibility that comes with its proper development, execution, and management. While the law entrusts actors in charge of the system – controllers – with the duty to "implement appropriate technical and organizational measures", opportunities for abuse remain for those who use the system (*Art. 25 GDPR – Data Protection by Design and by Default*, 2016).

One of these potential cases of abuse is copyright infringement with regards to the text input, as Section 2 of the German Copyright Law explicitly protects written work (*Act on Copyright and Related Rights (Urheberrechtsgesetz – UrhG)*, n.d.). A user may, for example, upload a text authored by someone else without the originator's consent or other legitimization to do so, and generate an audio file with the synthetic imitation of their own voice. This may falsely suggest ownership of the text and thereby constitute a copyright violation.

A second potential case is identity appropriation: By feeding another person's natural voice into the AI system without their explicit consent to create an artificial generator of their speech for any text amounts to deceptively assuming their identity. The General Right of Personality (APR) is a German legal institution that originated in 1954 and was eventually developed by case law. Derived from Article 2 I and Article 1 I of the Basic Law (*Grundgesetz*), the APR seeks to guarantee human dignity, the

---

52 These rights include, importantly, the claim to transparent information about the collection, processing, and storage of personal data "in a concise, transparent, intelligible and easily accessible form, using clear and plain language" (*Art. 12 GDPR – Transparent Information, Communication and Modalities for the Exercise of the Rights of the Data Subject*, 2016).

right of free development (Bundesrepublik Deutschland, n.d.-b, n.d.-a) and to protect an individual person's attributes from unauthorized public exposure or distribution when specific statutory rights such as the "right to one's image" (*§ 22 KunstUrhG - Einzelnorm*, n.d.) and the "right of name" (*§ 12 BGB - Einzelnorm*, n.d.) do not apply. Additionally, Section 201 of the German Criminal Code protects against unauthorized recordings of spoken word and distribution of such recordings (*German Criminal Code (Strafgesetzbuch – StGB)*, n.d.). Users of VocallyYours could use the voice recording of someone without their consent or a licensing agreement.

In the case of 'persons of contemporary history' (*Personen der Zeitgeschichte*), denoting individuals significantly related to current events or of long-standing public interest, their privacy and personality rights somewhat differ. However, when an identifiable attribute is used to evoke the well-known individual in connection with commercial value, previous German court decisions have largely ruled in favor of the person of contemporary history. For example, in the case *Heinz Ehrhardt*, the son of the deceased actor sued because of a radio commercial centered on an explicit imitation of his father's voice. The Court of Appeals of Hamburg correlated the case to protections of name and likeness in Section 22 of the German Art Copyright Act *(Kunsturhebergerecht)* and broadened them to include a protection for voice against emulation (Bergmann, 1999, p. 512).

Unlawful use of another person's voice might be compounded by fraudulent intentions. In 2019, a German energy company's subsidiary in Britain reported one of the first cases of an AI-generated voice heist. A director-level employee received a call in which he heard an identical copy of his German boss's voice, instructing him to wire 240,000 USD to an Hungarian account. The voice turned out to be a synthetic imitation as part of a financial fraud scheme. The firm's insurance company's spokeswoman described that "the software was able to imitate the voice, and not only the voice: the tonality, the punctuation, the German accent" (Harwell, 2019b). Evidently, VocallyYours' system offers, even exalts this exact functionality – and thus bears similar risks.

Less clear are the cases of parody and satire, as there have been decisions allowing for it when the spoof is recognizable – unless it amounts to defamation (Bergmann, 1999, p. 505). For example, should the text basis for an unauthorized synthetic speech output cause significant reputational damage to the owner of its audio basis, even if meant with parodic intent, the German Criminal Code protects against defamation and slander (*German Criminal Code (Strafgesetzbuch – StGB)*, n.d.).

Moreover, as the General Right of Personality is a personal instead of a property right, it is not transferable without a licensing fee. However, linked to commercial value, as the *Ehrhardt* decision shows, the protection of one's vocal likeness can be considered transferable and even descendible (Bergmann, 1999, p. 515). With a technology such as VocallyYours, an individual attribute like the human voice thus becomes a part of one's personality that is marketable.

Finally, the recent proposal for the EU's AI regulation, if it comes to pass, might bear significant consequences for the use of TTS systems such as VocallyYours. In its effort to prevent misconceptions of content, the proposal includes a disclosure requirement for AI systems that produce synthetic media of any kind which could "falsely appear to a person to be authentic or truthful ('deep fake')" (European Commission, 2021b, p. 69). If this regulation is enacted into law and applied by EU Member States, it would necessitate systems like VocallyYours to declare the audio output as clearly artificial whenever users interact with the material. In summary, several regulatory considerations are key to the ongoing development of the project, underlining the central importance of sociopolitical considerations for the deployment of synthetic voice generation more generally and the imitation of individual voices in particular.

7.6 Discussion

This application of the CODE framework to VocallyYours, a TTS system in the making, serves two major aims: First, it reveals how specific manifestations of people, their choices, technical possibilities, and social institutions are entangled and together configure this TTS technology. Second, it projects the system's potential scope of impacts, embedded in its particular context. Together they point towards several important steps in the upcoming design process that might ensure that the conception of the project is closely aligned with its outcomes, some of which I reflect on in this section.

For example, while the conception of this particular system is heavily influenced by the framing of a tool for journalism, the wide range of applications for TTS systems outside of this realm is evident and, in fact, challenges certain parts of its conception. Steps must be taken to warrant that the system might not be abused beyond its intended purposes. To avoid misinformation and confusion, crucially, outputs generated by VocallyYours should be declared as artificially generated. While the

EU proposal that includes such disclosure requirements is not yet enacted into law, the project could proactively prevent several nefarious uses by technically integrating clear communication about the synthetic nature of the files produced. Moreover, to address potential risks of identity fraud, verification mechanisms such as steganography watermarks are central.

Next, given the new potential for commercial licenses of one's own voice, the specific legal implications under the GDPR – or under potential future regulations that concern such synthetic media – must be clearly communicated to users, including how their data is used and what licensing one's audio likeness might entail. As vocal particularities can be considered identifying personal data, this system may inherently include the handling of sensitive material. Equally, questions about the processing and storing of the specific content within both the written and audio data, which could include personal information (eg. in the form of a love letter), must be addressed. Prior to deployment, several future decisions must consider the delicate reality of how people might engage with the system.

Additionally, to ensure that VocallyYours facilitates inclusive participation, future training data prior to launch should strive to be representative of a wide range of voices, accents, and prosodies. User interface considerations should account for accessibility affordances so that socioeconomic factors such as differing recording equipment or surroundings do not significantly affect the quality of the service. Finally, to avoid unwanted skewing of the training data through intentional or unintentional misuse, which could reduce the output standards, quality gate management should be put in place through batch learning.

As an exercise during the design process, a CODE analysis serves mainly as an anticipation of how various aspects of an AI system might interact with its environment to produce social outcomes and impacts. However, particularly the E dimension could in this case only be assessed through estimations based on existing research and responses to beta-tests. While the current status of evaluations, for example, serves as an indicator that the models perform decently in terms of naturalness perception by a specific set of beta audience, more research needs to be done in terms of trust perception and how the disclosure as AI-generated content might impact these impressions. Prior to the deployment of VocallyYours, the gap between such forecasts and the effects of real-life implementation cannot be fully gauged. Therefore, post-launch, a follow-up CODE assessment would produce further insights into the technology's actual Code Capital.

7.7 Conclusion

In this chapter, I applied the notion of Code Capital to better anticipate the potential implications of an AI system currently in development. To situate the particular study of synthetic voice generation, I first contextualized the potential uses for such a technology and the diverse concerns it raises. In reviewing, I underlined that TTS synthesis touches several foundations of interpersonal interaction as it automates human communication, challenging notions of authenticity, participation, and intimacy. Specifically, concerns about the handling of personal vocal data and the potential for abuse in the form of identity fraud emphasize that TTS systems can have broad societal effects, beneficial as well as detrimental, and are a timely case study for a Code Capital analysis. My application to one such project still in development, VocallyYours, spotlighted the necessity for careful consideration of the four CODE dimensions during the design phase. As it aims to imitate the specific tonality and conversational style of an individual in turning written input into personalized audio output, VocallyYours illustrates how choices about transparent communication, self-disclosure, identity verification mechanisms, user interface design, as well as quality configurations of training data and evaluation methods have decisive effects on system impacts. At this early stage, the CODE framework is a guide during development to sensitize key participants for the need to plan for contingencies and to encourage individuals' reflection on their areas of oversight. In the next chapter, I will synthesize my insights and offer final reflections on the applicability of Code Capital.

8. Conclusions

"To see things as they really are,
you must imagine them for what they might be"
Derrick Bell
Who's afraid of Critical Race Theory?, 1995

8.1 Summary

AI development and deployment need rethinking. An intellectual endeavor that originated across disciplines has grown into a vast field that capitalizes on technological progress, economic disruption, and social re-organization. While AI systems represent scientific breakthroughs due to unprecedented volumes of data and computing capacities, their wide-ranging ramifications have long been unmitigated and unexamined. My quest in this work was to develop an interdisciplinary notion to explain how individual AI systems emerge and come to have an influential impact on numerous human processes, micro interactions, and macro dynamics. Throughout the duration of my doctoral research, this topic has only increased in relevance. Recent advancements have produced ever more capable programs and expanded the areas of usage even further. Their potential societal leverage is increasing. Investment in and application of AI has intensified worldwide, as have calls for regulation and accountable management of unintended consequences.

Tracing back the study of sociotechnical systems brings to light a deepening understanding of the entangled relationship between all aspects of artifacts. If the social, technical, and material effectuate each other, a holistic assessment of an AI system must consider each and the sum of their parts. Rather than considering the technology as a deterministic force, AI management must include an appreciation of the active and passive contributions of relevant actors affecting and being affected by the system. Narratives and business models shape how sense is given to and made of the system. With the intangible nature of digital technologies, material features such as operational and visual decisions grow in significance. Their interaction with the human environment in which the system is embedded is particularly relevant, as can be seen in the example of data that are comprised of human behavior, histories, and social conventions of what gets measured. Finally, the system is embedded within environmental constraints and affordances through factors such as institutional boundaries, social norms, and natural resources. These layers affect the creation and dissemination of AI systems throughout their life cycle. Any notion seeking to capture AI's potential must take them into account.

These maturing descriptions of technologies resemble the storied history of the evolving socioeconomic interpretations of capital. Once of financial origin, the term has transformed into a moniker for various forms of powerful assets, from social to mental to erotic capital, that can be transferred into influential value in their arena. Capital has become a symbolic architecture for a repository of intangible leverage. Examining how digital technologies have altered means of production and dissemination, collective institutions, and individual behaviors show some fundamental shift in what is of value, how it is exchanged, and what novel business models arise. An economy driven by AI will become increasingly intangible-intensive not only in the economic sense but in the form of immaterial capital forces overall.

In connecting the two fields of sociotechnology and socioeconomics, I arrived at the original idea of Code Capital, which considers AI systems through the novel lens of capital. As a concept, Code Capital represents how the socially embedded configurations of an AI system manifest as the source of the system's value. It is an account of AI's potential impact in bespoke circumstances, bringing to the fore its inherent normative forces. Code Capital is intended as a notion to organize a widely dispersed discourse addressing a diversity of AI systems. To apply a Code Capital analysis, I introduced the concomitant CODE framework, guiding a systemic assessment along the dimensions of Conception, Operations, Data, and Environment to describe how resources and configurations inscribed within translate to socially embedded value, power, and consequences. Considering these four dimensions clarifies that humans have immense agency in shaping Code Capital. Together, the introduction of Code Capital as a concept and the related CODE framework comprises one of the major contributions of my doctoral work.

To further show their applicability, I used two case studies to show how the framework can be applied to a system either post-deployment or during the design process. My first case focused on technologies to analyze and classify facial features, an example of an AI system with significant current relevance: Research has exposed the risk of discriminatory effects in facial recognition technology (FRT) through bias in performance that disproportionately impacts women and people of color (Braca, 2017; Buolamwini & Gebru, 2018; Klare et al., 2012; Ngan & Grother, 2015). In parallel to other forms of surveillance technology, increasing applications of FRT by law enforcement have prompted debates about the balancing of privacy rights and security measures (McCoy, 2002; Milligan, 1999). Calls for regulation from researchers, governmental actors, as well as technology providers themselves abound. Grasping the implications of the technology is pertinent to several stakeholders. To contextualize my CODE analysis, I first presented partial results of my empirical study in four countries on the levels of and factors affecting social acceptance of FRT used in public. These AI systems are interpreted in different ways in the context of distinct sociopolitical backgrounds and norms. Between China, Germany, the UK and the U.S., expectations of heightened security or increased privacy violations vary. One common thread is that the perception of terrorist threats is a significant positive predictor across all four countries, which shows: Framing of when and why the technology is employed matters. In contributing this empirical study, I demonstrated how the environment sets the social, cultural, and regulatory stage for human-machine interaction and thus underlined the importance of analyzing these dimensions to gauge the Code Capital of a particular AI system. I then provided a CODE analysis of the project FacesOfTheRiot based on interviews with key participants as well my own investigation of material features and contextual circumstances. Exploring each dimension in turn, I discussed notions of accountability and surveillance, as well as the vastly different consequences for the operational choice of backend facial classification instead of a frontend retrieval option. Through this case study, I offered a detailed account of how one particular AI system emerged and how its individual parameters interact and beget each other to create its actual and potential impact. While the system has already been deployed as a publicly available website, the CODE analysis offers reflections on how certain decisions and practices have configured it and, importantly, provides contingency options for shaping it.

In my second case study, I examined text-to-speech (TTS) technologies. While they have been employed to assist people with various disabilities in the past, recent advances in natural language processing through neural networks have contributed to the rising challenge of synthetic media and fraudulent identities. Given the state of divergent regulations across the globe on the use of such individual vocal audio as personal data, anticipating the manifestations of TTS technology is important for researchers, practitioners, policymakers and users alike. To contextualize the CODE analysis, I surveyed the issues raised by TTS applications, including concerns of authenticity, participation, and intimacy. In choosing a project prior to its launch, VocallyYours, I illustrated how my framework can be used during the development process to better forecast and manage impact trajectories. The analysis engendered several insights for contingency planning that could aid sensegiving actors in how to proceed with the project. For example, while it has potential to be of significant use for journalists and vocal professionals in automating their work, the analysis showed that considerations of misuse, for example in the form of fraudulent voice imitations, should be of high priority for sensegiving actors. To prevent unintended consequences, verification mechanisms through, for instance, steganography methods should be central to the ongoing development process. Moreover, against the backdrop of increasing calls and proposed regulation for declaring AI-produced content that might reasonably be considered authentic, VocallyYours should include a disclosure feature to ensure that the line between automated and human speech, while approaching likeness in quality, is transparently communicated to users. Finally, pitfalls of unwanted bias should be avoided by representing the perspective and vocal features of a diversity of users. This second case study shows that using the CODE framework at this early stage in development allows taking stock of potential future implications and engaging in active contingency planning for how to actively steer them.

Both case studies were contributions to show how the novel concept of Code Capital can be applied to gain a more refined understanding of AI systems. As I chose projects from two central fields of current AI development and application, facial analysis and synthetic media generation, the tangible implications of my research are beginning to emerge.

8.2 Limitations

In the light of my interdisciplinary approach to the research challenge, I employed a mixed methodological approach to produce this dissertation. While it allowed a holistic examination of the implications of AI systems, this research had limitations.

First, both case studies were largely conducted during the COVID-19 pandemic including periods of complete lockdowns. This made safe in-person conversations impossible. Video interviews with relevant participants mitigated the consequences and allowed for real-time communication. As best as possible, I incorporated features of the system into these interactions to bring to the fore the entanglement between the social and the material (as described in Section 1.4.1). For example, I examined the website of FacesOfTheRiot together with its creator and scrutinized visualizations of VocallyYours' algorithmic model with the system's developers. However, in the case study of VocallyYours, I had originally planned to be closer involved in the development of the AI system to get more nuanced and rich impressions of the process. Again, because of the major restrictions of the pandemic, I was not able to spend substantial amounts of time with the technical team to observe their practices, including internal discussions, conflicts, and solution-finding, up close. If not for the sole option of video conversations, serendipitous referrals to or encounters with further important interviewees for both projects might have also been more likely. In the process of future applications of the CODE framework, more observations, and insights about enacted sociomaterial practices will enrich the analysis.

Second, the empirical cross-country study in Chapter 6 has a few limitations given its nature as a mobile- and desktop-based online surveys. For example, it could face a potential opt-in bias. Respondents who choose to take part in and follow through with such a questionnaire may already have a particular affinity with using technology, which could positively affect their stance towards innovations in this field, including the focus of this study. This effect may have been heightened by the virtual rewards individuals were promised for their participation, as they might have been more likely to associate the positivity of incentives with positivity towards FRT. More generally, given that it is an online survey, the study resembles the Internet-connected population in each respective setting, suggesting perhaps an already higher affinity with technology. In addition, since it was conducted in several national settings, some questions might have been understood or interpreted differently across countries. For example, as the implementation and use cases of FRT vary widely in the four contexts studied, mentions of the technology may conjure up diverse associations and scenarios. This could influence the connotation participants have when asked about its acceptability. In China, the authoritarian political context might be reflected in the reported levels of social acceptance, as dissent of technologies officially endorsed by the government can be difficult. Though participants were aware that any identifying data was anonymized and analyzed for research purposes only, we cannot exclude the possibility of intentionally skewed responses.

Third, a possible improvement to my research could have been to have the CODE framework challenged by an even broader audience of external experts. Since I developed the original idea in 2016, the concept of Code Capital as well as its analytical guide have gone through various iterations. Through my professional experiences with and insights into several examples of large-scale AI systems and, significantly, in the process of conducting the case studies, I consolidated the substantial parts. Additional discussions could have provided pointers for further hurdles in real-world application.

8.3 Discussion

AI systems constitute a new form of capital. Code Capital as a concept serves as a symbolic representation and the CODE framework as an analytical guide for various stakeholders to reveal how AI systems come to affect society. Given the current debate about how to assess, manage, and regulate these technologies, my doctoral contributions bridge relevant disciplines to offer a shared, holistic ontology, with both theoretical and practical ramifications.

8.3.1 Theoretical Implications

Among the several emerging strategies, frameworks, and concepts informing regulation, Code Capital can be a conceptual anchor for the sum of AI's impactful parts and its contingencies. One of the major benefits of Code Capital is that it combines theoretical approaches of sociotechnology with socioeconomics or rather a sociological interpretation of a once economic term. Drawing on both fields, which are themselves interdisciplinary to varying degrees, allowed me to develop Code Capital into an idea that addresses challenges from multiple realms relevant in the management of AI. Given the often wide gap between technology company executives, developers of AI systems, impact researchers, policymakers, and people using or affected by the system, this means bridging a divide that I have encountered during my doctoral work, too. As priorities and perspectives on the topic of AI diverge and terms overlap or contradict in meaning, it has become even more important to find a shared ground for discussion. Code Capital could thus represent a theoretical paradigm shift.

Code Capital is such a shift because, first, it acknowledges that any AI system has capital comprised of various sources, regardless of a linguistic threshold qualification as responsible, ethical, fair, or friendly. Systems do not merely have dichotomous, binary options for impact as either a game-changer or a job eliminator for an entire industry. Neither is any system exempt because of the veneer of objective technological progress or presumed beneficial effects. Instead, one of the central tasks is to become aware of the myriad contributors to impact and of contingencies and areas of potential oversight. Second, relatedly, this rethinking requires taking responsibility for each individual system's capital manifestations. Given the wide variability of the unknowns that affect an AI system – intentional abuse, unexpected user behavior or unplanned exogenous events – recognizing Code Capital demands considering contingencies and responses.

In arguing for the existence of other socialized forms of capital, their proponents draw parallels between socioeconomic features and the financial origins in terms of accumulation, reproducibility, and conversion. As these dimensions can be applied to Code Capital as well, I will consider them in turn to underline how my research has steadily deepened my thinking about the choice of this term.

8.3.1.1 Accumulation

Code Capital can be acquired by configuring the various intangible assets that flow into an AI system. Like with other forms of capital, it can be accumulated by taking steps to strategically assemble what is needed for one's stock of power to reach optimal potential. Owning your Code Capital means consciously aligning the four dimensions of C, O, D, E to activate maximum impact. It entails orienting operational choices and data configurations for an AI system in line with its conception and considerations of the overall ecosystem. This symbolic power can be used for multiple purposes. Like political capital, it can be used for one's own positive gain or negative effects on opponents. In the case of AI, this potential for beneficial and detrimental intent is ever present since "pretty much all technologies are dual-use to some degree: a hammer can hit a nail or break a bone" (Hutson, 2021). Moreover, similarly to psychological capital, awareness of the capital itself can boost competitiveness and returns (Luthans et al., 2007). Knowing the extent of your accumulated Code Capital results in more targeted momentum to employ it. Holding Code Capital means owning the choices and configurations that have been accrued.

8.3.1.2 Reproducibility

Capital in all its forms has controlling effects on human relations, both as a force inscribed in certain structures, vis insita, and as an active force, lex insita, because of disparate distribution and mechanisms of reproduction (Bourdieu, 1986). If it was more evenly divided, capital would lose some of its competitive value. As Bourdieu summarized, "the unequal distribution of capital, that is, the structure of the entire field, thus forms the basis for the specific effects of capital, namely the ability to appropriate profits and to enforce rules of the game that are as favorable as possible for capital and its reproduction" (Bourdieu, 2015, p. 58). For those who hold Code Capital, it is the imposition of the 'rules of the game' that are the most consequential benefits in addition to the appropriation of profits. Incumbents favor structures that tend to reproduce its unequal distribution. For example, technology leaders calling for regulation of AI on their terms engage in a way that may continue their control of the rules of the game by foregoing outright bans of certain technologies. Moreover, by setting the operational parameters including technical and material features, holders of Code Capital make decisions about what data to collect, prioritize, and monetize. With data reflecting particular sets of preferences and perspectives on the past or present, the notion of predicting the future is a literal reproduction: AI systems define and alter the world that users get the opportunity to participate in, based on past patterns, setting the classifiers that rule what factors should be optimized for. In that sense, holding Code Capital means not only owning literal data, but figurative authority to construct the choice architecture, or 'structure of the entire field', which will reinforce capital reproduction. Finally, given the potential for vast scalability of AI systems, Code Capital's effects can be spread at high speed – with 'virality' - and reproduction rates, whether of benefit, inequality, or otherwise, can be exponential. With its interdisciplinary dimensions bringing to the fore the inherent normative forces within AI systems, the concept of Code Capital thereby helps to expose these "hidden mechanisms of power" (Bourdieu, 2015).

8.3.1.3 Conversion

Like previous forms of socialized capital, Code Capital is convertible into other types as its value can translate into many different arenas (Fukuyama, 1995; Nahaphiet & Ghoshal, 1998). In the case of Code Capital this can happen in three ways. First, it can transfer into other capital iterations for those holding the Code Capital. For instance, computationally optimizing advertisement may translate to higher revenues, thereby generating financial capital. Ranking and recommending content represents authority over cultural capital in terms of knowledge, visibility, and popularity. Second, AI systems can act as a substitute for a lack of other capital. One example is insufficient human or intellectual capital to execute a task, which can be taken over by an AI system. This type of machine performance resembles the initial definition of artificial intelligence. Third, notably, AI systems have an influence on the capital stock of others. For example, employing facial analysis for a structured display of vast amounts of data can affect the reputational capital of the people featured. Social networks programmed to grow communities, enhance users' exposure, and facilitate social interactions, may expand or diminish other people's individual and collective social capital. In effect, this is the most original aspect of Code Capital: Its leverage over power dynamics in various social domains.

8.3.2 Practical Applications

A reckoning in the field of AI about implication management is overdue. In contrast to some other scientific realms, the recent academic work in computer science has often been deployed at massive scale on society without established ethics review boards for research. This impunity for unexamined consequences is particularly pertinent, because the rules of the game encoded in many AI systems become codes of conduct for millions of people as "algorithms alter our social systems, not just our technical ones; it's hard to patch a government that's become addicted to surveillance, or a public that can no longer trust what it reads, sees, or hears" (Hutson, 2021). In addition to the many recent calls for regulation, several major AI conference such as Neural Information Processing Systems (NeurIPS) have now begun to integrate considerations of societal impact into their review process. NeurIPS 2020, decided for the first time, like the Association for Computational Linguistics and the Association for the Advancement of Artificial Intelligence, that submissions required a broader impact statement, and a panel of ethics experts evaluated entries' undue risk of harm (Lin et al., 2020). One recent paper reflecting on this new requirement expressed serious concern about the quality of the submitted impact statements, as the authors quoted Arthur C Clarke to warn of *"failures of imagination* in AI infused system development and deployment" (Boyarskaya et al., 2020). Nonetheless, these developments demonstrate an acknowledgement in the computer science community: Given that published trained models can be used for the production of deployable systems, recognition of potential implications of application is necessary even at the research stage.

A recent study shows, however, that awareness and accountability among business leaders remains scant: In a survey for the 2021 FICO State of Responsible AI Report conducted with 100 global leaders from the financial services, insurance, retail, healthcare and pharma, manufacturing, public and utilities sectors, only 35 % responded that their respective organization made an effort to employ AI in a transparent and accountable manner. Meanwhile, 80 % reported struggling to establish processes for the appropriate use of AI, an overall picture illustrating that "awareness of AI ethics issues remains patchy" (*The State of Responsible AI*, 2021, p. 7). No consensus emerged about the specific responsibilities of companies, and, emphasizing the lacking appreciation of sociotechnical factors, only 6 % indicated that they ensure AI development teams are diverse (*The State of Responsible AI*, 2021, p. 14). This status quo underlines the urgent need for engagement from multiple stakeholders to acknowledge that "the responsible — ethical, legal and beneficial — development and use of AI is not about technology. It is about us: how we want our world to be" (Dignum, 2021, p. 500).

A Code Capital approach does exactly that: It impresses upon stakeholders that every AI system is socially embedded, from its genesis to its implications. As an interdisciplinary framework, a CODE analysis has the potential for individuals' reflection on their own intentions, logics of causality, choices of algorithmic models and material design, integration of sociopolitical insights, possible areas of oversight, downstream effects, and contingency planning. In contrast to qualifiers such as responsible, ethical, or fair AI, Code Capital is not the threshold itself, but instead the descriptor and tool that spotlights recognizing and addressing alignment disparities, paradoxes, and contradictions.

Specifically, the CODE framework serves as a two-fold analytical tool for business leaders, investors, developers, entrepreneurs, and policymakers. First, it can be used as a bespoke model to evaluate an AI system's sources of impact, contextualized by time and setting. Such an examination can and should occur at different points of a system's life cycle. Second, it may be used as an instrument for responsibly designing and employing an AI system by identifying and deliberately shaping outcomes, intended and unintended. Several stakeholders will benefit.

First, researchers from various fields could share the ontology of Code Capital and the CODE framework specifically to connect their disciplinary perspectives in the endeavor to appropriately assess AI systems. The four dimensions encapsulate, inter alia, socioeconomic, technical, ethical, psychological, legal, and cultural aspects. Depending on the specific type of technology and potential use cases, a Code Capital approach could make collaborations across fields particularly helpful. Research proposals and paper submissions that integrate a CODE analysis would indicate systematized self-inspection with regards to future implications. Major conferences could require such foresight.

Second, organizations and companies deploying AI systems are the locus for promoting a Code Capital analysis and encouraging a culture where foresight and contingency planning are valued. Code Capital can aid these sensegiving actors to plan for and negotiate the effects that, for example, an AI system developed for one setting may exert in another. Or how changes in material features, training data, the underlying business model, or external communication can affect sensemaking actors. Those entities who explicitly conduct and publish their assessment could be standard setters by publicly signaling their commitment to being held accountable. To be able to thoroughly employ the interdisciplinary investigations required by the CODE framework, companies need appropriately trained staff to complement technical expertise. Such role modeling could have additional positive effects on organizational reputation and employee engagement.

Third, users and people unwillingly affected by AI systems can use Code Capital as a way to question the technologies they interact with. The four dimensions might guide individuals to gain a more nuanced understanding than through the sweeping, binary judgments most commonly found in popular media today. As much as they can independently investigate, citizens can utilize Code Capital to become increasingly sensitized to methods of challenging ingrained AI-driven processes and structures.

Fourth, policy- and decisionmakers can integrate the concept and framework into aspects of their leadership and agenda-setting. Considerations along the four dimensions could factor into regulations, particularly with regards to benchmarks analyses such as the EU's recently proposed term of "high-risk" systems. Specifically, a CODE analysis could actively help entities such as the announced European Artificial Intelligence Board in determining whether, for example, systems that employ facial recognition qualify as high risk. Its analytical and explanatory nature might further help guide the policymaking community: "For law to meet the challenge of accelerating technology, it will need to change some core principles.

To the extent that we think of law as rules, we must reconceive it as a way of guiding change in rules" (Fairfield, 2021, p. 87). By spotlighting the contextual sociotechnical factors that contribute to making AI systems impactful, Code Capital could signpost further legal debates for necessary changes in rules. Moreover, to increase compliance, Code Capital could become conditionally tied to regulations. First, without a published, accessible CODE analysis including documentation along the four dimensions and contingency plans for various outcome trajectories, no AI system should be used to make or assist governmental decisions of public consequence. Second, funding from the many national investment plans in the field of AI could be dependent upon a thorough account of Code Capital. Similarly, private investors could require a Code Capital analysis including contingency plans as part of the valuation of AI systems.

8.4 Outlook for Further Research

My doctoral work contributed several insights on the societal implications of AI systems, which in turn highlight areas for future research. Given the timeliness of the overall topic, the following foci for further research are of particular importance. First, the CODE model is an instructive, evolving guide. While I consider the four dimensions of Conception, Operations, Data, and Environment to be integral parts of the framework, their subcategories can be expansive and must reflect the bespoke circumstances of each AI system. Research on further case studies would, on the one hand, test the framework's applicability and, on the other hand, help crystallize the range of important subcategories. In applying the CODE framework to AI systems by different providers acting in various societal arenas and across cultural settings, studies could question if there are subcategories that might be universally essential for every system. For example, given the scientific consensus about the state of climate development, should the question of sustainability be present in every analysis of the E dimension to account for the impact on natural resources? Or, in view of ample evidence of unwanted bias and discriminatory effects, should considerations of AI systems' influence on inequities and unequal structures be an immutable part of the same dimension? Further, are there other key subcategories that I missed to include or allude to?

Second, research could establish standards and guidelines for methods to include in the CODE analysis. Through my two case studies, I provided examples for the kinds of examinations that can engender ample insights.

But given the interdisciplinary nature of this research, more applications are needed to assemble a catalogue of possible methodologies that sufficiently cover all perspectives.

Third, given the rich existing literature on the interaction of digital technologies and capitalist structures, theoretical research could look further into how the notion of Code Capital fits into and enriches this discourse. Similarly, research in the field of computer science would benefit from including the Code Capital into research endeavors as a complementary sociotechnical lens.

Fourth, to increase comparability, research could consider the possibilities for proxy metrics to express, perhaps visually, the alignment of the four dimensions. While it might not be feasible or advisable to quantify Code Capital in any way, even a complex, ecological evaluation approach might benefit from expressing results by various means.

Finally, it is important to examine how the concept and framework I have presented here interacts with the ongoing and upcoming efforts to establish legal guidelines and binding regulations with regards to AI management around the world. For example, research on how Code Capital might be integrated into the proposed EU legislation would situate it in a policymaking realm of utmost current relevance.

8.5 Concluding Remarks

In her *Atlas of AI*, Kate Crawford calls for an account of the technology that goes beyond the technical breakthroughs, urging that "to understand how AI is fundamentally political, we need to go beyond neural nets and statistical pattern recognition to instead ask *what* is being optimized, and for *whom*, and *who* gets to decide. Then we can trace the implications of those choices" (Crawford, 2021, p. 9). Code Capital represents such an investigation of choices to enable tracing of implications. Given the wide-ranging application of AI today, it is paramount that these systems do not create new or exacerbate existing inequalities, undermine civil liberties, or superfluously exploit natural resources. On the contrary, we must ensure that AI systems are developed, deployed, and managed in a participatory manner with oversight so as to maximize social benefits. We must ensure that the Code Capital of the few does not leave the many at their mercy.

References

§ 12 BGB - Einzelnorm. (n.d.). Retrieved January 28, 2021, from https://www.gesetze-im-internet.de/bgb/__12.html

§ 22 KunstUrhG - Einzelnorm. (n.d.). Retrieved January 28, 2021, from https://www.gesetze-im-internet.de/kunsturhg/__22.html

Abdi, H., Valentin, D., Edelman, B., & O'Toole, A. J. (1995). More about the difference between men and women: Evidence from linear neural networks and the principal-component approach. *Perception, 24*(5), 539–562.

Act on Copyright and Related Rights (Urheberrechtsgesetz – UrhG). (n.d.). Retrieved January 28, 2021, from https://www.gesetze-im-internet.de/englisch_urhg/englisch_urhg.html

Adam, A. (2006). *Artificial knowing: Gender and the thinking machine*. Routledge.

Adams, R., & McIntyre, N. (2020, August 13). England A-level downgrades hit pupils from disadvantaged areas hardest. *The Guardian*. http://www.theguardian.com/education/2020/aug/13/england-a-level-downgrades-hit-pupils-from-disadvantaged-areas-hardest

Adobe. (2017, October 21). *#ProjectCloak: Adobe MAX 2017* [Video]. YouTube. https://www.youtube.com/watch?v=TzBZWBht02I

Adomavicius, G., Bockstedt, J. C., Curley, S. P., & Zhang, J. (2018). Effects of online recommendations on consumers' willingness to pay. *Information Systems Research, 29*(1), 84–102.

Adomavicius, G., & Tuzhilin, A. (2005). Toward the next generation of recommender systems: A survey of the state-of-the-art and possible extensions. *IEEE Transactions on Knowledge and Data Engineering, 17*(6), 734–749.

AFP. (2019, September 4). Smile-to-pay: Chinese shoppers turn to facial payment technology. *The Guardian*. https://www.theguardian.com/world/2019/sep/04/smile-to-pay-chinese-shoppers-turn-to-facial-payment-technology

Agarwal, S. (2021, March 11). India's new social media law spells trouble for tech giants. *Fast Company*. https://www.fastcompany.com/90613579/india-social-media-rules-twitter-facebook-free-speech

Aguiar, L., & Waldfogel, J. (2018). *Platforms, promotion, and product discovery: Evidence from spotify playlists* (NBER Working Papers 24713). National Bureau of Economic Research. https://economics.ucdavis.edu/events/papers/515Waldfogel.pdf

AI Ethics Lab. (2020). *TOOLBOX: Dynamics of AI Principles*. AI ETHICS LAB. https://aiethicslab.com/big-picture/

Ajder, H. (2019, June 16). The ethics of deepfakes aren't always black and white. *The Next Web*. https://thenextweb.com/podium/2019/06/16/the-ethics-of-deepfakes-arent-always-black-and-white/

Akrich, M. (1992). The de-scription of Technical Objects. In W. E. Bijker & J. Law (Eds.), *Shaping Technology, building society* (pp. 205–224). MIT Press. https://www.scribd.com/document/389890486/The-de-scription-of-Technical-Objects-Madeleine-Akrich

Akrich, M., & Latour, B. (1992). A Summary of a Convenient Vocabulary for the Semiotics of Human and Nonhuman Assemblies. In *Shaping Technology, Building Society*. MIT Press.

Alexander, C. P. (1983, May 30). The New Economy. *Time*. http://content.time.com/time/subscriber/article/0,33009,926013-1,00.html

Allyn, B. (2020, June 10). Amazon Halts Police Use Of Its Facial Recognition Technology. *NPR*. https://www.npr.org/2020/06/10/874418013/amazon-halts-police-use-of-its-facial-recognition-technology

Alper, M. (2017a). *Giving voice: Mobile communication, disability, and inequality*. MIT Press.

Alper, M. (2017b, July 21). Talking Like a "Princess": What Speaking Machines Say About Human Biases. *The New Inquiry*. https://thenewinquiry.com/blog/talking-like-a-princess-what-speaking-machines-say-about-human-biases/

Ananny, M. (2016). Toward an ethics of algorithms: Convening, observation, probability, and timeliness. *Science, Technology, & Human Values*, 41(1), 93–117.

Anderson, A., Maystre, L., Anderson, I., Mehrotra, R., & Lalmas, M. (2020). Algorithmic effects on the diversity of consumption on spotify. *Proceedings of The Web Conference 2020*, 2155–2165.

Anderson, C. (2012). The Impact of Social Media on Lodging Performance. *Cornell Hospitality Report*, 12(15), 6–11.

Anderson, CW. (2013). Towards a sociology of computational and algorithmic journalism. *New Media & Society*, 15(7), 1005–1021. https://doi.org/10.1177/1461444812465137

Angwin, J., Larson, J., Mattu, S., & Kirchner, L. (2016, May 23). Machine Bias. *ProPublica*. https://www.propublica.org/article/machine-bias-risk-assessments-in-criminal-sentencing

Anonymous. (2021). *Capitol Map*. http://capitolmap.com/

Arrieta, A. B., Díaz-Rodríguez, N., Del Ser, J., Bennetot, A., Tabik, S., Barbado, A., García, S., Gil-López, S., Molina, D., & Benjamins, R. (2020). Explainable Artificial Intelligence (XAI): Concepts, taxonomies, opportunities and challenges toward responsible AI. *Information Fusion*, 58, 82–115.

Arrieta-Ibarra, I., Goff, L., Jiménez-Hernández, D., Lanier, J., & Weyl, E. G. (2018). Should We Treat Data as Labor? Moving beyond" Free". *Aea Papers and Proceedings*, 108, 38–42.

Art. 4 GDPR – Definitions, European Commission (2016). https://gdpr-info.eu/art-4-gdpr/

Art. 5 GDPR – Principles relating to processing of personal data, European Commission (2016). https://gdpr-info.eu/art-5-gdpr/

Art. 6 GDPR – Lawfulness of processing, European Commission (2016). https://gdpr-info.eu/art-6-gdpr/

Art. 12 GDPR – Transparent information, communication and modalities for the exercise of the rights of the data subject, European Commission (2016). https://gdpr-info.eu/art-12-gdpr/

Art. 25 GDPR – Data protection by design and by default, European Commission (2016). https://gdpr-info.eu/art-25-gdpr/

Aru, O. E., & Gozie, I. (2013). Facial Verification Technology for Use In Atm Transactions. *American Journal of Engineering Research*, *2*(5), 188–193.

Audio Advertising—Austria. (n.d.). Statista Market Forecast. Retrieved January 20, 2021, from https://www.statista.com/outlook/20200/128/audio-advertising/austria?currency=eur

Audio Advertising—Germany. (n.d.). Statista Market Forecast. Retrieved January 20, 2021, from https://www.statista.com/outlook/20200/137/audio-advertising/germany

Audio Advertising—Switzerland. (n.d.). Statista Market Forecast. Retrieved January 20, 2021, from https://www.statista.com/outlook/20200/155/audio-advertising/switzerland

Azzi, C., & Ehrenberg, R. (1975). Household allocation of time and church attendance. *Journal of Political Economy*, *83*(1), 27–56.

Bai, X., Cambazoglu, B. B., Gullo, F., Mantrach, A., & Silvestri, F. (2017). Exploiting search history of users for news personalization. *Information Sciences*, *385*, 125–137.

Baker, J. (2016, August 22). Germany eyes facial recognition tech for airports, train stations. *Ars Technica*. https://arstechnica.com/tech-policy/2016/08/germany-facial-recognition-tech-airports-train-stations/

Baker, P., & Potts, A. (2013). 'Why do white people have thin lips?' Google and the perpetuation of stereotypes via auto-complete search forms. *Critical Discourse Studies*, *10*(2), 187–204.

Bandura, A. (1986). Social foundations of thought and action. *Englewood Cliffs, N.J., Prentice-Hall.*

Banfield, E. (1961). *Political Influence*. The Free Press of Glencoe.

Barad, K. (2003). Posthumanist performativity: Toward an understanding of how matter comes to matter. *Signs: Journal of Women in Culture and Society*, *28*(3), 801–831.

Barad, K. (2007). *Meeting the universe halfway: Quantum physics and the entanglement of matter and meaning*. Duke University Press.

Barassi, V. (2019). Datafied citizens in the age of coerced digital participation. *Sociological Research Online*, *24*(3), 414–429.

Barfield, W. (2018). Liability for autonomous and artificially intelligent robots. *Paladyn, Journal of Behavioral Robotics*, *9*(1), 193–203.

Barocas, S., & Selbst, A. D. (2016). Big data's disparate impact. *Calif. L. Rev.*, *104*(3), 671–732.

Baron, J. N., & Hannan, M. T. (1994). The impact of economics on contemporary sociology. *Journal of Economic Literature*, *32*(3), 1111–1146.

Barr, A. (2015, July 1). Google Mistakenly Tags Black People as 'Gorillas,' Showing Limits of Algorithms. *WSJ*. https://blogs.wsj.com/digits/2015/07/01/google-mista kenly-tags-black-people-as-gorillas-showing-limits-of-algorithms/

Bates, J. (2009). Airport Security: CCTV Takes Off. *International Airport Review*, *13*(4), 21–24.

Bathaee, Y. (2017). The artificial intelligence black box and the failure of intent and causation. *Harv. JL & Tech.*, *31*(2), 889–937.

Bayerische Landeszentrale für neue Medien. (2020). *Online-Audio-Monitor 2020*. Bayerische Landeszentrale für neue Medien. https://www.online-audio-monitor. de/wp-content/uploads/Bericht-OAM_2020_010920_FINAL_V3.pdf

Becker, G. (1962). Investment in human capital: A theoretical analysis. *Journal of Political Economy*, *70*(5), 9–49.

Bell, D. (1976). The coming of the post-industrial society. *The Educational Forum*, *40*(4), 574–579.

Bell, D. A. (1995). Who's afraid of critical race theory. *U. Ill. L. Rev.*, 893.

Bellman, R. (1978). *An introduction to artificial intelligence: Can computers think?* Boyd & Fraser Publishing Company.

Bender, E. M., Gebru, T., McMillan-Major, A., & Shmitchell, S. (2021). On the Dangers of Stochastic Parrots: Can Language Models Be Too Big? 🦜. *Proceedings of the 2021 ACM Conference on Fairness, Accountability, and Transparency*, 610–623.

Benitez-Quiroz, C. F., Srinivasan, R., Feng, Q., Wang, Y., & Martinez, A. M. (2017). EmotioNet Challenge: Recognition of facial expressions of emotion in the wild. *ArXiv Preprint:1703.01210 [Cs]*. http://arxiv.org/abs/1703.01210

Benjamin, R. (2019). *Race after technology: Abolitionist tools for the new jim code*. Polity.

Berdux, S. (2015). "Eine kempelensche Sprechmaschine". New insights in speaking machines in the late 18th and early 19th centuries. *HSCR@ INTERSPEECH*, 50–51. https://www.isca-speech.org/archive/hscr_2015/papers/hs15_050.pdf

Berg, F., Koelbel, J. F., & Rigobon, R. (2019). *Aggregate confusion: The divergence of ESG ratings*. MIT Sloan School of Management.

Bergmann, S. (1999). Publicity Rights in the United States and Germany: A Comparative Analysis. *Loyola of Los Angeles Entertainment Law Journal*, *19*(3), 45.

Berinsky, A. J., Huber, G. A., & Lenz, G. S. (2012). Evaluating online labor markets for experimental research: Amazon.com's Mechanical Turk. *Political Analysis*, *20*(3), 351–368.

Bialek, C. (2020, July 29). Audio-Markt: Nachfrage nach Podcasts und Hörbüchern wächst in der Coronazeit rasant. *Handelsblatt*. https://www.handelsblatt.com/un ternehmen/it-medien/audio-markt-nachfrage-nach-podcasts-und-hoerbuechern -waechst-in-der-coronazeit-rasant/26047506.html

Big Brother Watch UK Team. (2019, August 16). *Facial Recognition 'Epidemic' in the UK – Big Brother Watch*. https://bigbrotherwatch.org.uk/all-media/facial-recogniti on-epidemic-in-the-uk/

Bijker, W. E., Hughes, T. P., & Pinch, T. (Eds.). (1987). *The Social construction of technological systems: New directions in the sociology and history of technology.* MIT Press.

Bimber, B. (1990). Karl Marx and the Three Faces of Technological Determinism. *Social Studies of Science, 20*(2), 333–351. JSTOR. https://doi.org/10.1177/0306312 90020002006

Birch, K., Cochrane, D., & Ward, C. (2021). Data as asset? The measurement, governance, and valuation of digital personal data by Big Tech. *Big Data & Society, 8*(1), 1–15.

Bodén, L. (2013). Seeing red? The agency of computer software in the production and management of students' school absences. *International Journal of Qualitative Studies in Education, 26*(9), 1117–1131.

Böhm-Bawerk, E. von. (1890). *Capital and interest.* Macmillan.

Bollier, D. (2010). *The promise and peril of big data.* Aspen Institute. https://www.asp eninstitute.org/publications/promise-peril-big-data/

Bolukbasi, T., Chang, K.-W., Zou, J. Y., Saligrama, V., & Kalai, A. T. (2016). Man is to computer programmer as woman is to homemaker? Debiasing word embeddings. *Advances in Neural Information Processing Systems, 29*, 4349–4357.

Bonham, J. (2021, January 25). Their faces should be published. Every last one of them should be charged, tried and convicted of sedition. #FacesOfTheRiot https://t.co/YCABCnCMGv [Tweet]. *@b0nham_J.* https://twitter.com/b0nham_J/ status/1353711411139137537

Bostrom, N. (2014). *Superintelligence: Paths, Dangers, Strategies.* Oxford University Press.

Bourdieu, P. (1977). *Outline of a Theory of Practice.* Cambridge University Press.

Bourdieu, P. (1983). Ökonomisches Kapital, kulturelles Kapital, soziales Kapital. In R. Kreckel (Ed.), *Soziale Ungleichheiten* (pp. 183–198). Schwartz.

Bourdieu, P. (1986). The Forms of Capital. In J. Richardson (Ed.), *Handbook of Theory and Reseqarch for the Sociology of Education* (pp. 241–258). Greenwood.

Bourdieu, P. (2015). *Die verborgenen Mechanismen der Macht* (M. Steinrücke, Ed.). VSA Verlag.

Bowles, S., & Gintis, H. (2002). Social Capital And Community Governance. *The Economic Journal, 112*(483), 419–436.

Bowyer, K. W. (2004). Face recognition technology: Security versus privacy. *IEEE Technology and Society Magazine, 23*(1), 9–19.

Boyarskaya, M., Olteanu, A., & Crawford, K. (2020). Overcoming Failures of Imagination in AI Infused System Development and Deployment. *ArXiv:2011.13416 [Cs].* http://arxiv.org/abs/2011.13416

boyd, danah, & Crawford, K. (2012). Critical Questions for Big Data. *Information, Communication & Society, 15*(5), 662–679. https://doi.org/10.1080/1369118X.201 2.678878

Braca, A. (2017). *An investigation into Bias in Facial Recognition using Learning Algorithms* [Master's Thesis]. National College of Ireland.

Brey, P., & Søraker, J. H. (2009). Philosophy of computing and information technology. In A. Meijers (Ed.), *Philosophy of technology and engineering sciences* (pp. 1341–1407). Elsevier.

Brivot, M., & Gendron, Y. (2011). Beyond panopticism: On the ramifications of surveillance in a contemporary professional setting. *Accounting, Organizations and Society, 36*(3), 135–155. https://doi.org/10.1016/j.aos.2011.03.003

Brown, T. B., Mann, B., Ryder, N., Subbiah, M., Kaplan, J., Dhariwal, P., Neelakantan, A., Shyam, P., Sastry, G., Askell, A., Agarwal, S., Herbert-Voss, A., Krueger, G., Henighan, T., Child, R., Ramesh, A., Ziegler, D. M., Wu, J., Winter, C., … Amodei, D. (2020). Language Models are Few-Shot Learners. *ArXiv Preprint ArXiv:2005.14165.* http://arxiv.org/abs/2005.14165

Brundage, M., Avin, S., Wang, J., Belfield, H., Krueger, G., Hadfield, G., Khlaaf, H., Yang, J., Toner, H., & Fong, R. (2020). Toward trustworthy AI development: Mechanisms for supporting verifiable claims. *ArXiv Preprint ArXiv:2004.07213.*

Brunelli, R., & Poggio, T. (1993). Face recognition: Features versus templates. *IEEE Transactions on Pattern Analysis and Machine Intelligence, 15*(10), 1042–1052.

Brynjolfsson, E., Eggers, F., & Gannamaneni, A. (2018). Using Massive Online Choice Experiments to Measure Changes in Well-being. *National Bureau of Economic Research Working Paper Series.* https://www.nber.org/papers/w24514.pdf

Buchanan, R. A. (2005). History of Technology. In *Encyclopedia Britannica: History of technology.* https://www.britannica.com/technology/history-of-technology

Buckley, O., & Nurse, J. R. (2019). The language of biometrics: Analysing public perceptions. *Journal of Information Security and Applications, 47*, 112–119.

Bundesrepublik Deutschland. (n.d.-a). *Art 1 GG - Einzelnorm.* Grundgesetz. Retrieved January 28, 2021, from https://www.gesetze-im-internet.de/gg/art_1.html

Bundesrepublik Deutschland. (n.d.-b). *Art 2 GG - Einzelnorm.* Grundgesetz. Retrieved January 28, 2021, from https://www.gesetze-im-internet.de/gg/art_2.html

Bundesverband Digitale Wirtschaft. (2020, December 2). Online-Audio-Umsätze in Deutschland verdoppeln sich innerhalb von nur drei Jahren / Podcast-Umsätze steigen 2020 von neun auf 14 Millionen Euro. *BDVW News.* https://www.bvdw. org/der-bvdw/news/detail/artikel/online-audio-umsaetze-in-deutschland-verdopp eln-sich-innerhalb-von-nur-drei-jahren-podcast-umsaetze/

Bunge, M. (1999). *Social science under debate: A philosophical perspective.* University of Toronto Press.

Buolamwini, J., & Gebru, T. (2018). Gender shades: Intersectional accuracy disparities in commercial gender classification. *Conference on Fairness, Accountability and Transparency, 81*, 77–91.

Burgess, M. (2019, June 17). Inside the urgent battle to stop UK police using facial recognition. *Wired UK.* https://www.wired.co.uk/article/uk-police-facial-recognit ion

Burns, T. (Ed.). (1969). *Industrial Man: Selected Readings.* Penguin. https://trove.nla. gov.au/version/43718768

Burrell, J. (2016). How the machine 'thinks': Understanding opacity in machine learning algorithms. *Big Data & Society, 3*(1), 2053951715622512.

Buschak, D. M. (1999). Increases in natural speech production following experience with synthetic speech. *Journal of Special Education Technology*, 14(2), 44–53.

Butler, J. (1997). *The psychic life of power: Theories in subjection*. Stanford University Press.

Butler, J. (2021). *Excitable speech: A politics of the performative*. Routledge.

Caliskan, A., Bryson, J. J., & Narayanan, A. (2017). Semantics derived automatically from language corpora contain human-like biases. *Science*, 356(6334), 183–186.

Callaway, E. (2020). 'It will change everything': DeepMind's AI makes gigantic leap in solving protein structures. *Nature*, 588(7837), 203–204. https://doi.org/10.103 8/d41586-020-03348-4

Callon, M. (1987). Society in the Making: The Sudy of Technology as a Tool for Sociological Analysis. In W. E. Bijker, T. Hughes, & T. Pinch (Eds.), *The Social Construction of Technological Systems* (pp. 83–103). MIT Press.

Cameron, D. (2021, January 11). Every Deleted Parler Post, Many With Users' Location Data, Has Been Archived. *Gizmodo*. https://gizmodo.com/every-deleted -parler-post-many-with-users-location-dat-1846032466

Campbell-Dollaghan, K. (2016, November 14). The Algorithmic Democracy. *Co.Design*. https://www.fastcodesign.com/3065582/the-algorithmic-democracy

Campbell-Wilson, G. (2020, April 29). RIP Lyrebird AI—which alternatives should I try? *Replica Blog*. https://blog.replicastudios.com/lyrebird-alternatives/?gclid=Cj wKCAiAl4WABhAJEiwATUnEF47s26mvFyibN2kWb6VLjjYY9aALrRqJv8W15 sB6moCioASnZnKV5hoCnJAQAvD_BwE

Cannan, E. (1921). Early History of the Term Capital. *The Quarterly Journal of Economics*, 35(3), 469–481. JSTOR. https://doi.org/10.2307/1884097

Carstensen, T. (2021a). *Parler Videos*. Capitol Terrorist Attack. https://www.tommyc arstensen.com/terrorism/index.html

Carstensen, T. (2021b). @ParlerVideos I am an anti-fascist! I tweet mostly in English and Danish USDK I block anonymous profiles and those using ad hominem arguments 🏴. *@hologram_stan*. https://twitter.com/carstensenpol

Cassell, J., & Bickmore, T. (2000). External manifestations of trustworthiness in the interface. *Communications of the ACM*, 43(12), 50–56.

Castells, M. (2011). *The rise of the network society* (Vol. 12). John Wiley & Sons.

Cave, S., Craig, C., Dihal, K., Dillon, S., Montgomery, J., Singler, B., & Taylor, L. (2018). *Portrayals and perceptions of AI and why they matter*. The Royal Society. https://royalsociety.org/-/media/policy/projects/ai-narratives/AI-narratives-works hop-findings.pdf

Cave, S., Dihal, K., & Dillon, S. (2020). *AI narratives: A history of imaginative thinking about intelligent machines*. Oxford University Press.

Center, J. L. (1998). Practical application of facial recognition: Automated facial recognition access control system. In H. Wechsler, P. Philips, V. Bruce, F. F. Soulié, & T. S. Huang (Eds.), *Face Recognition* (Vol. 163, pp. 402–411). Springer.

Char, D. S., Abràmoff, M. D., & Feudtner, C. (2020). Identifying ethical considerations for machine learning healthcare applications. *The American Journal of Bioethics*, *20*(11), 7–17.

Char, D. S., Shah, N. H., & Magnus, D. (2018). Implementing machine learning in health care—Addressing ethical challenges. *The New England Journal of Medicine*, *378*(11), 981–983.

Charniak, E. (1985). *Introduction to artificial intelligence*. Pearson Education India.

Chavan, M. (2009). The balanced scorecard: A new challenge. *Journal of Management Development*, *28*(5), 393–406.

Chawla, R. (2019). Deepfakes: How a pervert shook the world. *International Journal of Advance Research and Development*, *4*(6), 4–8.

Chee, F. Y. (2020, January 16). EU mulls five-year ban on facial recognition tech in public areas. *Reuters*. https://www.reuters.com/article/uk-eu-ai-idINKBN1ZF2QN

Chen, A. (2019, March 25). *Tech journalist Clive Thompson examines the people behind the software changing the world*. The Verge. https://www.theverge.com/201 9/3/25/18277279/clive-thompson-coders-silicon-valley-software-engineers-progra mming-interview-books

Cheney-Lippold, J. (2016). Jus Algoritmi: How the National Security Agency Remade Citizenship. *International Journal of Communication*, *10*, 1721–1742.

Chitika Insights. (2013). *The value of Google result positioning*. Chitika Insights.

Chu, X., Ilyas, I. F., Krishnan, S., & Wang, J. (2016). Data cleaning: Overview and emerging challenges. *Proceedings of the 2016 International Conference on Management of Data*, 2201–2206.

Cialdini, R. B., & Goldstein, N. J. (2004). Social influence: Compliance and conformity. *Annu. Rev. Psychol.*, *55*(1), 591 621.

Citron, D. K., & Pasquale, F. (2014). The Scored Society: Due Process for Automated Predictions. *WASHINGTON LAW REVIEW*, *89*(1), 1–33.

Clark, A., & Chalmers, D. (1998). The extended mind. *Analysis*, *58*(1), 7–19.

Clark, J. (1886). Capital and its earnings. *Publications of the American Economic Association*, *3*(2), 9–69.

Clarke, R. (2019). Principles and business processes for responsible AI. *Computer Law & Security Review*, *35*(4), 410–422.

Cohen, A. J., & Harcourt, G. C. (2003). Retrospectives Whatever Happened to the Cambridge Capital Theory Controversies? *Journal of Economic Perspectives*, *17*(1), 199–214. https://doi.org/10.1257/089533003321165010

Cohen, G. A. (1978). *Karl Marx's Theory of History*. Clarendon Press. https://press.pr inceton.edu/titles/320.html

Cohen, J. E. (2017). Law for the Platform Economy. *UCDL Rev.*, *51*, 133–204.

Cohen, Z. C., & Wild, W. (2021, April 28). Internal emails reveal Capitol security officials dismissed warnings about troubling social media posts before January 6 riot. *CNN*. https://www.cnn.com/2021/04/28/politics/capitol-security-emails-soci al-media-riot/index.html

Coleman, J. (1988). Social Capital in the Creation of Human Capital. *American Journal of Sociology*, *94*(1). https://www.jstor.org/stable/2780243?seq=1#metadata _info_tab_contents

Collins, H. (1981). Stages in the Empirical Programme of Relativism. *Social Studies of Science*, *11 (1)*, 3–10.

Corrado, C. A., Hulten, C. R., & Sichel, D. E. (2006). Intangible Capital and Economic Growth. *National Bureau of Economic Research Working Paper Series*, *11948*. https://doi.org/10.3386/w11948

Crawford, K. (2021). *The Atlas of AI*. Yale University Press.

Creator of FacesOfTheRiot. (2021, February 23). *Personal Communication* [Personal communication].

Danaher, J. (2016). The Threat of Algocracy: Reality, Resistance and Accommodation. *Philosophy & Technology*, *29*(3), 245–268. https://doi.org/10.1007/s13347-015-0211-1

Data Ethics Commission. (2019). *Opinion of the Data Ethics Commission*. Bundesministerium der Justiz und für Verbraucherschutz. https://www.bmjv.de/S haredDocs/Downloads/DE/Themen/Fokusthemen/Gutachten_DEK_EN.pdf?__ blob=publicationFile&v=2

Datta, A., Tschantz, M. C., & Datta, A. (2015). Automated experiments on ad privacy settings. *Proceedings on Privacy Enhancing Technologies*, *2015*(1), 92–112.

Davis, K. (2012). *Ethics of Big Data: Balancing risk and innovation*. O'Reilly Media.

Dawson, M., & Foster, J. B. (1996). Virtual Capitalism: The Political Economy of the Information Highway. *Monthly Review*, *48*(3), 40–58.

De Swarte, T., Boufous, O., & Escalle, P. (2019). Artificial intelligence, ethics and human values: The cases of military drones and companion robots. *Artificial Life and Robotics*, *24*(3), 291–296.

De Visser, E. J., Monfort, S. S., McKendrick, R., Smith, M. A., McKnight, P. E., Krueger, F., & Parasuraman, R. (2016). Almost human: Anthropomorphism increases trust resilience in cognitive agents. *Journal of Experimental Psychology: Applied*, *22*(3), 331–349.

DeepMind. (2020, November 30). AlphaFold: A solution to a 50-year-old grand challenge in biology. *DeepMind Blog*. /blog/article/alphafold-a-solution-to-a-50-year-old-grand-challenge-in-biology

del Rio, J. S., Moctezuma, D., Conde, C., de Diego, I. M., & Cabello, E. (2016). Automated border control e-gates and facial recognition systems. *Computers & Security*, *62*, 49–72.

Delcker, J. (2018, September 13). Big Brother in Berlin. *POLITICO*. https://www.poli tico.eu/article/berlin-big-brother-state-surveillance-facial-recognition-technology/

Delcker, J. (2021, May 6). Opinion: Trump's Facebook ban could have global impact. *Deutsche Welle*. https://www.dw.com/en/opinion-trumps-facebook-ban-c ould-have-global-impact/a-57442639

Dencik, L., Hintz, A., & Cable, J. (2016). Towards data justice? The ambiguity of anti-surveillance resistance in political activism. *Big Data & Society*, *3*(2), 1–12.

DeSanctis, G., & Poole, M. S. (1994). Capturing the complexity in advanced technology use: Adaptive structuration theory. *Organization Science*, 5(2), 121–147.

Desmedt, Y., Hou, S., & Quisquater, J.-J. (1998). Audio and optical cryptography. *International Conference on the Theory and Application of Cryptology and Information Security*, 392–404.

Diakopoulos, N., & Johnson, D. (2019). *Anticipating and Addressing the Ethical Implications of Deepfakes in the Context of Elections* (SSRN Scholarly Paper ID 3474183). Social Science Research Network. https://doi.org/10.2139/ssrn.3474183

Digital News Initiative. (n.d.). Digital News Initiative. Retrieved January 8, 2021, from https://newsinitiative.withgoogle.com/

Dignum, V. (2021). AI — the people and places that make, use and manage it. *Nature*, 593(7860), 499–500. https://doi.org/10.1038/d41586-021-01397-x

Dijkstra, J. J., Liebrand, W. B. G., & Timminga, E. (1998). Persuasiveness of expert systems. *Behavior & Information Technology*, 17(3), 155–163.

DiMaggio, P. (1979). Reproduction in Education, Society and Culture. By Pierre Bourdieu, Jean-Claude Passeron and Richard Nice; Outline of a Theory of Practice. By Pierre Bourdieu and Richard Nice. *American Journal of Sociology*, 84(6), 1460–1474.

DNI Final Impact Report. (2020). Digital News Initiative. https://newsinitiative.with google.com/dnifund/documents/46/DNI_Fund_Impact_Report_v3.pdf

DNI Terms and Conditions. (n.d.). Digital News Initiative. Retrieved January 8, 2021, from https://newsinitiative.withgoogle.com/dnifund/documents/22/DNI -App-TC-02082018.pdf

Donde, J. (2017, September 21). Self-Driving Cars Will Kill People. Who Decides Who Dies? *WIRED*. https://www.wired.com/story/self-driving-cars-will-kill-peopl e-who-decides-who-dies/

Doyle, A. (2011). Revisiting the synopticon: Reconsidering Mathiesen's 'The Viewer Society' in the age of Web 2.0. *Theoretical Criminology*, 15(3), 293–299.

Drucker, P. F. (1992, September). The New Society of Organizations. *Harvard Business Review*. https://hbr.org/1992/09/the-new-society-of-organizations

D'Souza, D. (2002). *The virtue of prosperity: Finding values in an age of technoafflu-ence*. Simon and Schuster.

Dudley, H., & Tarnoczy, T. H. (1950). The speaking machine of Wolfgang von Kempelen. *The Journal of the Acoustical Society of America*, 22(2), 151–166.

Durkin, E. (2019, May 30). New York tenants fight as landlords embrace facial recognition cameras. *The Guardian*. https://www.theguardian.com/cities/2019/m ay/29/new-york-facial-recognition-cameras-apartment-complex

Dzindolet, M. T., Peterson, S. A., Pomranky, R. A., Pierce, L. G., & Beck, H. P. (2003). The role of trust in automation reliance. *International Journal of Human-Computer Studies*, 58(6), 697–718.

Economist. (2017, May 6). Data is giving rise to a new economy. *The Economist*. https://www.economist.com/briefing/2017/05/06/data-is-giving-rise-to-a-new-eco nomy

Eitel-Porter, R. (2021). Beyond the promise: Implementing ethical AI. *AI and Ethics*, *1*(1), 73–80.

Ellul, J. (1904). *The Technological Society*. Vintage Book.

Epstein, R., & Robertson, R. (2015). The search engine manipulation effect (SEME) and its possible impact on the outcomes of elections. *Proceedings of the National Academy of Sciences*, *112*, E4512–E4521.

Espinoza, J., & Murgia, M. (2020, February 11). EU backs away from call for blanket ban on facial recognition tech. *Financial Times*. https://www.ft.com/content/ff798944-4cc6-11ea-95a0-43d18ec715f5

EU High-Level Expert Group on AI. (2019). *Ethics guidelines for trustworthy AI*. European Commission. https://ec.europa.eu/digital-single-market/en/news/ethics-guidelines-trustworthy-ai

Eubanks, V. (2018). *Automating inequality: How high-tech tools profile, police, and punish the poor*. St. Martin's Press.

European Commission. (2021a). *Announcement: Proposal for a Regulation laying down harmonised rules on artificial intelligence (Artificial Intelligence Act)*. https://ec.europa.eu/newsroom/dae/items/709090

European Commission. (2021b). *Proposal for a Regulation laying down harmonised rules on artificial intelligence (Artificial Intelligence Act)*. https://ec.europa.eu/newsroom/dae/items/709090

Evans, M. P. (2007). Analysing Google rankings through search engine optimization data. *Internet Research*, *17*(1), 21–37.

Evelyn, K. (2021, January 8). Capitol attack: The five people who died. *The Guardian*. http://www.theguardian.com/us-news/2021/jan/08/capitol-attack-police-officer-five-deaths

Eyal, N. (2014). *Hooked: How to Build Habit-Forming Products* (R. Hoover, Ed.). Portfolio.

Faces of the Riot. (2021). https://facesoftheriot.com/

Fairfield, J. A. (2021). *Runaway Technology: Can Law Keep Up?* Cambridge University Press.

Fanta, A. (2018, September 26). *The Publishers' Patron*. Tech Transparency Project. https://www.techtransparencyproject.org/articles/publishers-patron-how-googles-news-initiative-redefining-journalism

Faulkner, P., & Runde, J. (2012). On sociomateriality. *Materiality and Organizing: Social Interaction in a Technological World*, 49–66.

Faulkner, Philip, & Runde, J. (2011). The social, the material, and the ontology of non-material technological objects. *European Group for Organizational Studies (EGOS) Colloquium, Gothenburg*, *985*, 4–8.

Federal Buerau of Investigation. (2021). *FBI Most Wanted: Capitol Violence*. Federal Bureau of Investigation. https://www.fbi.gov/wanted/capitol-violence

Federal Trade Commission. (2020, January 28). *You Don't Say: An FTC Workshop on Voice Cloning Technologies*. https://www.ftc.gov/news-events/events-calendar/you-dont-say-ftc-workshop-voice-cloning-technologies

Ferry, G. (2015). Ada Lovelace: In search of "a calculus of the nervous system." *The Lancet, 386*(10005), 1731. https://doi.org/10.1016/S0140-6736(15)00686-8

Fetter, F. (1937). Capital. In E. R. A. Seligman & A. Johnson (Eds.), *Encyclopedia Of The Social Sciences Vol-III (1937)* (pp. 187–190). Macmillan. http://archive.org/details/in.ernet.dli.2015.14950

Fischer, C. (1994). *America Calling*. University of California Press. https://www.ucpress.edu/book/9780520086470/america-calling

Fisher, I. (1904). Precedents of Defining Capital. *Quarterly Journal of Economics, 18*(3), 386–408.

Fisher, I. (1906). *The nature of capital and income*. Macmillan. http://archive.org/details/natureofcapitali00fishuoft

Fiss, P. C., & Zajac, E. J. (2006). The symbolic management of strategic change: Sensegiving via framing and decoupling. *Academy of Management Journal, 49*(6), 1173–1193.

Fletcher, J. (2018). Deepfakes, artificial intelligence, and some kind of dystopia: The new faces of online post-fact performance. *Theatre Journal, 70*(4), 455–471.

Floridi, L. (2014). *The fourth revolution: How the infosphere is reshaping human reality*. Oxford University Press.

Floridi, L. (2019). Establishing the rules for building trustworthy AI. *Nature Machine Intelligence, 1*(6), 261–262.

Floridi, L., & Chiriatti, M. (2020). GPT-3: Its nature, scope, limits, and consequences. *Minds and Machines, 30*(4), 681–694.

Forster, Y., Naujoks, F., & Neukum, A. (2017). Increasing anthropomorphism and trust in automated driving functions by adding speech output. *2017 IEEE Intelligent Vehicles Symposium (IV)*, 365–372.

Foucault, M. (1977). *Discipline and punish: The birth of the prison*. Penguin Books.

Foucault, M. (1984). On the genealogy of ethics: An overview of work in progress. *The Foucault Reader, 340*, 372.

Fouquet, H. (2019, October 3). France Set to Roll Out Nationwide Facial Recognition ID Program. *Bloomberg*. https://www.bloomberg.com/news/articles/2019-10-03/french-liberte-tested-by-nationwide-facial-recognition-id-plan

Franck, G. (1998). *Die Ökonomie der Aufmerksamkeit*. Carl Hanser.

Friedman, B., & Nissenbaum, H. (2017). *Bias in computer systems*. Routledge.

Fuchs, C. (2010). Labor in Informational Capitalism and on the Internet. *The Information Society, 26*(3), 179–196.

Fuchs, C. (2013). Capitalism or information society? The fundamental question of the present structure of society. *European Journal of Social Theory, 16*(4), 413–434.

Fuchs, C. (2019). Karl Marx in the age of big data capitalism. In D. Chandler & C. Fuchs (Eds.), *Digital Objects, Digital Subjects: Interdisciplinary Perspectives on Capitalism, Labour and Politics in the Age of Big Data* (pp. 53–71). University of Westminster Press.

Fuegi, J., & Francis, J. (2003). Lovelace & Babbage and the creation of the 1843'notes'. *IEEE Annals of the History of Computing, 25*(4), 16–26.

Fukuyama, F. (1995). *Trust: The Social Virtues and the Creation of Prosperity*. The Free Press.

Fukuyama, F. (2000). *Social Capital and Civil Society* (SSRN Scholarly Paper ID 879582). Social Science Research Network. https://papers.ssrn.com/abstract=879582

Fussell, S. (2019, June 28). The Strange Politics of Facial Recognition. *The Atlantic*. https://www.theatlantic.com/technology/archive/2019/06/democrats-and-republicans-passing-soft-regulations/592558/

Garrahan, M., & Khan, M. (2018, June 26). Google criticised for push against EU copyright reform. *Financial Times*. https://www.ft.com/content/a8031d7a-78a0-11e8-bc55-50daf11b720d

Garvie, C. (2019, May 16). *Garbage In. Garbage Out. Face Recognition on Flawed Data*. Flawed Face Data. https://www.flawedfacedata.com

Garvie, C., Bedoya, A. M., & Jonathan, F. (2016). *The Perpetual Line-Up: Unregulated police face recognition in America*. Georgetown Law Center on Privacy & Technology. https://www.perpetuallineup.org/

Gasser, U. (2017, June 26). AI and the Law: Setting the Stage. *Medium*. https://medium.com/berkman-klein-center/ai-and-the-law-setting-the-stage-48516fda1b11

Gates, K. A. (2011). *Our biometric future: Facial recognition technology and the culture of surveillance* (Vol. 2). NYU Press.

German Criminal Code (Strafgesetzbuch – StGB). (n.d.). Retrieved January 28, 2021, from https://www.gesetze-im-internet.de/englisch_stgb/englisch_stgb.html#p1842

Gholipour, B. (n.d.). New AI Tech Can Mimic Any Voice. *Scientific American*. Retrieved January 14, 2021, from https://www.scientificamerican.com/article/new-ai-tech-can-mimic-any-voice/

Gibson, W. (2010, August 31). Opinion | Google's Earth. *The New York Times*. https://www.nytimes.com/2010/09/01/opinion/01gibson.html

Giddens, A. (1984). *The Constitution of Society*. Wiley.

Gillespie, T. (2014). The Relevance of Algorithms. In T. Gillespie, P. J. Boczkowski, & K. A. Foot (Eds.), *Media Technologies* (pp. 167–194). The MIT Press. https://doi.org/10.7551/mitpress/9780262525374.003.0009

Gioia, D. A., & Chittipeddi, K. (1991). Sensemaking and sensegiving in strategic change initiation. *Strategic Management Journal*, *12*(6), 433–448.

Glaser, B. G., & Strauss, A. L. (2017). *Discovery of grounded theory: Strategies for qualitative research*. Routledge.

Goguen, J. (1997). Towards a social, ethical theory of information. In G. C. Bowker, S. L. Star, W. Turner, & L. Gasser (Eds.), *Social science, technical systems and cooperative work: Beyond the great divide* (pp. 27–56). Psychology Press.

Gong, L. (2008). How social is social responses to computers? The function of the degree of anthropomorphism in computer representations. *Computers in Human Behavior*, *24*(4), 1494–1509. https://doi.org/10.1016/j.chb.2007.05.007

Goodfellow, I. J., Pouget-Abadie, J., Mirza, M., Xu, B., Warde-Farley, D., Ozair, S., Courville, A., & Bengio, Y. (2014). Generative adversarial networks. *ArXiv Preprint ArXiv:1406.2661.*

Graham, S., & Wood, D. (2003). Digitizing Surveillance: Categorization, Space, Inequality. *Critical Social Policy, 23*(2), 227–248. https://doi.org/10.1177/0261018303023002006

Gray, M. (2003). Urban Surveillance and Panopticism: Will we recognize the facial recognition society? *Surveillance & Society, 1*(3), 314–330. https://doi.org/10.24908/ss.v1i3.3343

Greenberg, A. (2021, January 20). This Site Published Every Face From Parler's Capitol Riot Videos. *Wired.* https://www.wired.com/story/faces-of-the-riot-capitol-insurrection-facial-recognition/

Greene, J. (2020, June 11). Microsoft won't sell police its facial-recognition technology, following similar moves by Amazon and IBM. *Washington Post.* https://www.washingtonpost.com/technology/2020/06/11/microsoft-facial-recognition/

Greig, J. (2021, May 26). One year after Amazon, Microsoft and IBM ended facial recognition sales to police, smaller players fill void. *ZDNet.* https://www.zdnet.com/article/one-year-after-amazon-microsoft-and-ibm-ended-facial-recognition-sales-to-police-smaller-players-fill-void/

Grevatt, N. (2018). *Google's Duplex and Deception through Power and Dignity* [Final Paper, University of Virginia]. https://aipavilion.github.io/docs/papers/duplex.pdf

Greve, J. (2021, March 2). FBI chief calls Capitol attack "domestic terrorism" and defends US intelligence. *The Guardian.* http://www.theguardian.com/us-news/2021/mar/02/fbi-christopher-wray-capitol-attack-domestic-terrorism

Grimshaw, M. (2009). The audio Uncanny Valley: Sound, fear and the horror game. *Audio Mostly*, 21–26.

Grossmann, M. (1972). On the concept of healthcapital and the demand for health. *Journal of Political Economy, 80*(2), 223–255.

Groth, O., Nitzberg, M. J., & Russell, S. (2019, August 15). AI Algorithms Need FDA-Style Drug Trials. *Wired.* https://www.wired.com/story/ai-algorithms-need-drug-trials/

Habermas, J. (1970). Technology and science as "ideology." In *Toward a Rational Society* (pp. 81–122). Beacon.

Haenlein, M., & Kaplan, A. (2019). A brief history of artificial intelligence: On the past, present, and future of artificial intelligence. *California Management Review, 61*(4), 5–14.

Haggerty, K., & Ericson, R. (2000). The surveillant assemblage. *British Journal of Sociology, 51*(4), 605–622. https://doi.org/10.1080/00071310020015280

Hakim, C. (2010). Erotic capital. *European Sociological Review, 26*(5), 499–518.

Halpern, S. (2021, May 2). Facebook and the Normalization of Deviance. *The New Yorker.* https://www.newyorker.com/news/daily-comment/facebook-and-the-normalization-of-deviance

Hamann, S. (2016, July 18). Kriminalität: So will die Polizei Einbrüche in NRW voraussagen. *RP ONLINE*. http://www.rp-online.de/nrw/panorama/predictive-po licing-so-sagt-die-polizei-einbrueche-in-nrw-voraus-aid-1.6097807

Hamm, J., Kohler, C. G., Gur, R. C., & Verma, R. (2011). Automated facial action coding system for dynamic analysis of facial expressions in neuropsychiatric disorders. *Journal of Neuroscience Methods*, 200(2), 237–256.

Hanifan, L. J. (1916). The rural school community center. *Annals of the American Academy of Political and Social Science*, 67, 130–138.

Hansen, A. H. (1921). The Technological Interpretation of History. *The Quarterly Journal of Economics*, 36(1), 72–83. https://doi.org/10.2307/1883779

Hao, K. (2020, August 14). A college kid created a fake, AI-generated blog. It reached #1 on Hacker News. *MIT Technology Review*. https://www.technologyrev iew.com/2020/08/14/1006780/ai-gpt-3-fake-blog-reached-top-of-hacker-news/

Hao, K. (2021, April 13). Big Tech's guide to talking about AI ethics. *MIT Technolo gy Review*. https://www.technologyreview.com/2021/04/13/1022568/big-tech-ai-e thics-guide/

Harari, Y. N. (2016). *Homo Deus: A brief history of tomorrow*. Random House.

Harwell, D. (2019a, July 7). FBI, ICE find state driver's license photos are a gold mine for facial-recognition searches. *Washington Post*. https://www.washingtonp ost.com/technology/2019/07/07/fbi-ice-find-state-drivers-license-photos-are-gold -mine-facial-recognition-searches/

Harwell, D. (2019b, September 5). An artificial-intelligence first: Voice-mimicking software reportedly used in a major theft. *Washington Post*. https://www.washing tonpost.com/technology/2019/09/04/an-artificial-intelligence-first-voice-mimicki ng-software-reportedly-used-major-theft/

Haskel, J., & Westlake, S. (2018). *Capitalism without capital: The rise of the intangible economy*. Princeton University Press.

Haugeland, J. (1989). *Artificial intelligence: The very idea*. MIT Press.

Hayles, N. K. (2008). *How we became posthuman: Virtual bodies in cybernetics, litera ture, and informatics*. University of Chicago Press.

Healy, J., Nicholson, D., & Pekarek, A. (2017). Should we take the gig economy seriously? *Labour & Industry: A Journal of the Social and Economic Relations of Work*, 27(3), 232–248.

Heilbroner, R. L. (1967). Do Machines Make History? *Technology and Culture*, 8(3), 335–345. JSTOR. https://doi.org/10.2307/3101719

Hern, A. (2018, May 11). Google's "deceitful" AI assistant to identify itself as a robot during calls. *The Guardian*. http://www.theguardian.com/technology/2018 /may/11/google-duplex-ai-identify-itself-as-robot-during-calls

Hian, L. B., Chuan, S. L., Trevor, T. M. K., & Detenber, B. H. (2004). Getting to know you: Exploring the development of relational intimacy in computer-medi ated communication. *Journal of Computer-Mediated Communication*, 9(3), 9–24.

Hibbard, B. (2014). Ethical artificial intelligence. *ArXiv Preprint ArXiv:1411.1373*.

Hill, K. (2020a, January 18). The Secretive Company That Might End Privacy as We Know It. *The New York Times*. https://www.nytimes.com/2020/01/18/technology/clearview-privacy-facial-recognition.html

Hill, K. (2020b, March 5). Before Clearview Became a Police Tool, It Was a Secret Plaything of the Rich. *The New York Times*. https://www.nytimes.com/2020/03/05/technology/clearview-investors.html

Hill, K. (2020c, June 24). Wrongfully Accused by an Algorithm. *The New York Times*. https://www.nytimes.com/2020/06/24/technology/facial-recognition-arrest.html

Hill, K. (2020d, December 29). Another Arrest, and Jail Time, Due to a Bad Facial Recognition Match. *The New York Times*. https://www.nytimes.com/2020/12/29/technology/facial-recognition-misidentify-jail.html

Hill, K. (2021a, February 3). Clearview AI's Facial Recognition App Called Illegal in Canada. *The New York Times*. https://www.nytimes.com/2021/02/03/technology/clearview-ai-illegal-canada.html

Hill, K. (2021b, February 27). How One State Managed to Actually Write Rules on Facial Recognition. *The New York Times*. https://www.nytimes.com/2021/02/27/technology/Massachusetts-facial-recognition-rules.html

Hill, K. (2021c, March 18). What Happens When Our Faces Are Tracked Everywhere We Go? *The New York Times*. https://www.nytimes.com/interactive/2021/03/18/magazine/facial-recognition-clearview-ai.html

Hill, K. (2021d, March 18). What We Learned About Clearview AI and Its Secret 'Co-Founder.' *The New York Times*. https://www.nytimes.com/2021/03/18/technology/clearview-facial-recognition-ai.html

Hines, D., Saris, R. N., & Throckmorton-Belzer, L. (2002). Pluralistic ignorance and health risk behaviors: Do college students misperceive social approval for risky behaviors on campus and in media? *Journal of Applied Social Psychology*, 32(12), 2621–2640.

Hirsh, R. F., & Sovacool, B. K. (2006). Technological systems and momentum change: American electric utilities, restructuring, and distributed generation. *The Journal of Technology Studies*, 72–85. https://doi.org/10.21061/jots.v32i2.a.2

Hjelmaas, E., & Low, B. K. (2001). Face detection: A survey. *Computer Vision and Image Understanding*, 83(3), 236–274.

Hodgson, G. M. (2014). What is capital? Economists and sociologists have changed its meaning: should it be changed back? *Cambridge Journal of Economics*, 38(5), 1063–1086. https://doi.org/10.1093/cje/beu013

Hoffmann, E. T. A. (1967). The Sandman. In R. Robertson (Trans.), *The Golden Pot and Other Tales* (pp. 85–118). Oxford University Press.

Hollan, J., Hutchins, E., & Kirsh, D. (2000). Distributed cognition: Toward a new foundation for human-computer interaction research. *ACM Transactions on Computer-Human Interaction (TOCHI)*, 7(2), 174–196.

Holmes, D. (2001). From Iron Gaze to Nursing Care: Mental Health Nursing in the Era of Panopticism. *Journal of Psychiatric and Mental Health Nursing*, 8(1), 7–15.

Huang, T., Xiong, Z., & Zhang, Z. (2005). Face recognition applications. In S. Z. Li & A. K. Jain (Eds.), *Handbook of Face Recognition* (pp. 371–390). Springer.

Huber, B. M., & Comstock, M. (2017, July 27). ESG Reports and Ratings: What They Are, Why They Matter. *The Harvard Law School Forum on Corporate Governance*. https://corpgov.law.harvard.edu/2017/07/27/esg-reports-and-ratings-what-t hey-are-why-they-matter/

Huff, C., & Tingley, D. (2015). "Who are these people?" Evaluating the demographic characteristics and political preferences of MTurk survey respondents. *Research & Politics*, 2(3), 1–15. https://doi.org/10.1177/2053168015604648

Hughes, T. (1983). *Networks of Power: Electrification in Western Society, 1880-1930*. The John Hopkins University Press.

Hughes, T. (1986). The Seamless Web: Technology, Science, Etcetera, Etcetera. *Social Studies of Science*, 16(2), 281–292.

Hughes, T. (1987). The Evolution of Large Technological Systems. In W. E. Bijker, T. Hughes, & T. Pinch (Eds.), *The Social Construction of Technological Systems* (pp. 50–82). MIT Press.

Hughes, T. (1989). *American Genesis: A century of invention and technological enthusiasm, 1870-1970*. University of Chicago Press.

Hultin, L. (2019). On becoming a sociomaterial researcher: Exploring epistemological practices grounded in a relational, performative ontology. *Information and Organization*, 29(2), 91–104. https://doi.org/10.1016/j.infoandorg.2019.04.004

Hutson, M. (2021, February 15). Who Should Stop Unethical A.I.? *The New Yorker*. https://www.newyorker.com/tech/annals-of-technology/who-should-stop-unethi cal-ai

Hvistendahl, M. (2016, September 27). Can 'predictive policing' prevent crime before it happens? *Science*. http://www.sciencemag.org/news/2016/09/can-predict ive-policing-prevent-crime-it-happens

Icelandic Institute for Intelligent Machines. (2015). *Ethics Policy*. https://www.iiim.i s/ethics-policy/

International Network of Privacy Law Professionals. (2020, October 26). Facial recognition technologies from a Swedish data protection perspective. *INPLP Latest News*. https://inplp.com/latest-news/article/facial-recognition-technologies -from-a-swedish-data-protection-perspective/

International Standards Organization. (2015). *Societal security—Business continuity management systems—Guidelines for business impact analysis (ISO Standard No ISO/TS 22317)*. International Standards Organization. https://www.iso.org/obp/ ui/#iso:std:iso:ts:22317:ed-1:v1:en

International Standards Organization. (2018). *Risk management—Guidelines (ISO Standard No. 31000:2018)*. International Standards Organization. https://www.is o.org/obp/ui/#iso:std:iso:31000:en

International Standards Organization. (2020). *Guidance for the governance of organizations (ISO Standard No. ISO 37000)*. International Standards Organization. https://www.iso.org/cms/render/live/en/sites/isoorg/contents/data/standard/06/5 0/65036.html

Introna, L. D., & Nissenbaum, H. (2000). Shaping the Web: Why the politics of search engines matters. *The Information Society, 16*(3), 169–185.

Introna, L. D., & Nissenbaum, H. (2010). *Facial Recognition Technology: A survey of policy and implementation issues*. NYU Center for Catastrophe Preparedness and Response. https://nissenbaum.tech.cornell.edu/papers/facial_recognition_report.pdf

Introna, L., & Wood, D. (2004). Picturing algorithmic surveillance: The politics of facial recognition systems. *Surveillance & Society, 2*(2/3), 177–198.

Jackman, T. (2021, January 28). Police union says 140 officers injured in Capitol riot. *Washington Post*. https://www.washingtonpost.com/local/public-safety/police-union-says-140-officers-injured-in-capitol-riot/2021/01/27/60743642-60e2-11eb-9430-e7c77b5b0297_story.html

Jaiman, A. (2020, August 27). Debating the ethics of deepfakes. *Observer Research Foundation*. https://www.orfonline.org/expert-speak/debating-the-ethics-of-deepfakes/

Jasanoff, S., & Kim, S.-H. (2009). Containing the Atom: Sociotechnical Imaginaries and Nuclear Power in the United States and South Korea. *Minerva, 47*(2), 119–146.

Jennings, R. (2021, January 14). Scraped Parler data is truly revealing. *Tech Beacon*. https://techbeacon.com/security/scraped-parler-data-reveals-countless-capitol-perps

Joerges, B. (1988). Large Technical Systems: Concepts and issues. In R. Mayntz & T. P. Hughes (Eds.), *The Development of Large Technical Systems* (pp. 9–36). Campus.

Johnson. (2020, June 25). Congress introduces bill that bans facial recognition use by federal government. *VentureBeat*. https://venturebeat.com/2020/06/25/congress-introduces-bill-that-bans-facial-recognition-use-by-federal-government/

Johnson, C. (2015, November 16). *From Idea to Execution: Spotify's Discover Weekly* [PowerPoint slides]. https://www.slideshare.net/MrChrisJohnson/from-idea-to-execution-spotifys-discover-weekly

Johnson, D., & Wiles, J. (2003). Effective affective user interface design in games. *Ergonomics, 46*(13–14), 1332–1345.

Jones, A., & Jenkins, K. (2008). Indigenous Discourse and "the Material" A Post-interpretivist Argument. *International Review of Qualitative Research, 1*(2), 125–144.

Jumper, J., Evans, R., Pritzel, A., Green, T., Figurnov, M., Tunyasuvunakool, K., Ronneberger, O., Bates, R., Zidek, A., & Bridgland, A. (2020). High accuracy protein structure prediction using deep learning. In *Critical Assessment of Techniques for Protein Structure Prediction* (pp. 22–24). Abstract Book. https://predictioncenter.org/casp14/doc/CASP14_Abstracts.pdf

Kallinikos, J. (2010). *Governing through technology: Information artefacts and social practice*. Springer.

Kaplan, R. S. (2009). Conceptual foundations of the balanced scorecard. In A. G. Hopwood, C. S. Chapman, & M. D. Shields (Eds.), *Handbooks of management accounting research* (Vol. 3, pp. 1253–1269). Elsevier Science.

Kaplan, R. S., & Norton, D. P. (1998). Putting the balanced scorecard to work. *The Economic Impact of Knowledge, 27*(4), 315–324.

Karapapa, S., & Borghi, M. (2015). Search engine liability for autocomplete suggestions: Personality, privacy and the power of the algorithm. *International Journal of Law and Information Technology, 23*(3), 261–289.

Karras, T., Laine, S., & Aila, T. (2019). A style-based generator architecture for generative adversarial networks. *Proceedings of the IEEE/CVF Conference on Computer Vision and Pattern Recognition*, 4401–4410.

Karras, T., Laine, S., Aittala, M., Hellsten, J., Lehtinen, J., & Aila, T. (2020). Analyzing and improving the image quality of stylegan. *Proceedings of the IEEE/CVF Conference on Computer Vision and Pattern Recognition*, 8110–8119.

Kasy, M., & Abebe, R. (2021). Fairness, equality, and power in algorithmic decision-making. *Proceedings of the 2021 ACM Conference on Fairness, Accountability, and Transparency*, 576–586.

Katz, M. L., & Shapiro, C. (1985). Network externalities, competition, and compatibility. *The American Economic Review, 75*(3), 424–440.

Katz, M. L., & Shapiro, C. (1994). Systems competition and network effects. *Journal of Economic Perspectives, 8*(2), 93–115.

Kauflin, J., Gara, A., & Klebnikov, S. (2020, August 19). *The Inside Story Of Robinhood's Billionaire Founders, Option Kid Cowboys And The Wall Street Sharks That Feed On Them*. Forbes. https://www.forbes.com/sites/jeffkauflin/2020/08/19/the-inside-story-of-robinhoods-billionaire-founders-option-kid-cowboys-and-the-wall-street-sharks-that-feed-on-them/

Kember, S. (2003). Cyberfeminism and Artificial Life. *FEMINIST THEORY, 4*(3), 369–370.

Kenney, M., & Zysman, J. (2016). The rise of the platform economy. *Issues in Science and Technology, 32*(3), 61.

Kharpal, A. (2020, January 28). Big Tech's calls for more regulation offers a chance for them to increase their power. *CNBC*. https://www.cnbc.com/2020/01/28/big-techs-calls-for-ai-regulation-could-lead-to-more-power.html

Klare, B. F., Burge, M. J., Klontz, J. C., Bruegge, R. W. V., & Jain, A. K. (2012). Face recognition performance: Role of demographic information. *IEEE Transactions on Information Forensics and Security, 7*(6), 1789–1801.

Klein, S., & Kao, J. (2021, January 17). Why We Published More Than 500 Videos Taken by Parler Users of the Capitol Riot. *ProPublica*. https://www.propublica.org/article/why-we-published-parler-users-videos-capitol-attack?token=T9DMO_4oncWnPFNlubLC6K7JtywmqAu3

Kline, R. R. (2015). Technological Determinism. In *International Encyclopedia of the Social & Behavioral Sciences* (pp. 109–112). Elsevier. https://doi.org/10.1016/B978-0-08-097086-8.85034-5

Knight, W. (2017a). The dark secret at the heart of aI. *Technology Review, 120*(3), 54–61.

Knight, W. (2017b, November 4). The Dark Secret at the Heart of AI. *MIT Technology Review*. https://www.technologyreview.com/s/604087/the-dark-secret-at-the-heart-of-ai/

Korolova, A. (2010). Privacy violations using microtargeted ads: A case study. *2010 IEEE International Conference on Data Mining Workshops*, 474–482.

Kostka, G. (2019). China's social credit systems and public opinion: Explaining high levels of approval. *New Media & Society, 21*(7), 1565–1593.

Kostka, G., Steinacker, L., & Meckel, M. (2021a). Between security and convenience: Facial recognition technology in the eyes of citizens in China, Germany, the United Kingdom, and the United States. *Public Understanding of Science, 21*(5), 556–572.

Kostka, G., Steinacker, L., & Meckel, M. (2021b). Between security and convenience: Facial recognition technology in the eyes of citizens in China, Germany, the United Kingdom, and the United States. *Public Understanding of Science*, 09636625211001555. https://doi.org/10.1177/09636625211001555

Kotler, P. (2010). The prosumer movement. In *Prosumer Revisited* (pp. 51–60). Springer.

Kranzberg, M. (1986). Technology and History: "Kranzberg's Laws." *Technology and Culture, 27*(3), 544–560. https://doi.org/10.2307/3105385

Krol, K., Parkin, S., & Sasse, M. A. (2016). " I don't like putting my face on the Internet!": An acceptance study of face biometrics as a CAPTCHA replacement. *2016 IEEE International Conference on Identity, Security and Behavior Analysis (ISBA)*, 1–7.

Kurwa, R. (2019). Building the Digitally Gated Community: The Case of Nextdoor. *Surveillance & Society, 17*(1/2), 111–117.

Kurzweil, R., Richter, R., Kurzweil, R., & Schneider, M. L. (1990). *The age of intelligent machines* (Vol. 579). MIT Press.

Kuss, P., & Leenes, R. (2020). The Ghost in the Machine-Emotionally Intelligent Conversational Agents and the Failure to Regulate'Deception by Design'. *SCRIPTed, 17*(2), 320–358.

Lambert, T. A., Kahn, A. S., & Apple, K. J. (2003). Pluralistic ignorance and hooking up. *Journal of Sex Research, 40*(2), 129–133.

Lambrecht, A., & Tucker, C. (2019). Algorithmic Bias? An Empirical Study of Apparent Gender-Based Discrimination in the Display of STEM Career Ads. *Management Science, 65*(7), 2966–2981.

Latour, B. (1990). Technology is Society Made Durable. *The Sociological Review, 38*(1_suppl), 103–131.

Latour, B. (2017). On Actor-Network Theory. A Few Clarifications, Plus More Than a Few Complications. *Philosophical Literary Journal Logos, 27*(1), 173–197. https://doi.org/10.22394/0869-5377-2017-1-173-197

Lattimore, R., & Baskin, L. (2011). *The Iliad of Homer*. University of Chicago Press.

Law, J. (1987). Technology and Heterogeneous Engineering: The Case of Portuguese Expansion. In *The Social Construction of Technological Systems* (pp. 111–134). MIT Press.

Law, J. (2001). Notes on the Theory of the Actor Network: Ordering, Strategy and Heterogeneity. In *Organizational Studies: Critical Perspectives on Business and Management*. Routledge.

Leavy, S. (2018). Gender bias in artificial intelligence: The need for diversity and gender theory in machine learning. *Proceedings of the 1st International Workshop on Gender Equality in Software Engineering*, 14–16.

Lecher, C. (2019, July 10). Congress faces 'hard questions' on facial recognition as activists push for ban. *The Verge*. https://www.theverge.com/2019/7/10/20688932/congress-facial-recognition-hearing-ban

Lee, E. A. (2017). *Plato and the Nerd: The Creative Partnership of Humans and Technology*. MIT Press.

Lee, K.-F. (2017, June 24). The Real Threat of Artificial Intelligence. *The New York Times*. https://www.nytimes.com/2017/06/24/opinion/sunday/artificial-intelligence-economic-inequality.html

Leibold, J. (2020). Surveillance in China's Xinjiang region: Ethnic sorting, coercion, and inducement. *Journal of Contemporary China*, 29(121), 46–60.

Lenglet, M. (2011). Conflicting Codes and Codings: How Algorithmic Trading Is Reshaping Financial Regulation. *Theory, Culture & Society*, 28(6), 44–66. https://doi.org/10.1177/0263276411417444

Leonardi, P. M. (2007). Activating the informational capabilities of information technology for organizational change. *Organization Science*, 18(5), 813–831.

Leonardi, P. M. (2011). When flexible routines meet flexible technologies: Affordance, constraint, and the imbrication of human and material agencies. *MIS Quarterly*, 35(1), 147–167.

Leonardi, P. M. (2012). Materiality, sociomateriality, and socio-technical systems: What do these terms mean? How are they different? Do we need them. In P. M. Leonardi, B. A. Nardi, & J. Kallinikos (Eds.), *Materiality and Organizing: Social Interaction in a Technological World* (pp. 25–48). Oxford University Press. https://ssrn.com/abstract=2129878 or http://dx.doi.org/10.2139/ssrn.2129878

Leonardi, P. M. (2013). Theoretical foundations for the study of sociomateriality. *Information and Organization*, 23(2), 59–76.

Leong, N., & Belzer, A. (2016). The new public accommodations: Race discrimination in the platform economy. *Geo. LJ*, 105, 1271.

Leporini, B., Buzzi, M. C., & Buzzi, M. (2012). Interacting with mobile devices via VoiceOver: Usability and accessibility issues. *Proceedings of the 24th Australian Computer-Human Interaction Conference*, 339–348.

Lessig, L. (1999). *Code: And Other Laws of Cyberspace*. Basic Books.

Lessig, L. (2006). *Code 2.0*. Basic Books. http://codev2.cc/download+remix/Lessig-Codev2.pdf

Lev, B. (2004). Sharpening the intangibles edge. *Harvard Business Review*, 109–116.

Levy, S. (2010, December 27). The AI Revolution Is On. *Wired*. https://www.wired.com/2010/12/ff-ai-essay-airevolution/

Li, J. (2019, October 3). Getting a new mobile number in China will involve a facial-recognition test. *Quartz*. https://qz.com/1720832/china-introduces-facial-re cognition-step-to-get-new-mobile-number/

Liakin, D., Cardoso, W., & Liakina, N. (2017). The pedagogical use of mobile speech synthesis (TTS): Focus on French liaison. *Computer Assisted Language Learning, 30*(3–4), 325–342. https://doi.org/10.1080/09588221.2017.1312463

Lin, H.-T., Balcan, M. F., Hadsell, R., & Ranzato, M. (2020, October 16). What we learned from NeurIPS 2020 reviewing process. *Medium*. https://neuripsconf.med ium.com/what-we-learned-from-neurips-2020-reviewing-process-e24549eea38f

Liu, Y., Kohlberger, T., Norouzi, M., Dahl, G. E., Smith, J. L., Mohtashamian, A., Olson, N., Peng, L. H., Hipp, J. D., & Stumpe, M. C. (2019). Artificial Intelligence-Based Breast Cancer Nodal Metastasis Detection: Insights Into the Black Box for Pathologists. *Archives of Pathology & Laboratory Medicine, 143*(7), 859–868. https://doi.org/10.5858/arpa.2018-0147-OA

Lomas, N. (2021, February 12). Sweden's data watchdog slaps police for unlawful use of Clearview AI. *TechCrunch*. https://social.techcrunch.com/2021/02/12/swed ens-data-watchdog-slaps-police-for-unlawful-use-of-clearview-ai/

Lovelace, A. & Steinacker, L. (2033). How we built the analytical engine - finally. *Morals & Machines*, 13(3), 67-89.

Luhmann, N. (2018). Unterwachung. In *Schriften zur Organisation 1* (pp. 415–424). Springer.

Luo, X., Tong, S., Fang, Z., & Qu, Z. (2019). Frontiers: Machines vs. humans: The impact of artificial intelligence chatbot disclosure on customer purchases. *Marketing Science*, 38(6), 937–947.

Luthans, F., Youssef, C. M., & Avolio, B. (2007). *Psychological capital: Developing the human competitive edge*. Oxford University Press.

Lyons, M. J., Budynek, J., & Akamatsu, S. (1999). Automatic classification of single facial images. *IEEE Transactions on Pattern Analysis and Machine Intelligence*, 21(12), 1357–1362. https://doi.org/10.1109/34.817413

MacKenzie, D. (1984). Marx and the Machine. *Technology and Culture*, 25(3), 473–502. https://doi.org/10.2307/3104202

Malle, B. F., Magar, S. T., & Scheutz, M. (2019). AI in the sky: How people morally evaluate human and machine decisions in a lethal strike dilemma. In M. I. Aldinhas Ferreira, J. Silva Sequeira, V. Gurvinder, O. Tokhi, & E. Kadar (Eds.), *Robotics and well-being* (pp. 111–133). Springer.

Mann, M., & Smith, M. (2017). Automated facial recognition technology: Recent developments and approaches to oversight. *UNSWLJ*, 40(1), 121–145.

Manokha, I. (2018). Surveillance, Panopticism, and Self-Discipline in the Digital Age. *Surveillance & Society*, 16(2), 219–237. https://doi.org/10.24908/ss.v16i2.8346

Manovich, L. (2011). Trending: The promises and the challenges of big social data. *Debates in the Digital Humanities*, 2(1), 460–475.

Manyika, J., Lund, S., Bughin, J., Robinson, K., Mischke, J., & Mahajan, D. (2016). Independent work: Choice, necessity, and the gig economy. *McKinsey Global Institute*, 1–16.

Maras, M.-H., & Alexandrou, A. (2019). Determining authenticity of video evidence in the age of artificial intelligence and in the wake of Deepfake videos. *The International Journal of Evidence & Proof*, 23(3), 255–262.

Marche, S. (2021, April 30). The Computers Are Getting Better at Writing, Thanks to Artificial Intelligence. *The New Yorker*. https://www.newyorker.com/culture/cultural-comment/the-computers-are-getting-better-at-writing

Marcus, J. (2020, February 20). How Technology Is Changing the Future of Higher Education. *The New York Times*. https://www.nytimes.com/2020/02/20/education/learning/education-technology.html

Markoff, J. (2011, October 10). U.S. Intelligence Unit Aims to Build a 'Data Eye in the Sky.' *The New York Times*. https://www.nytimes.com/2011/10/11/science/11predict.html

Martinez-Martin, N. (2019). What Are Important Ethical Implications of Using Facial Recognition Technology in Health Care? *AMA Journal of Ethics*, 21(2), 180–187.

Marx, K. (1971). *The Poverty of Philosophy*. Progress Publishers.

Marx, K. (2010a). *Capital: A Critique of Political Economy—Volume II* (F. Engels, Ed.). Progress Publishers. https://libcom.org/files/Capital-Volume-II.pdf

Marx, K. (2010b). *Capital: A Critique of Political Economy—Volume III* (F. Engels, Ed.). Progress Publishers. https://www.marxists.org/archive/marx/works/download/pdf/Capital-Volume-III.pdf

Marx, K. (2015). *Capital: A Critique of Political Economy—Volume I*. Progress Publishers. https://www.marxists.org/archive/marx/works/download/pdf/Capital-Volume-I.pdf

Marx, K., & Engels, F. (1970). *The German Ideology* (C. Arthur, Ed.). International Publishers Co.

Marx, L. (1994). The Idea of "Technology" and Postmodern Pessimism. In Y. Ezrahi, E. Mendelsohn, & H. Segal (Eds.), *Technology, Pessimism, and Postmodernism* (pp. 11–28). Springer Netherlands. https://doi.org/10.1007/978-94-011-0876-8_2

Marx, L., & Smith, M. R. (1994). Introduction. In M. R. Smith & L. Marx (Eds.), *Does Technology Drive History?: The Dilemma of Technological Determinism*. MIT Press.

Massachusetts State Government. (2020, December 31). *Governor Baker Signs Police Reform Legislation*. https://www.mass.gov/news/governor-baker-signs-police-reform-legislation

Mathiesen, T. (1997). The viewer society: Michel Foucault's "Panopticon" revisited. *Theoretical Criminology*, 1(2), 215–234.

McCarthy, J., Minsky, M. L., Rochester, N., & Shannon, C. E. (2006). A proposal for the dartmouth summer research project on artificial intelligence, august 31, 1955. *AI Magazine*, 27(4), 12–12.

McClurg, A. J. (2007). In the face of danger: Facial recognition and the limits of privacy law. *Harvard Law Review*, 120(7), 1870–1891.

McCorduck, P. (2004). *Machines who think: A personal inquiry into the history and prospects of artificial intelligence.* CRC Press.

McCormack, D. (2003). Can Corporate America Secure Our Nation-An Analysis of the Identix Framework for the Regulation and Use of Facial Recognition Technology. *BUJ Sci. & Tech. L.*, *9*, 128.

McCoy, S. (2002). O'Big Brother Where Art Thou?: The Constitutional Use of Facial-Recognition Technology. *The John Marshall Journal of Information Technology & Privacy Law*, *20*(3), 471–493.

McKinlay, A., & Starkey, K. (1997). *Foucault, Management and Organization Theory: From Panopticon to Technologies of Self.* SAGE.

McMullan, T. (2015, July 23). What does the panopticon mean in the age of digital surveillance? *The Guardian.* https://www.theguardian.com/technology/2015/jul/2 3/panopticon-digital-surveillance-jeremy-bentham

Meckel, M., & Steinacker, L. (2021). Hybrid reality: The rise of deepfakes and diverging truths. *Morals & Machines*, *1*(1), 10–20.

Menebrea, L. F., & Lovelace, A. (1842). *Sketch of the Analytical Engine Invented by Charles Babbage.* R. & J. E. Taylor. https://johnrhudson.me.uk/computing/Mena brea_Sketch.pdf

Metcalfe, B. (2013). Metcalfe's law after 40 years of ethernet. *Computer*, *46*(12), 26–31.

Metcalfe, R. (1995). Metcalfe's law. *Infoworld*, *2*.

Metz, R. (2019, July 17). Beyond San Francisco, more cities are saying no to facial recognition. *CNN.* https://www.cnn.com/2019/07/17/tech/cities-ban-facial-recog nition/index.html

Miailhe, N. (2017). Understanding the Rise of Artificial Intelligence. Introduction. *Field Actions Science Reports. The Journal of Field Actions*, Special Issue 17, 5.

Midler v. Ford Motor Co. 549 F. 2d 460 (9th Cir.). (1988). https://cyber.harvard.edu/p eople/tfisher/1988%20Midler.pdf

Milan, S. (2015). When Algorithms Shape Collective Action: Social Media and the Dynamics of Cloud Protesting. *Social Media + Society*, *1*(2), 1–10. https://doi.org/ 10.1177/2056305115622481

Miller, R. W. (1984). *Analyzing Marx.* Princeton University Press. https://press.princ eton.edu/titles/1565.html

Milligan, C. S. (1999). Facial recognition technology, video surveillance, and privacy. *S. Cal. Interdisc. LJ*, *9*, 295.

Mittelstadt, B. (2019). Principles alone cannot guarantee ethical AI. *Nature Machine Intelligence*, *1*(11), 501–507.

Mittelstadt, B. D., Allo, P., Taddeo, M., Wachter, S., & Floridi, L. (2016). The ethics of algorithms: Mapping the debate. *Big Data & Society*, *3*(2), 1–21. https:// doi.org/10.1177/2053951716679679

Mori, M., MacDorman, K. F., & Kageki, N. (2012). The uncanny valley [from the field]. *IEEE Robotics & Automation Magazine*, *19*(2), 98–100.

Morris, M. R. (2020). AI and accessibility. *Communications of the ACM*, *63*(6), 35–37.

Morse, J. (2019, October 9). California just scored a major privacy win against facial-recognition tech. *Mashable*. https://mashable.com/article/california-facial-recognition-tech-body-cam-ban/

Moses, L. B., & Chan, J. (2018). Algorithmic prediction in policing: Assumptions, evaluation, and accountability. *Policing and Society*, *28*(7), 806–822. https://doi.org/10.1080/10439463.2016.1253695

Mozur, P. (2019, April 17). One Month, 500,000 Face Scans: How China Is Using A.I. to Profile a Minority. *The New York Times*. https://www.nytimes.com/2019/04/14/technology/china-surveillance-artificial-intelligence-racial-profiling.html

Mozur, P., Kang, C., Satariano, A., & McCabe, D. (2021, April 20). A Global Tipping Point for Reining In Tech Has Arrived. *The New York Times*. https://www.nytimes.com/2021/04/20/technology/global-tipping-point-tech.html

Mueller, B., Renken, U., & van Den Heuvel, G. (2016). Get your act together: An alternative approach to understanding the impact of technology on individual and organizational behavior. *ACM SIGMIS Database: The DATABASE for Advances in Information Systems*, *47*(4), 67–83.

Mueller, M. (1989). The switchboard problem: Scale, signaling, and organization in manual telephone switching, 1877-1897. *Technology and Culture*, *30*(3), 534–560.

Murgia, M. (2019, August 12). London's King's Cross uses facial recognition in security cameras. *Financial Times*. https://www.ft.com/content/8cbcb3ae-babd-11e9-8a88-aa6628ac896c

Mutch, A. (2013). Sociomateriality—Taking the wrong turning? *Information and Organization*, *23*(1), 28–40.

Nahaphiet, J., & Ghoshal, S. (1998). Social capital, intellectual capital, and the organizational advantage. *Academy of Management Review*, *23*(2), 242–266.

Nakamura, L. (2013). *Cybertypes: Race, ethnicity, and identity on the Internet*. Routledge.

Naker, S., & Greenbaum, D. (2017). Now you see me: Now you still do: Facial recognition technology and the growing lack of privacy. *BUJ Sci. & Tech. L.*, *23*, 88–123.

Nass, C., Steuer, J., & Tauber, E. R. (1994). Computers are social actors. *Proceedings of the SIGCHI Conference on Human Factors in Computing Systems*, 72–78.

NBC News. (2021, September 2). *House Impeachment Managers Play Video Of Capitol Riot During Impeachment Trial*. https://www.youtube.com/watch?v=ERIbhsCzZwk

Neyman, C. J. (2017). A survey of addictive software design. *Digital Commons@Cal Poly*.

Ngan, M., & Grother, P. J. (2015). *Face recognition vendor test (FRVT) performance of automated gender classification algorithms*. US Department of Commerce, National Institute of Standards and Technology. https://nvlpubs.nist.gov/nistpubs/ir/2015/NIST.IR.8052.pdf

Nguyen, T. T., Nguyen, C. M., Nguyen, D. T., Nguyen, D. T., & Nahavandi, S. (2019). Deep learning for deepfakes creation and detection. *ArXiv Preprint ArXiv:1909.11573, 1*.

Nietzsche, F. (1910). *Human, all too human* (Zimmern, Trans.). T.N. Foulis.

Nilsson, N. J. (1998). *Artificial intelligence: A new synthesis*. Morgan Kaufmann.

Nitzan, J., & Bichler, S. (2009). *Capital as power*. Routledge.

Ogburn, W. F. (1936). Technology and Governmental Change. *The Journal of Business of the University of Chicago, 9*(1), 1–13. JSTOR.

O'Neil, C. (2017). *Weapons of Math Destruction: How Big Data Increases Inequality and Threatens Democracy*. Penguin.

Oppermann, R. (2002). User-interface design. In H. H. Adelsberger & J. M. Palowski (Eds.), *Handbook on information technologies for education and training* (pp. 233–248). Springer.

Orlikowski, W. J. (2000). Using technology and constituting structures: A practice lens for studying technology in organizations. *Organization Science, 11*(4), 404–428.

Orlikowski, W. J. (2007). Sociomaterial practices: Exploring technology at work. *Organization Studies, 28*(9), 1435–1448.

Orlikowski, W. J., & Scott, S. V. (2008). Sociomateriality: Challenging the separation of technology, work and organization. *Academy of Management Annals, 2*(1), 433–474.

Orlikowski, W. J., & Scott, S. V. (2015). The algorithm and the crowd: Considering the materiality of service innovation. *MIS Quarterly, 39*(1), 201–216.

Orlikowski, W. J., Walsham, G., Jones, M. R., & DeGross, J. I. (1996). *Information technology and changes in organizational work*. Springer Science & Business Media.

Owuor, J., & Larkan, F. (2017). Assistive Technology for an Inclusive Society for People with Intellectual Disability. *Studies in Health Technology and Informatics, 242*, 805–812.

Pace, J. (2018). The concept of digital capitalism. *Communication Theory, 28*(3), 254–269.

Page, L., Brin, S., Motwani, R., & Winograd, T. (1998). *The PageRank Citation Ranking: Bringing Order to the Web*. Stanford InfoLab. http://ilpubs.stanford.edu:8090/422/1/1999-66.pdf

Paine, T. L., Khorrami, P., Chang, S., Zhang, Y., Ramachandran, P., Hasegawa-Johnson, M. A., & Huang, T. S. (2016). Fast wavenet generation algorithm. *ArXiv Preprint ArXiv:1611.09482*.

Pal, D., Arpnikanondt, C., Funilkul, S., & Varadarajan, V. (2019). User experience with smart voice assistants: The accent perspective. *2019 10th International Conference on Computing, Communication and Networking Technologies (ICCCNT)*, 1–6.

Paluck, E. L. (2009). What's in a norm? Sources and processes of norm change. *Journal of Personality and Social Psychology, 96*(3), 594–600. https://doi.org/10.1037/a0014688

Paluck, E. L., & Green, D. P. (2009). Prejudice reduction: What works? A review and assessment of research and practice. *Annual Review of Psychology, 60,* 339–367.

Paluck, E. L., & Shepherd, H. (2012). The salience of social referents: A field experiment on collective norms and harassment behavior in a school social network. *Journal of Personality and Social Psychology, 103*(6), 899–915. https://doi.org/10.1037/a0030015

Parkhi, O. M., Vedaldi, A., & Zisserman, A. (2015). Deep Face Recognition. *Proceedings of the British Machine Vision Conference 2015, 80,* 41.1-41.12. https://doi.org/10.5244/C.29.41

Partnership On AI. (2016). *Tenets.* Partnership on AI. https://www.partnershiponai.org/tenets/

Pasinetti, L. L., Fisher, F. M., Felipe, J., McCombie, J. S. L., & Greenfield, R. L. (2003). Cambridge Capital Controversies. *The Journal of Economic Perspectives, 17*(4), 227–232.

Pasquale, F. (2016a). *The Black Box Society.* Harvard University Press.

Pasquale, F. (2016b). Two narratives of platform capitalism. *Yale L. & Pol'y Rev., 35,* 309.

Pennachin, C., & Goertzel, B. (2007). Contemporary approaches to artificial general intelligence. In B. Goertzel & C. Pennachin (Eds.), *Artificial general intelligence* (pp. 1–30). Springer.

Perkowitz, S. (2021). The Bias in the Machine: Facial Recognition Technology and Racial Disparities. *MIT Case Studies in Social and Ethical Responsibilities of Computing.* https://mit-serc.pubpub.org/pub/bias-in-machine/release/1

Pettman, D. (2016). *Infinite distraction.* John Wiley & Sons.

Phillips, P., Barnes, S., Zigan, K., & Schegg, R. (2016). Understanding the Impact of Online Reviews on Hotel Performance: An Empirical Analysis. *Journal of Travel Research, 56*(2), 235–249. https://doi.org/10.1177/0047287516636481

Picard, R. (2002). Affective medicine: Technology with emotional intelligence. *Studies in Health Technology and Informatics,* 69–84.

Pichai, S. (2020, January 20). Why Google thinks we need to regulate AI. *Financial Times.* https://www.ft.com/content/3467659a-386d-11ea-ac3c-f68c10993b04

Pickering, A. (2010). *The mangle of practice: Time, agency, and science.* University of Chicago Press.

Pidd, H. (2020, August 14). "Punishment by statistics": The father who foresaw A-level algorithm flaws. *The Guardian.* http://www.theguardian.com/education/2020/aug/14/punishment-by-statistics-the-father-who-foresaw-a-level-algorithm-flaws

Piketty, T. (2014). *Capital in the twenty-first century.* Harvard University Press.

Pinch, T., & Bijker, W. E. (1987). The Social Construction of Facts and Artifacts: Or How the Sociology of Science and the Sociology of Technology Might Benefit Each Other. In W. E. Bijker & T. P. Hughes (Eds.), *The Social Construction of Technological Systems* (pp. 17–50). MIT Press.

Platform for the Information Society. (2018). *Artificial Intelligence Impact Assessment*. Platform for the Information Society. https://static1.squarespace.com/stati c/5b7877457c9327fa97fef427/t/5c368c611ae6cf01ea0fba53/1547078768062/Artifi cial+Intelligence+Impact+Assessment++English.pdf

Pomerantz, S., & Raby, R. (2020). Bodies, hoodies, schools, and success: Post-human performativity and smart girlhood. *Gender and Education, 32*(8), 983–1000.

Poole, D., Mackworth, A., & Goebel, R. (1998). *Computational intelligence: A logical approach*. Oxford University Press.

Porter, J. (2021, February 24). *Australia passes law requiring Facebook and Google to pay for news content*. The Verge. https://www.theverge.com/2021/2/24/22283777/ australia-new-media-bargaining-code-facebook-google-paying-news

Prassl, J. (2018). *Humans as a service: The promise and perils of work in the gig economy*. Oxford University Press.

Prentice, D. A., & Miller, D. T. (1996). Pluralistic ignorance and the perpetuation of social norms by unwitting actors. In M. P. Zanna (Ed.), *Advances in experimental social psychology* (Vol. 28, pp. 161–209). Academic Press.

Press Association. (2019, March 30). Mark Zuckerberg calls for stronger regulation of internet. *The Guardian*. http://www.theguardian.com/technology/2019/mar/3 0/mark-zuckerberg-calls-for-stronger-regulation-of-internet

Prokoshyna, N., Szlichta, J., Chiang, F., Miller, R. J., & Srivastava, D. (2015). Combining quantitative and logical data cleaning. *Proceedings of the VLDB Endowment, 9*(4), 300–311.

Purdy, G. (2010). ISO 31000: 2009—setting a new standard for risk management. *Risk Analysis: An International Journal, 30*(6), 881–886.

Puschmann, T., & Alt, R. (2016). Sharing economy. *Business & Information Systems Engineering, 58*(1), 93–99.

Putnam, R. D. (1993). What makes democracy work? *National Civic Review, 82*(2), 101–107. https://doi.org/10.1002/ncr.4100820204

Putnam, R. D. (2000). *Bowling alone: America's declining social capital*. Simon and Schuster.

Qiu, L., & Benbasat, I. (2005). An investigation into the effects of Text-To-Speech voice and 3D avatars on the perception of presence and flow of live help in electronic commerce. *ACM Transactions on Computer-Human Interaction (TOCHI), 12*(4), 329–355.

Rahwan, I. (2018). Society-in-the-loop: Programming the algorithmic social contract. *Ethics and Information Technology, 20*(1), 5–14. https://doi.org/10.1007/s106 76-017-9430-8

Rahwan, I., Cebrian, M., Obradovich, N., Bongard, J., Bonnefon, J.-F., Breazeal, C., Crandall, J. W., Christakis, N. A., Couzin, I. D., Jackson, M. O., Jennings, N. R., Kamar, E., Kloumann, I. M., Larochelle, H., Lazer, D., McElreath, R., Mislove, A., Parkes, D. C., Pentland, A. 'Sandy,' … Wellman, M. (2019). Machine behaviour. *Nature, 568*(7753), 477–486. https://doi.org/10.1038/s41586-019-1138-y

Ramiller, N. C., & Chiasson, M. (2008). The service behind the service: Sensegiving in the service economy. In M. Barrett, E. Davidson, E. Middleton, & J. DeGross (Eds.), *Information Technology in the Service Economy: Challenges and Possibilities for the 21st Century* (pp. 117–126). Springer.

Reid, E. M. (1991). *Electropolis: Communication and community on internet relay chat* [Honours Thesis, University of Melbourne, Department of History]. http://www.aluluei.com/electropolis.htm

Reisman, D., Schultz, J., Crawford, K., & Whittaker, M. (2018). Algorithmic impact assessments: A practical framework for public agency accountability. *AI Now Institute*. https://ainowinstitute.org/aiareport2018.pdf

H.R. 7356: Facial Recognition and Biometric Technology Moratorium Act of 2020, U.S. Congress (2020) (testimony of Pramila Rep. Jayapal). https://www.govtrack.us/congress/bills/116/hr7356

Reynolds, D. A. (2009). Gaussian Mixture Models. In S.Z. Li (Ed.), *Encyclopedia of Biometrics* (pp. 659–663). Springer.

Ribeiro, M. H., Ottoni, R., West, R., Almeida, V. A., & Meira Jr, W. (2020). Auditing radicalization pathways on YouTube. *Proceedings of the 2020 Conference on Fairness, Accountability, and Transparency*, 131–141.

Rich, E., Knight, K., & Nair, S. B. (2009). *Artificial intelligence third edition*. McGraw-Hill.

Richardson, L. (2015). Performing the sharing economy. *Geoforum*, *67*, 121–129.

Ringrose, K. (2019). Law Enforcement's Pairing of Facial Recognition Technology with Body-Worn Cameras Escalates Privacy Concerns. *Va. L. Rev. Online*, *105*, 57.

Ritzer, G. (2015). Prosumer capitalism. *The Sociological Quarterly*, *56*(3), 413–445.

Ritzer, G., Dean, P., & Jurgenson, N. (2012). The coming of age of the prosumer. *American Behavioral Scientist*, *56*(4), 379–398.

Robertson, R. E., Jiang, S., Lazer, D., & Wilson, C. (2019). Auditing autocomplete: Suggestion networks and recursive algorithm interrogation. *Proceedings of the 10th ACM Conference on Web Science*, 235–244.

Rogers, B. (2016). Employment rights in the platform economy: Getting back to basics. *Harv. L. & Pol'y Rev.*, *10*, 479.

Rolls Royce. (2020, December). *The Aletheia Framework*. Rolls Royce. https://www.rolls-royce.com/sustainability/ethics-and-compliance/the-aletheia-framework.aspx

Romer, P. M. (1990). Endogenous Technological Change. *Journal of Political Economy*, *98*(5, Part 2), S71–S102. https://doi.org/10.1086/261725

Roscher, W. (1870). Die romantische Schule der Nationalökonomik in Deutschland. *Zeitschrift Für Die Gesamte Staatswissenschaft / Journal of Institutional and Theoretical Economics*, 57–105.

Rowley, H. A., Baluja, S., & Kanade, T. (1998). Neural network-based face detection. *IEEE Transactions on Pattern Analysis and Machine Intelligence*, *20*(1), 23–38.

Rudin, C., Waltz, D., Anderson, R. N., Boulanger, A., Salleb-Aouissi, A., Chow, M., Dutta, H., Gross, P. N., Huang, B., & Ierome, S. (2011). Machine learning for the New York City power grid. *IEEE Transactions on Pattern Analysis and Machine Intelligence, 34*(2), 328–345.

Russell, S. (2019, October 8). How to Stop Superhuman A.I. Before It Stops Us. *The New York Times*. https://www.nytimes.com/2019/10/08/opinion/artificial-intelligence.html

Russell, S., & Norvig, P. (2010). *Artificial Intelligence: A modern approach* (3rd edition). Pearson Education.

Sadowski, J. (2019). When data is capital: Datafication, accumulation, and extraction. *Big Data & Society, 6*(1), 1–12.

Sætra, H. S. (2020). A shallow defence of a technocracy of artificial intelligence: Examining the political harms of algorithmic governance in the domain of government. *Technology in Society, 62*(101283), 1–10.

Salin, E. D., & Winston, P. H. (1992). Machine learning and artificial intelligence: An introduction. *Analytical Chemistry, 64*(1), 49A-60A.

Samatas, M. (2005). Studying surveillance in Greece: Methodological and other problems related to an authoritarian surveillance culture. *Surveillance & Society, 3*(2), 181–197.

Sambasivan, N., & Holbrook, J. (2018). Toward responsible AI for the next billion users. *Interactions, 26*(1), 68–71.

Sandberg, S., & Pedersen, W. (2011). *Street capital: Black cannabis dealers in a white welfare state*. The Policy Press.

Sandler, M., & Howard, A. (2018, April 3). MobileNetV2: The Next Generation of On-Device Computer Vision Networks. *Google AI Blog*. http://ai.googleblog.com/2018/04/mobilenetv2-next-generation-of-on.html

Sandler, M., Howard, A., Zhu, M., Zhmoginov, A., & Chen, L.-C. (2018). Mobilenetv2: Inverted residuals and linear bottlenecks. *Proceedings of the IEEE Conference on Computer Vision and Pattern Recognition*, 4510–4520.

Satariano, A. (2019, September 4). Police Use of Facial Recognition Is Accepted by British Court. *The New York Times*. https://www.nytimes.com/2019/09/04/business/facial-recognition-uk-court.html

Saygin, A. P., Cicekli, I., & Akman, V. (2000). Turing test: 50 years later. *Minds and Machines, 10*(4), 463–518.

Scassa, T. (2018). Information Law in the Platform Economy: Ownership, Control, and Reuse of Platform Data. In D. McKee, F. Makela, & T. Scassa (Eds.), *Law and the «Sharing Economy»: Regulating Online Market Platforms* (pp. 321–356). University of Ottawa Press.

Schermer, B. W. (2011). The limits of privacy in automated profiling and data mining. *Computer Law & Security Review, 27*(1), 45–52.

Scheuerman, M. K., Paul, J. M., & Brubaker, J. (2019). How Computers See Gender: An Evaluation of Gender Classification in Commercial Facial Analysis and Image Labeling Services. *Proceedings of the ACM on Human-Computer Interaction, 3*, 1–33.

Scheuerman, M. K., Wade, K., Lustig, C., & Brubaker, J. R. (2020). How We've Taught Algorithms to See Identity: Constructing Race and Gender in Image Databases for Facial Analysis. *Proceedings of the ACM on Human-Computer Interaction*, 4(CSCW1), 1–35.

Schiller, D. (2000). *Digital capitalism: Networking the global market system*. MIT Press.

Schiller, D., & Mosco, V. (2001). *Continental Order? Integrating North America for Cybercapitalism*. Rowman and Littlefield.

Schmidt, E., Work, B., Catz, S., Chien, S., Darby, C., Ford, K., Griffiths, J.-M., Horvitz, E., Jassy, A., & Mark, W. (2021). *National Security Commission on Artificial Intelligence (AI)*. National Security Commission on Artificial Intelligence. https://www.nscai.gov/wp-content/uploads/2021/03/Full-Report-Digital-1.pdf

Schor, J. (2016). Debating the sharing economy. *Journal of Self-Governance and Management Economics*, 4(3), 7–22.

Schor, J. B., & Attwood-Charles, W. (2017). The "sharing" economy: Labor, inequality, and social connection on for-profit platforms. *Sociology Compass*, 11(8), e12493.

Schultz, T. W. (1961). Investment in Human Capital. *The American Economic Review*, 51(1), 1–17.

Schumpeter, J. (1954). *History of Economic Analysis* (E. B. Schumpeter, Ed.). Routledge.

Schwartz, O. (2018, September 26). Love in the time of AI: Meet the people falling for scripted robots. *The Guardian*. https://www.theguardian.com/technology/2018/sep/26/mystic-messenger-dating-simulations-sims-digital-intimacy

Seeger, A.-M., & Heinzl, A. (2018). Human versus machine: Contingency factors of anthropomorphism as a trust-inducing design strategy for conversational agents. In F. D. Davis, R. Riedl, P. vom Brocke, P. Léger, & A. B. Randolph (Eds.), *Information systems and neuroscience* (pp. 129–139). Springer.

Seelman, K. D. (1993). Assistive technology policy: A road to independence for individuals with disabilities. *Journal of Social Issues*, 49(2), 115–136.

Segura, M. S., & Waisbord, S. (2019). Between data capitalism and data citizenship. *Television & New Media*, 20(4), 412–419.

Sengupta, A. (2020, November 16). Election polls were a disaster this year. Here's how AI could help. *Fast Company*. https://www.fastcompany.com/90575531/ai-election-polling

Senior, A. W., Evans, R., Jumper, J., Kirkpatrick, J., Sifre, L., Green, T., Qin, C., Žídek, A., Nelson, A. W., & Bridgland, A. (2020). Improved protein structure prediction using potentials from deep learning. *Nature*, 577(7792), 706–710.

Shaw, W. H. (1979). "The Handmill Gives You the Feudal Lord": Marx's Technological Determinism. *History and Theory*, 18(2), 155–176. JSTOR. https://doi.org/10.2307/2504754

Shelley, M. W. (1869). *Frankenstein, or, The Modern Prometheus*. Sever, Francis, & Company.

Shen, J., Pang, R., Weiss, R. J., Schuster, M., Jaitly, N., Yang, Z., Chen, Z., Zhang, Y., Wang, Y., & Skerrv-Ryan, R. (2018). Natural tts synthesis by conditioning wavenet on mel spectrogram predictions. *2018 IEEE International Conference on Acoustics, Speech and Signal Processing (ICASSP)*, 4779–4783.

Shergill, G. S., Sarrafzadeh, A., Diegel, O., & Shekar, A. (2008). Computerized Sales Assistants: The application of computer technology to measure consumer interest-a conceptual framework. *Journal of Electronic Commerce Research*, 9(2), 176–191.

Sherif, M. (1936). The psychology of social norms. *Harper.*

Shilton, K. (2015). " That's Not An Architecture Problem!": Techniques and Challenges for Practicing Anticipatory Technology Ethics. *IConference 2015 Proceedings.*

Shilton, K. (2018). Engaging values despite neutrality: Challenges and approaches to values reflection during the design of internet infrastructure. *Science, Technology, & Human Values*, 43(2), 247–269.

Siau, K., & Wang, W. (2020). Artificial intelligence (AI) ethics: Ethics of AI and ethical AI. *Journal of Database Management (JDM)*, 31(2), 74–87.

Siegel, E. (2013). *Predictive Analytics: The Power to Predict Who Will Click, Buy, Lie, or Die.* Wiley.

Silverman, C. (2016, November 16). This Analysis Shows How Viral Fake Election News Stories Outperformed Real News On Facebook. *BuzzFeed News.* https://www.buzzfeednews.com/article/craigsilverman/viral-fake-election-news-outperformed-real-news-on-facebook

Similar companies to VocaliD. (2021). Venture Radar. https://www.ventureradar.com/similar/VocaliD/34420c6a-e53f-46ae-870b-cef6bc01008a

Simonite, T. (2019, September 3). Behind the Rise of China's Facial-Recognition Giants. *Wired.* https://www.wired.com/story/behind-rise-chinas-facial-recognition-giants/

Simonite, T. (2020, July 22). AI Text Generator GPT-3 Is Learning Our Language—Fitfully. *WIRED.* https://www.wired.com/story/ai-text-generator-gpt-3-learning-language-fitfully/

Simonite, T. (2021, March 16). The Departure of 2 Google AI Researchers Spurs More Fallout. *WIRED.* https://www.wired.com/story/departures-2-google-ai-researchers-spur-fallout/

Sinha, N., Bhowmick, A., & Kishore, B. (2015). Encrypted information hiding using audio steganography and audio cryptography. *International Journal of Computer Applications*, 112(5), 49–53.

Sismondo, S. (2009). *An Introduction to Science and Technology Studies* (2nd ed.). Wiley-Blackwell.

Skitka, L. J., Mosier, K. L., & Burdick, M. (1999). Does automation bias decision-making? *International Journal of Human-Computer Studies*, 51(5), 991–1006.

Slaney, M., & Casey, M. (2008). Locality-sensitive hashing for finding nearest neighbors [lecture notes]. *IEEE Signal Processing Magazine*, 25(2), 128–131.

Slater, D. (2013). *Love in times of algorithms: What technology does to meeting and mating*. Current.

Smaradottir, B. F., Haaland, J. A., & Martinez, S. G. (2018). User evaluation of the smartphone screen reader VoiceOver with visually disabled participants. *Mobile Information Systems*, *2018*. https://doi.org/10.1155/2018/6941631

Smith, Aaron. (2019, September 5). More Than Half of U.S. Adults Trust Law Enforcement to Use Facial Recognition Responsibly. *Pew Research Center: Internet, Science & Tech*. https://www.pewinternet.org/2019/09/05/more-than-half-of-u-s-adults-trust-law-enforcement-to-use-facial-recognition-responsibly/

Smith, Adam. (1804). *An Inquiry Into the Nature and Causes of the Wealth of Nations, Volume 1* (Vol. 1). Oliver D Cooke.

Solow, R. M. (2017). Thomas Piketty Is Right. In H. Boushey, J. B. DeLong, & M. Steinbaum (Eds.), *After Piketty* (pp. 48–59). Harvard University Press. https://doi.org/10.4159/9780674978195-003

Sotala, K. (2020, July 18). Collection of GPT-3 results. *LESSWRONG*. https://www.lesswrong.com/posts/6Hee7w2paEzHsD6mn/collection-of-gpt-3-results

Sovacool, B. K., & Hess, D. J. (2017). Ordering theories: Typologies and conceptual frameworks for sociotechnical change. *Social Studies of Science*, *47*(5), 703–750. https://doi.org/10.1177/0306312717709363

Srnicek, N. (2017). *Platform capitalism*. John Wiley & Sons.

St. Vincent, S. (2019, June 21). Facial Recognition Technology in US Schools Threatens Rights. *Human Rights Watch*. https://www.hrw.org/news/2019/06/21/facial-recognition-technology-us-schools-threatens-rights

Star, S. L. (1999). The ethnography of infrastructure. *American Behavioral Scientist*, *43*(3), 377–391.

Statista. (2018). *Nachrichteninhalte—Aufmerksamkeitsquellen in Deutschland 2016*. Statista. https://de.statista.com/statistik/daten/studie/550868/umfrage/aufmerksamkeitsquellen-fuer-nachrichteninhalte/

Statista. (2021, January). *Search engines: Market share of desktop and mobile search in Germany 2021*. Statista. https://www.statista.com/statistics/445974/search-engines-market-share-of-desktop-and-mobile-search-germany/

Statt, N. (2018, May 10). Google now says controversial AI voice calling system will identify itself to humans. *The Verge*. https://www.theverge.com/2018/5/10/17342414/google-duplex-ai-assistant-voice-calling-identify-itself-update

Steinacker, L., Kostka, G., Meckel, M., Guo, D., & Suter, V. (2020, May). *Facing the public: A cross-national analysis of social norms and communication about facial recognition technologies*. International Communication Association 2020, Australia. https://www.alexandria.unisg.ch/259127/

Steinacker, L., Meckel, M., Kostka, G., & Borth, D. (2020). Facial Recognition: A cross-national Survey on Public Acceptance, Privacy, and Discrimination. *ArXiv Preprint ArXiv:2008.07275*.

Steinbicker, J. (2001). *Zur Theorie der Informationsgesellschaft*. Springer.

Steiner, C. (2013). *Automate This: How algorithms took over markets, our jobs, and the world*. Penguin Random House.

Stern, S. E., Dumont, M., Mullennix, J. W., & Winters, M. L. (2007). Positive prejudice toward disabled persons using synthesized speech: Does the effect persist across contexts? *Journal of Language and Social Psychology*, 26(4), 363–380.

Stern, S. E., Mullennix, J. W., & Wilson, S. J. (2002). Effects of perceived disability on persuasiveness of computer-synthesized speech. *Journal of Applied Psychology*, 87(2), 411–417.

Stöcker, C., & Preuss, M. (2020). Riding the Wave of Misclassification: How We End up with Extreme YouTube Content. *International Conference on Human-Computer Interaction*, 359–375.

Stone, D., Jarrett, C., Woodroffe, M., & Minocha, S. (2005). *User interface design and evaluation*. Elsevier.

Stone, P., Brooks, R., Brynjolfsson, E., Calo, R., Etzioni, O., Hager, G., Hirschberg, J., Kalyanakrishnan, S., Kamar, E., Kraus, S., Leyton-Brown, K., Parkes, D. C., Press, W., Saxenian, A., Shah, J., Tambe, M., & Teller, A. (2016). *One hundred year study on Artificial Intelligence: AI and life in 2030*. Stanford University. ai100.standford.edu

Strauss, A., & Corbin, J. (1998). *Basics of qualitative research techniques*. Citeseer.

Striphas, T. (2015). Algorithmic culture. *European Journal of Cultural Studies*, 18(4–5), 395–412. https://doi.org/10.1177/1367549415577392

Strubell, E., Ganesh, A., & McCallum, A. (2019). Energy and policy considerations for deep learning in NLP. *ArXiv Preprint ArXiv:1906.02243*.

Suarez-Villa, L. (2000). *Invention and the Rise of Technocapitalism*. Rowman & Littlefield.

Suarez-Villa, L. (2013). *Technocapitalism*. http://www.technocapitalism.com/Introduction.htm

Suchman, L. (1987). *Plans and Situated Actions: The Problem of Human-Machine Communication*. Cambridge University Press.

Suchman, L. (2007). *Human-machine reconfigurations: Plans and situated actions* (2nd Edition). Cambridge University Press.

Svenmarck, P., Luotsinen, L., Nilsson, M., & Schubert, J. (2018). Possibilities and challenges for artificial intelligence in military applications. *Proceedings of the 2018 NATO Big Data and Artificial Intelligence for Military Decision Making Specialists' Meeting*, 1–15.

Sweeney, L. (2013). Discrimination in online ad delivery. *ArXiv Preprint ArXiv:1301.6822*.

Taigman, Y., Yang, M., Ranzato, M., & Wolf, L. (2014). DeepFace: Closing the Gap to Human-Level Performance in Face Verification. *Proceedings of the IEEE Conference on Computer Vision and Pattern Recognition*, 1701–1708. https://www.cv-foundation.org/openaccess/content_cvpr_2014/html/Taigman_DeepFace_Closing_the_2014_CVPR_paper.html

Takeishi, A., & Lee, K.-J. (2005). Mobile music business in Japan and Korea: Copyright management institutions as a reverse salient. *The Journal of Strategic Information Systems*, 14(3), 291–306. https://doi.org/10.1016/j.jsis.2005.07.005

Tan, B., Shen, X., & Zhai, C. (2006). Mining long-term search history to improve search accuracy. *Proceedings of the 12th ACM SIGKDD International Conference on Knowledge Discovery and Data Mining*, 718–723.

Tandoc, E. C., Lim, Z. W., & Ling, R. (2018). Defining "Fake News": A typology of scholarly definitions. *Digital Journalism*, 6(2), 137–153. https://doi.org/10.1080/2 1670811.2017.1360143

Tankard, M. E., & Paluck, E. L. (2016). Norm Perception as a Vehicle for Social Change: Vehicle for Social Change. *Social Issues and Policy Review*, 10(1), 181–211. https://doi.org/10.1111/sipr.12022

Tankard, M. E., & Paluck, E. L. (2017). The Effect of a Supreme Court Decision Regarding Gay Marriage on Social Norms and Personal Attitudes. *Psychological Science*, 28(9), 1334–1344. https://doi.org/10.1177/0956797617709594

Tans, G. (2018, October 11). For Businesses Big and Small, AI is the Great Equalizer. *Linkedin*. https://www.linkedin.com/pulse/businesses-big-small-ai-great-equal izer-gillian-tans

Tao, Q., & Veldhuis, R. (2010). Biometric authentication system on mobile personal devices. *IEEE Transactions on Instrumentation and Measurement*, 59(4), 763–773.

Tariq, S., Jeon, S., & Woo, S. S. (2021). Am I a Real or Fake Celebrity? Measuring Commercial Face Recognition Web APIs under Deepfake Impersonation Attack. *ArXiv Preprint ArXiv:2103.00847*.

Taylor, L. (2017). What is data justice? The case for connecting digital rights and freedoms globally. *Big Data & Society*, 4(2), 1–14.

Taylor, P. (2009). *Text-to-speech synthesis*. Cambridge University Press.

Tene, O., & Polonetsky, J. (2013). Big data for all: Privacy and user control in the age of analytics. *Nw. J. Tech. & Intell. Prop.*, 11(5), 240–272.

Thaler, R. H., Sunstein, C. R., & Balz, J. P. (2013). Choice architecture. In E. Shafir (Ed.), *The behavioral foundations of public policy* (pp. 428–439). Princeton University Press.

The Royal Society. (2017). *Machine learning: The power and promise of computers that learn by example*. The Royal Society. https://royalsociety.org/-/media/policy/proje cts/machine-learning/publications/machine-learning-report.pdf

The State of Responsible AI: 2021. (2021). FICO. https://www.fico.com/en/resource-a ccess/download/36776?access_token_9f4fd=3a3e8333dc8922948bee98cd1fd89cb 11e2585415f725da6adf63342cb6e18d0

Thelen, K. A. (2018). Regulating Uber: The politics of the platform economy in Europe and the United States. *Perspectives on Politics*, 16(4), 938–953.

Thompson, C. (2014). *Smarter Than You Think: How Technology is Changing Our Minds for the Better*. Harper Collins Australia.

Thompson, C. (2019). *Coders: The making of a new tribe and the remaking of the world*. Penguin Press.

Thrift, N. (1998). Virtual Capitalism: The Globalisation of Reflexive Business Knowledge. In J. Carrier & D. Miller (Eds.), *Virtualism: A New Political Economy* (pp. 161–186). Berg Publishers.

Tiernan, E. (2021, February 17). Massachusetts' New Police Reform Law Misses First Deadline. *Governing.* https://www.governing.com/now/Massachusetts-New-Police-Reform-Law-Misses-First-Deadline.html

TradeCNBC. (2021, January 25). I wish @CNN cared as much about the riots that happened all summer. This #FacesOfTheRiot show is scary, like a McCarthy hearing, or Russian dissenter hunt [Tweet]. *@TradeCNBC.* https://twitter.com/TradeCNBC/status/1353549611638652929

Tréguer, P. (2018, May 30). Meaning andOorigin of 'to be unable to run a whelk stall.' *Word Histories.* https://wordhistories.net/2018/05/30/unable-run-whelkstall/

Trouvain, J., & Brackhane, F. (2011). Wolfgang von Kempelen's speaking machine as an instrument for demonstration and research. *Proceedings of the 17th International Conference of Phonetic Sciences*, 164–167.

Tufekci, Z. (2014). Engineering the public: Big data, surveillance and computational politics. *First Monday*, 19(7). https://doi.org/10.5210/fm.v19i7.4901

Tufekci, Z. (2018). YouTube, the great radicalizer. *The New York Times.* https://www.nytimes.com/2018/03/10/opinion/sunday/youtube-politics-radical.html

Turing, A. M. (1950). Computing Machinery and Intelligence. *Mind, LIX*(236), 433–460. https://doi.org/10.1093/mind/LIX.236.433

Tutt, A. (2017). An FDA for algorithms. *Admin. L. Rev.*, 69, 83–123.

UBI Hologram. (2021, January 24). Any #Facesoftheriot bounty hunters out there? We're looking for a guy that owes us some money ... What the hell: I'll toss another $100 on the pile. [Tweet]. *@hologram_stan.* https://twitter.com/hologram_stan/status/1353420876662755329

United Nations Environment Programme. (2020). *Principles for Responsible Investment Report 2020.* PRI. https://www.unpri.org/download?ac=10948

U.S. Federal Trade Commission. (2021, April 19). *Aiming for truth, fairness, and equity in your company's use of AI.* Federal Trade Commission. https://www.ftc.gov/news-events/blogs/business-blog/2021/04/aiming-truth-fairness-equity-your-companys-use-ai

U.S. podcast advertising revenue 2019. (2020, July). Statista. https://www.statista.com/statistics/760791/us-podcast-advertising-revenue/

Vaccari, C., & Chadwick, A. (2020). Deepfakes and disinformation: Exploring the impact of synthetic political video on deception, uncertainty, and trust in news. *Social Media + Society*, 6(1), 1–13.

Vallas, S. P. (2019). Platform capitalism: What's at stake for workers? *New Labor Forum*, 28(1), 48–59.

van Heek, J., Arning, K., & Ziefle, M. (2016). The Surveillance Society: Which Factors Form Public Acceptance of Surveillance Technologies? In M. Helfert, C. Klein, B. Donnellan, & O. Gusikhin (Eds.), *Smart Cities, Green Technologies, and Intelligent Transport Systems* (pp. 170–191). Springer.

Van Hoof, J., Kort, H. S., Markopoulos, P., & Soede, M. (2007). Ambient intelligence, ethics and privacy. *Gerontechnology*, 6(3), 155–163.

Veblen, T. (1908a). On the nature of capital. *Quarterly Journal of Economics*, 23(1), 104–136.

Veblen, T. (1908b). Professor Clark's economics. *Quarterly Journal of Economics*, 22(2), 147–195.

Venkatesh, Morris, Davis, & Davis. (2003). User Acceptance of Information Technology: Toward a Unified View. *MIS Quarterly*, 27(3), 425. https://doi.org/10.230 7/30036540

Venkatesh, V., Thong, J. Y. L., & Xu, X. (2012). Consumer Acceptance and Use of Information Technology: Extending the Unified Theory of Acceptance and Use of Technology. *MIS Quarterly*, 36(1), 157–178. https://doi.org/10.2307/41410412

Vincent, J. (2016, June 29). Satya Nadella's rules for AI are more boring (and relevant) than Asimov's Three Laws. *The Verge*. https://www.theverge.com/2016/ 6/29/12057516/satya-nadella-ai-robot-laws

Vincent, J. (2020, July 27). This is what a deepfake voice clone used in a failed fraud attempt sounds like. *The Verge*. https://www.theverge.com/2020/7/27/21339898/ deepfake-audio-voice-clone-scam-attempt-nisos

Vincent, J. (2021a, April 14). The EU is considering a ban on AI for mass surveillance and social credit scores. *The Verge*. https://www.theverge.com/2021/4/14/22 383301/eu-ai-regulation-draft-leak-surveillance-social-credit

Vincent, J. (2021b, April 21). FBI used facial recognition to identify a Capitol rioter from his girlfriend's Instagram posts. *The Verge*. https://www.theverge.com/2021 /4/21/22395323/fbi-facial-recognition-us-capital-riots-tracked-down-suspect

Viola, P., & Jones, M. (2001). Rapid object detection using a boosted cascade of simple features. *Proceedings of the 2001 IEEE Computer Society Conference on Computer Vision and Pattern Recognition*, 1, I–I.

Viola, P., & Jones, M. J. (2004). Robust Real-Time Face Detection. *International Journal of Computer Vision*, 57(2), 137–154.

Vocally Yours (Round 5). (2018). Digital News Initiative. https://newsinitiative.withg oogle.com//dnifund/dni-projects/vocally-yours-round-5/

Voiceitt: Home. (2021). Voiceitt. https://voiceitt.com/

Von Kempelen, W. (1791). *Mechanismus der menschlichen Sprache nebst der Beschreibung einer sprechenden Machine*. Degen.

Wagner, E. L., Newell, S., & Piccoli, G. (2010). Understanding project survival in an ES environment: A sociomaterial practice perspective. *Journal of the Association for Information Systems*, 11(5), 276–297.

Wajcman, J. (2002). Addressing Technological Change: The Challenge to Social Theory. *Current Sociology*, 50(3), 347–363. https://doi.org/10.1177/001139210205 0003004

Walther, J. B. (1996). Computer-mediated communication: Impersonal, interpersonal, and hyperpersonal interaction. *Communication Research*, 23(1), 3–43.

Walther, J. B. (2007). Selective self-presentation in computer-mediated communication: Hyperpersonal dimensions of technology, language, and cognition. *Computers in Human Behavior*, 23(5), 2538–2557.

Walther, J. B., Van Der Heide, B., Ramirez, A., Burgoon, J. K., & Peña, J. (2015). Interpersonal and hyperpersonal dimensions of computer-mediated communication. In S. S. Sundar (Ed.), *The handbook of the psychology of communication technology* (pp. 1–22). Wiley & Sons.

Wang, Yilun, & Kosinski, M. (2018). Deep neural networks are more accurate than humans at detecting sexual orientation from facial images. *Journal of Personality and Social Psychology, 114*(2), 246.

Wang, Yuxuan, Skerry-Ryan, R. J., Stanton, D., Wu, Y., Weiss, R. J., Jaitly, N., Yang, Z., Xiao, Y., Chen, Z., Bengio, S., Le, Q., Agiomyrgiannakis, Y., Clark, R., & Saurous, R. A. (2017). Tacotron: Towards End-to-End Speech Synthesis. *ArXiv:1703.10135 [Cs]*. http://arxiv.org/abs/1703.10135

Wardle, C., & Derakhshan, H. (2017). *Information disorder: Toward an interdisciplinary framework for research and policy making*. Council of Europe. https://rm.co e.int/information-disorder-toward-an-interdisciplinary-framework-for-researc/16 8076277c

Waytz, A., Heafner, J., & Epley, N. (2014). The mind in the machine: Anthropomorphism increases trust in an autonomous vehicle. *Journal of Experimental Social Psychology, 52*, 113–117.

Weber, M. (1968). *Economy and Society: An outline of interpretive sociology*. University of California Press.

Weber, S., & Stanton, C. (2019, October 2). The World Isn't Ready for AI to Upend the Global Economy. *Carnegie Endowment for International Peace*. https://carnegieendowment.org/2019/10/02/world-isn-t-ready-for-ai-to-upend-global-eco nomy-pub-79961

Webster, F. (2014). *Theories of the information society*. Routledge.

Weick, K. E., Sutcliffe, K. M., & Obstfeld, D. (2005). Organizing and the process of sensemaking. *Organization Science, 16*(4), 409–421.

West, S. M. (2019). Data capitalism: Redefining the logics of surveillance and privacy. *Business & Society, 58*(1), 20–41.

Wiener, N. (1988). *The human use of human beings: Cybernetics and society*. Da Capo Press.

Wiener, N. (2019). *Cybernetics or Control and Communication in the Animal and the Machine*. MIT Press.

Wing, J. M. (2020). Trustworthy AI. *ArXiv Preprint ArXiv:2002.06276*.

Winner, L. (1977). *Autonomous technology: Technics-out-of-control as a theme in political thought* (9. printing). MIT Press.

Wood, A. J., Graham, M., Lehdonvirta, V., & Hjorth, I. (2019). Good gig, bad gig: Autonomy and algorithmic control in the global gig economy. *Work, Employment and Society, 33*(1), 56–75.

Wood, S. G., Moxley, J. H., Tighe, E. L., & Wagner, R. K. (2018). Does Use of Text-to-Speech and Related Read-Aloud Tools Improve Reading Comprehension for Students With Reading Disabilities? A Meta-Analysis. *Journal of Learning Disabilities, 51*(1), 73–84. https://doi.org/10.1177/0022219416688170

Woodward, J. D., Horn, C., Gatune, J., & Thomas, A. (2003). *Biometrics: A look at facial recognition*. RAND.

Woolgar, S. (1991). The Turn to Technology in Social Studies of Science. *Science, Technology, & Human Values, 16*(1), 20–50. JSTOR. https://doi.org/10.1177/0162 24399101600102

Woolley, B. (2015). *The Bride of Science: Romance, reason and Byron's daughter*. Pan Macmillan.

Wu, X., & Zhang, X. (2016). Responses to Critiques on Machine Learning of Criminality Perceptions (Addendum of arXiv: 1611.04135). *ArXiv Preprint ArXiv:1611.04135*.

Yamamoto, R., Song, E., & Kim, J.-M. (2020). Parallel WaveGAN: A fast waveform generation model based on generative adversarial networks with multi-resolution spectrogram. *ICASSP 2020-2020 IEEE International Conference on Acoustics, Speech and Signal Processing (ICASSP)*, 6199–6203.

Yong, S. (2013). *Panopticism Technique in Crime Prevention Through Environmental Design* (SSRN Scholarly Paper ID 3001563). Social Science Research Network. https://papers.ssrn.com/abstract=3001563

Young, A. (1998). *Towards an Interim Statistical Framework: Selecting the Core Components of Intangible Investment*. OECD Secretariat.

Zarkadakis, G. (2015). *In Our Own Image: Will artificial intelligence save or destroy us?* Random House.

Zhang, D., Mishra, S., Brynjolfsson, E., Etchemendy, J., Ganguli, D., Grosz, B., Lyons, T., Manyika, J., Niebles, J. C., & Sellitto, M. (2021). *The AI Index 2021 Annual Report*. Human-Centered AI Institute, Stanford University. https://arxiv.org/pdf/2103.06312.pdf

Zhang, J.-X., Ling, Z.-H., & Dai, L.-R. (2018). Forward attention in sequence-to-sequence acoustic modeling for speech synthesis. *2018 IEEE International Conference on Acoustics, Speech and Signal Processing (ICASSP)*, 4789–4793.

Zielke, T., & Wolfer, R. C. (2008). Facing up to gambling addicts. *Biometric Technology Today, 16*(3), 10–11.

Zimmer, M. (2010). "But the data is already public": On the ethics of research in Facebook. *Ethics and Information Technology, 12*(4), 313–325.

Zou, J., & Schiebinger, L. (2018). *AI can be sexist and racist—It's time to make it fair*. Nature Publishing Group.

Zuboff, S. (1988). *In the age of the smart machine: The future of work and power*. Basic Books.

Zuboff, S. (2015). Big other: Surveillance capitalism and the prospects of an information civilization. *Journal of Information Technology, 30*(1), 75–89. https://doi.org/10.1057/jit.2015.5

Zuboff, S. (2016, March 5). Google as a Fortune Teller: The Secrets of Surveillance Capitalism. *Frankfurter Allgemeine Zeitung*. https://www.faz.net/1.4103616

Zuboff, S. (2019). *The age of surveillance capitalism: The fight for a human future at the new frontier of power*. Profile Books.

Appendix

Table A: Ordered logit regression, weighted; dependent variable: social acceptance of FRT in public

	TOTAL	CHINA	GERMANY	UK	US
AGE	0.00400**	0.00695	0.00042	0.00247	0.01023***
	(0.00180)	(0.00484)	(0.00358)	(0.00339)	(0.00366)
GENDER	-0.08896*	0.00598	-0.20971**	-0.10834	0.00739
	(0.04606)	(0.09362)	(0.09382)	(0.09307)	(0.09572)
EDUCATION					
MEDIUM	0.25815**	0.30059	0.51652***	0.00630	-0.34853
	(0.10351)	(0.24525)	(0.19545)	(0.17221)	(0.23558)
HIGH	0.49870***	0.60922**	0.59164***	0.31901*	-0.03548
	(0.11129)	(0.25556)	(0.22217)	(0.18750)	(0.25031)
PRIVACY THREAT					
MAYBE	-1.19227***	-0.88714***	-1.47814***	-1.25455***	-1.13848***
	(0.06499)	(0.12911)	(0.13558)	(0.12816)	(0.13783)
YES	-2.56136***	-2.05615***	-2.83184***	-2.73087***	-2.24377***
	(0.09095)	(0.19423)	(0.17812)	(0.19148)	(0.17547)
DON'T KNOW	-1.10769***	-0.61900***	-1.65456***	-1.14611***	-1.14786***
	(0.08928)	(0.18081)	(0.19379)	(0.18921)	(0.17015)
CONSEQUENCES					
CONVENIENCE	0.39866***	0.65575***	-0.21672*	0.61789***	0.48929***
	(0.05601)	(0.10862)	(0.12242)	(0.13169)	(0.11290)
PRIVACY VIOLATIONS	-0.47910***	-0.30679***	-0.51169***	-0.53786***	-0.50424***
	(0.05638)	(0.11384)	(0.11292)	(0.11722)	(0.11150)
EFFICIENCY	0.38049***	0.27139***	0.26869**	0.48286***	0.48989***
	(0.05647)	(0.10358)	(0.12690)	(0.11988)	(0.12034)
DISCRIMINATION	-0.39427***	-0.15615	-0.57354***	-0.29403**	-0.20140
	(0.07769)	(0.30014)	(0.14208)	(0.13921)	(0.14378)
SECURITY	0.71487***	0.77954***	0.90220***	0.61509***	0.62676***
	(0.05372)	(0.10211)	(0.10722)	(0.12419)	(0.11347)
SURVEILLANCE	0.15870***	-0.26568**	0.39048***	0.22459**	0.13438
	(0.04934)	(0.10949)	(0.10508)	(0.10463)	(0.09962)
NONE OF THE ABOVE	0.21330*	0.91277***	0.06282	0.22159	0.20214
	(0.11358)	(0.34577)	(0.25441)	(0.20607)	(0.20929)

continued on the next page

ISSUE CONCERN					
VIOLATION OF RULES	0.06854	0.01662	0.15430	-0.06003	0.10645
AND REGULATIONS	(0.05191)	(0.10302)	(0.10442)	(0.11323)	(0.10658)
CRIME	-0.00350	0.01879	0.18941	-0.15639	0.00426
	(0.06169)	(0.11331)	(0.12497)	(0.13409)	(0.13524)
TERRORIST THREATS	0.27710***	0.05836	0.53743***	0.36463***	0.29392**
	(0.05478)	(0.11117)	(0.10782)	(0.11341)	(0.12003)
BORDER CONTROL	0.02710	0.05025	0.03798	0.09390	0.07452
	(0.05257)	(0.11220)	(0.11135)	(0.10449)	(0.10537)
SOCIALLY	0.17819***	-0.08294	0.36925***	0.14626	0.07795
UNACCEPTABLE BEHAVIOR	(0.05030)	(0.10296)	(0.10088)	(0.11036)	(0.11076)
NONE OF THE ABOVE	0.16217*	0.00412	0.32852*	-0.07788	0.35713*
	(0.09183)	(0.18155)	(0.17772)	(0.20161)	(0.19948)
CUT1	-2.45276***	-2.84157***	-2.28142***	-2.83727***	-2.32633***
CONSTANT	(0.15142)	(0.35387)	(0.29993)	(0.29328)	(0.32109)
CUT2	-0.90108***	-0.71077**	-0.74262**	-1.36520***	-0.83437***
CONSTANT	(0.14857)	(0.32728)	(0.29838)	(0.28760)	(0.31508)
CUT3	0.54876***	0.76550**	0.70624**	0.15652	0.62404**
CONSTANT	(0.14808)	(0.32551)	(0.29969)	(0.28672)	(0.31392)
CUT4	2.70489***	3.11178***	3.17540***	2.27897***	2.40178***
CONSTANT	(0.15249)	(0.33614)	(0.31234)	(0.29421)	(0.32154)
OBSERVATIONS	6633	1651	1677	1685	1620

STANDARD ERRORS IN PARENTHESES
P <0.10, ** P <0.05, *** P <0.01